The Misuse of Drugs

The Misuse of Drugs

British Medical Association

harwood academic publishers

Australia • Canada • China • France • Germany • India
Japan • Luxembourg • Malaysia • The Netherlands • Russia
Singapore • Switzerland • Thailand • United Kingdom

Copyright ©1997 British Medical Association.
Published in The Netherlands by Harwood Academic Publishers.

Amsteldijk 166
1st Floor
1079 LH Amsterdam
The Netherlands

British Library Cataloguing in Publication Data

A catalogue record for this book is available from the British Library.

ISBN 90-5702-260-5 (soft cover)

Contents

3 The role of the medical profession   67

4 Constraints on current practice   109

Board of Science and Education

This report was prepared under the auspices of the Board of Science and Education of the British Medical Association whose membership for 1996/97 was

Working Party

A working party with the following membership was set up to advise the Board of Science and Education

Professor John Strang   Professor of Addictions, National Addiction Centre,
                          The Maudsley/Institute of Psychiatry, London
Dr T A N Waller   General Practitioner, Ipswich (retired June 1996) and
                          Suffolk County Specialist in Substance Misuse.

Acknowledgements

The Association is indebted to the Working Party members for so generously giving of their time and expertise and is particularly grateful to the Department of Health, Over-Count Drugs Advice Agency, and the Driver and Vehicle Licensing Agency for their kind permission to reproduce extracts and data from their publications. The Association is also grateful for the specialist help provided by the BMA Committees and many outside experts and organisations, and would particularly like to thank:

The ISDD (Institute for the Study of Drug Dependence); Dr John W Mack, Consultant Psychiatrist, Hackney Drug Dependency Unit, London; Mr John Ramsey, Research Fellow, Head of Toxicology Unit, St George's Hospital Medical School; Dr Nigel South, Reader in Sociology, Director of Health and Social Services Institute, University of Essex; and the Standing Conference on Drug Abuse (SCODA).

Introduction

The British Medical Association (BMA) is the professional organisation representing the medical profession in the UK. It was established in 1832 'to promote the medical and allied sciences, and to maintain the honour and interests of the profession'. The Board of Science and Education, a standing committee of the Association, supports this aim by acting as an interface between the profession, the government and the public. Its main purpose is to contribute to the improvement of public health, and it has developed policies on a wide range of issues, such as alcohol, smoking, infectious diseases, complementary medicine, pesticides and transport.

In 1994 the BMA's Annual Representative Meeting adopted a resolution, requesting that the Board of Science and Education:

i)   *Prepare an authoritative statement on the relative risks of drugs of addiction including the principal controlled drugs, tobacco and alcohol;*

ii)   *Advise on the role of the medical profession in relation to:*
       a) drug misusers who wish to discontinue their habit;
       b) drug misusers who wish to continue their habit;
       c) arrangements which exist, or might exist in the future, for supplying drugs to either of the above categories of drug misuser;

iii)   *Consider the benefits or otherwise of decriminalisation or legalisation of some or all controlled drugs.*

Over the last decade the BMA has produced a number of policy documents which address the major issues surrounding tobacco and alcohol use. The relative risks of smoking, alcohol and other drugs were considered in the Board of Science and Education report *Living with risk* (1990)[1]. The health consequences of heavy drinking among the young were addressed in *Young people and alcohol* (1986)[2] and the contribution of alcohol to driving and other accidents was considered in *The drinking driver* (1988)[3] and *The BMA guide to alcohol and accidents* (1989).[4] *Alcohol: guidelines on sensible drinking* (1995) provides advice on the consumption of alcohol

1

supported by a review of the evidence for the effects of alcohol on health[5] and the leaflet *Driving impairment through alcohol and other drugs* considers the effects on driving of illegal and prescribed drugs, and appropriate blood alcohol limits.[6] The Board has published a number of reports on smoking which have developed BMA policy in this area and the BMA maintains a high profile in campaigns to ban smoking in public places and tobacco advertising.

Throughout this century, drug misuse has concerned politicians, doctors and the public to varying degrees at any given time. Historically the attention devoted to illicit drug misuse has not always related directly to the size or severity of the problem, but concern shown at today's drug use coincides with a real increase in overall levels of drug-taking observed since the late 1970s, particularly amongst young people.[7,8] In addition, patterns of drug use have changed. There has been an increase in polydrug use, including the use of licit and illicit drugs together, and the arrival of the 'rave' scene with 'dance drugs' such as LSD, ecstasy and amphetamine forms part of an increase in recreational and experimental drug use. The dance scene has also witnessed the phenomenon of 'designer drugs', where new compounds are synthesized solely for misuse and with the aim of avoiding legislation in some countries. In view of these recent developments it is timely to consider the problems presented by illicit drug use.

The term 'drug misuse' covers a wide range of drug using activity, such as 'experimentation', weekend 'rave' drug use, and heroin dependence. Professionals, drug misusers and the public may all have different perceptions of what constitutes 'problem drug use'. The report therefore defines the problem in terms of what constitutes a problem to the user and to society.

Since the success of pioneering work in improving public health in the nineteenth century, it has been acknowledged that non-medical factors such as housing and employment have a direct impact on human health. In 1980 this was the subject of political attention with the publication of the 'Black Report'.[9] The BMA too has contributed to the debate on poverty and health through its discussion paper *Deprivation and ill-health* (1987),[10] and the policy documents *Inequalities in health* (1994)[11] and *Strategies for national renewal*, the BMA's commentary on the report of the Commission on Social Justice (1996)[12]. The health of drug users may be affected by many aspects of their lives and there is now a developing understanding that tackling the non-medical problems in drug users' lives can be an effective way of improving their health.

Scope and purpose of the report

To fulfill the Annual Representative Meeting's request, the Board established a working party of experts, both medical and non-medical, to review the evidence and prepare a report. The report has two main purposes: to provide information for medical and non-medical professionals already involved with, or considering caring for drug misusers and also, to raise awareness among health care purchasers and in government of how to deliver the best and most appropriate services for drug misusers.

To provide an 'authoritative statement on the relative risks of drugs of addiction including the principal controlled drugs, tobacco and alcohol', as requested in part *i)* of the Annual Representative Meeting's resolution, is not currently possible due to the incomplete nature of the evidence. However, to provide a basis for discussion and practical information for doctors, the report reviews the evidence on individual and social problems arising from drug misuse. Areas where further research is required are identified so that such a statement may be possible in the future.

Due to the extensive work already carried out by the BMA on the relative risks of tobacco and alcohol, these topics were not included in the remit for this present study, but it should be remembered that although drug misuse poses risks to the user and to others, from a public health perspective it remains a small problem in relation to the medical harm caused by alcohol and tobacco. It has been estimated that every year in the UK tobacco leads to at least 120,000 premature deaths,[13] and alcohol to between 28,000 and 33,000 deaths.[14]

Since the last century doctors have been the main professional group involved in the care of drug misusers, but today many medical professionals feel that drug misusers, and their wider problems require a range of expertise and experience. Sharing patient management between professionals and others from various fields and specialties should ensure that all aspects of treatment are targeted where they can be of greatest benefit, with all disciplines employing their skills where they are most effective.

As the major professional organisation representing doctors in the UK, the BMA is in a position to focus on those areas of drug misuse to which doctors can make the most direct and positive contribution, and to recognise when particular problems are best managed by other professionals and agencies. Part *ii)* of the Annual Representative Meeting's resolution refers to those who are already taking drugs, and therefore treatment rather than prevention of drug misuse forms the main focus of this report. The majority of patients presenting to treatment services are users of opiates, benzodiazepines and amphetamines, a high proportion of whom inject.[15] Their treatment is therefore considered in most detail.

In considering part *iii)* of the Annual Representative Meeting resolution, the BMA felt that in this report questions regarding the legalisation or decriminalisation of controlled drugs should be considered only with regard to their therapeutic use by patients for particular medical conditions. As a subject of wide public and professional interest, the potential therapeutic benefits of cannabis and cannabinoids have therefore been reviewed and are published in a separate discussion document. However, the main arguments regarding decriminalisation and legalisation of all drugs are outlined in Appendix I for discussion.

Considering what doctors can do for drug misusers inevitably leads to the question of which treatments are most effective. Whilst not attempting to duplicate the work of the Department of Health's Task Force to Review Services for Drug Misusers[16], this report examines some of the major questions surrounding current drug treatment and ways in which medical professionals can improve the general health of their drug using patients aside from their drug misuse.

1

Setting the scene

In the context of this report the term 'drug' is used to refer to a substance illicitly used for its psychoactive or performance enhancing effects. This definition includes the 'traditional' illegal psychoactive substances such as cannabis and heroin. It also covers legal psychoactive substances such as tranquillisers which are used for purposes other than those for which they were licensed, and the misuse of substances such as volatile compounds from domestic products such as butane from cigarette lighter refills which may include ingredients that have psychoactive properties. For ease of reference in this report, anabolic steroids are also termed 'drugs'. Although not misused for their psychoactive effects, they are now included within the Misuse of Drugs Act.

The legal framework

The Acts

There are two main statutes regulating the availability of drugs in the UK. The Medicines Act 1968 governs the manufacture and supply of pharmaceutical products of *all* kinds, most of which are legal drugs. Its enforcement rarely affects the general public, and it divides pharmaceuticals into three categories – 'Prescription Only', sold with prescriptions by pharmacists; 'Pharmacy Medicines', sold without prescriptions by pharmacists; and 'General Sales List', sold without prescriptions from any shop.

The second of the two statutes, The Misuse of Drugs Act 1971, is intended to prevent the non-medical use of certain drugs, some of which, because they have legitimate medical uses, are also covered by The Medicines Act (eg, temazepam and heroin). Offences under the Misuse of Drugs Act 1971 overwhelmingly involve the general public, and drugs subject to it are known as 'controlled' drugs.

Offences and penalties

The law defines a series of offences, including unlawful supply, intent to supply, import or export, unlawful production and, perhaps the most frequently committed offence, unlawful possession. In 1995 93,600 people were found guilty, cautioned or dealt with by 'compounding' for drug offences, of which nearly 90% were for unlawful possession. ('Compounding' is a penalty introduced in 1982 where a penalty is paid in lieu of prosecution for cases involving the importation of small quantities of cannabis for personal use).[1]

Under the Act, offences involving different classes of drugs attract varying penalties. Both for possession and supply of any drug, there is a possibility of an unlimited fine, but prison sentences are graded. Class A includes cocaine, heroin, morphine, LSD and ecstasy among others, and Class B drugs prepared for injection; their possession may result in up to a seven year sentence. Possession of Class B drugs which include amphetamines, barbiturates, cannabis and codeine may result in a five year sentence, and Class C drugs (pemoline, chlorphentermine, buprenorphine and benzodiazepines) a two year sentence. Supply or trafficking attract stiffer maximum penalties — sentences ranging from up to life for a Class A drug, to 14 years for a Class B, to 5 years for a Class C. However, most offenders are neither fined nor imprisoned, but cautioned — in total, 48,688 were cautioned in 1995 compared to 7,490 sentenced to immediate custody and 20,599 fined.[2]

Solvents are not classified under the Act, the only offence being to sell solvents to someone under 18 if there is reasonable cause to believe they intend to misuse them. In Scotland, if someone under 16 is found misusing volatile substances, they can be reported to the 'Reporter of the Children's Panel' and may subsequently be taken into care. Full details of this legislation are provided in Chapter 4.

Development of UK policy relating to drug misuse

Opium and later morphine and heroin were freely available in Britain and in other countries during the 19th century. The first moves to control opium (and its preparations), morphine, and cannabis came in 1868, until which time they were available over the counter without any form of restriction. Opiates were widely used both on medical prescription and as self-medication by those without access to medical treatment, for pain relief and to promote sleep.[3] Heroin was first controlled by the 1920 Dangerous Drugs Act and Britain's first defined policy on drug misuse was set out by the Rolleston Committee in 1926. This allowed the medical profession considerable scope and flexibility with regard to the treatment of drug dependence and in particular gave general practitioners control of the prescription of drugs. Those who needed treatment for their addiction at this time were mainly described as anxious middle aged professional people who had become addicted to opiate drugs, usually injectable morphine which had been prescribed to them for pain relief. The numbers were small and they were enabled to live useful and productive lives by the maintenance of their prescription. This became known as the 'British System'.

The Rolleston Committee was highly influential in defining addiction as a medical problem (as opposed to a moral one) as it advised that the prescription of heroin to an addict was within the remit of medical practice if in doing so the addict was allowed to live a normal, useful life.

Until the 1950s there were so few heroin addicts in Britain that nearly all of them were known personally to the Home Office Drugs Branch Inspectorate, which checked the pharmacy records from time to time.[4] As the name suggests, the prescribing permitted under the British System was distinctive from most other western industrialised countries. With the exception of Switzerland and the Netherlands, treatments involving the prescription of heroin and injectables were almost unknown and until recently Britain's doctors were given considerable clinical discretion.

In the early 1960s the picture changed. Newspaper reports were emerging of large numbers of young people taking drugs hedonistically. The Ministry of Health brought together an interdepartmental committee under Sir Russell Brain (the first Brain Committee) to examine the problem, but it reported in 1961 that the drug situation in Britain gave little cause for concern. However reports continued to appear in the press and the number of known heroin addicts rose from 62 in 1958 to 342 in 1964. The Brain Committee was therefore reconvened and reporting in 1965 accepted that a new young, unstable, non-therapeutic group of drug takers had emerged and that a handful of London doctors were prescribing dangerous drugs in excessive amounts to this group. The main reason for the escalation of the problem was thought to be overprescribing by unscrupulous, uninformed, or vulnerable doctors open to blackmail.

The second Brain Committee recommended that a number of treatment centres should be set up, run by psychiatrists with a special interest in the problem. GPs were allowed to treat drug users if they so wished, but only doctors with a special licence from the Home Office should be allowed to prescribe heroin and cocaine. This formalised the relationship between government and the medical profession, and ushered in the controls of the Addicts Index, under which doctors were obliged to notify the Home Office of any patients they consider to be addicted to one of 14 drugs.

The Drug Dependence Units or Clinics (DDUs or DDCs) were set up from 1968-70, mostly in the London area, and the treatment of drug misuse became a specialty, with GPs being discouraged from taking an active role. There were not enough specialist services to cover the whole country and GPs were still allowed by law to treat drug dependence with any drug apart from heroin and cocaine (dipipanone, an opioid analgesic in a preparation with the antihistamine cyclizine, was added to this list in 1984). Nevertheless, most drug-taking in the late 1960s and 1970s was concentrated in inner city areas where there was usually access to a DDU. The shift in emphasis towards specialisation and the movement away from treatment by the primary care services, meant that skills were not developed in this field by GPs and other generic professionals. Furthermore the training of this group in the problems and treatment of drug misuse received little attention. These developments culminated in the 1971 Misuse of Drugs Act, which also established the Advisory Council on the Misuse of Drugs.

In the late 1970s statistics from a number of sources showed that drug misuse in the UK was increasing rapidly, and this trend has continued since that time, despite all efforts to stem it. This has led to a reversal of UK policy. The first indication of this was the publication in 1982 of the *Treatment and rehabilitation* report of the Advisory Council on the Misuse of Drugs (ACMD). This stated "Given the widening geographical distribution of problem drug-taking and the increased variety of drugs misused, we are aware that it would be unreasonable to expect future hospital services to be developed to the point where they could provide comprehensive cover in all districts, particularly where access to specialist services is poor. We see therefore a possible role for some doctors outside the specialist services to play a role in the treatment of problem drug takers, but with strict safeguards".

Following this advice, the Medical Working Group on Drug Dependence was set up to prepare *Guidelines of good clinical practice in the treatment of drug misuse*. This working group consisted of representatives from the General Medical Council, the Royal College of General Practitioners, the Royal College of Psychiatrists, the Joint Consultants' Committee of the British Medical Association, the BMA General Medical Services Committee, and the Association of Independent Doctors in Addiction. In 1984 these *Guidelines* were published and under its guidance for General Medical Practitioners the document began: 'General practitioners are increasingly likely to see patients presenting with drug related problems in view of the increasing incidence of opioid addiction. We wish to encourage as many general practitioners as possible to treat these patients and to help them in every possible way...'. Thus, with the full consent of the medical profession's official bodies, including the BMA and its General Medical Services Committee, general practitioners were once more to be encouraged to treat drug misusers, and the *Guidelines* and subsequently the 1991 updated version,[5] have been sent to every GP in the country.

Yet in spite of the continued attempts to involve GPs, with the exception of one or two areas in the country, only a minority of GPs have been involved. Ways have been sought to remedy this situation. In 1985 the social services committee recommended that services for drug users should attract an 'item of service' fee for general practitioners. In 1986 Glanz published a survey of British GPs which found that they would probably play a more active role in the treatment of opiate drug users if more backup resources were available.[6] This encouraged the Advisory Council on the Misuse of Drugs (ACMD) to recommend in its 1988 report, *AIDS and drug misuse. Part 1*, that there should be further expansion of the number of community based drug services, which had been established in the mid-80s, with the aim of such a service being set up in every health district.[7] In the ensuing 2 years new community drug teams were established in all remaining health districts in England to support GPs who wished to treat their drug misusing patients. In 1989 the ACMD published its *AIDS and drug misuse. Part 2* report, which stated "We have concluded that a working party should be set up to consider urgently how GP involvement with drug misusers can be increased; and in particular to consider the desirability and practicability of offering financial or other incentives to GPs in respect of the treatment of drug misuse, following approved training". This recommendation was not taken up at the time, but following an initiative in Glasgow, where remuneration was given to GPs who treated drug misusers,[8] a number of other health districts have taken a similar approach. However, with the increasing burden of work passed to GPs, there has been a groundswell of opinion against the treatment of the problems of drug misuse by GPs. GP representatives have made a case to Government that such treatment should lie outside their obligatory workload (core General Medical Services) and be separately remunerated as a specialist activity.[9]

Apart from the move away from specialist to generic involvement with drug users, there have been other quite major changes in British policy over the past 2 decades, although the overall policy has consistently been a two-pronged approach: to reduce the supply of drugs via efforts by the police and customs and excise and to reduce demand through education, treatment, and rehabilitation and other community initiatives. After the setting up of the DDUs, prescribing was commonly undertaken for stimulant users, but this practice was almost completely abandoned after the first year of the operation of the DDUs. But, with the current upsurge of amphetamine use in the country and the known high risks of spreading HIV infection among injecting amphetamine users both by the sharing of injecting equipment and by 'unsafe' sexual activity, consideration once again is being given to carefully controlled prescribing for this group of drug misusers.[10] Also after the DDUs were set up, the 'British System' of maintenance prescribing for opiate users went through a number of changes. In the period 1968 to the early 1970s injectable heroin was widely prescribed by specialist psychiatrists at the DDUs. In the early 1970s there was a switch to injectable methadone maintenance, which was thought to be a safer drug. In the mid-1970s there was a general switch to oral methadone maintenance (a safer route of administration). By the early 1980s, maintenance prescribing was widely abandoned in favour of short-term detoxification to achieve abstinence, commonly over a period of 3 to 6 months. Yet in a few places the 'British System' could still be found and indeed the 1984 *Guidelines of good clinical practice in the treatment of drug misuse*,[11] which concurred with short-term prescribing, also stated 'longer term detoxification may be more suitable for patients with 5 years or more drug use...'. The updated 1991 *Guidelines* advanced on this and described 4 patterns of prescribing: rapid withdrawal (over a short period of a few weeks); gradual withdrawal (over a longer period of a few months); maintenance to abstinence (longer term withdrawal); and maintenance (stabilisation). The latter being a 'specialist form of treatment best provided by, or in consultation with, a specialist drug misuse service'.

The emergence of HIV and the risk of transmission through the sharing of injecting equipment led to a renewed preference for prescribing oral substitute drugs. Patients who had been injecting were prescribed oral methadone over the longer term (maintenance to abstinence) especially as good quality international evidence of benefit continued to mount.[12,13] The prevention of HIV transmission became especially important when it was recognised that the expected future wave of heterosexual transmission of this virus would largely occur via index cases from the drug using community, and that, if the virus could be prevented from infecting large numbers of drug users, then the wave of heterosexual infection of HIV would be much reduced. In 1985 the discovery of a high prevalence of HIV infection among Edinburgh and Dundee drug users[14] changed attitudes dramatically although other UK cities had no such problem.[15] In response to the practice developed in a few general practices in Edinburgh of supplying clean injecting equipment to drug users[16] in 1986, the McClelland Committee, at the Scottish Home and Health Department, made the radical recommendation that needle exchanges should be established in Scotland.[17] This was followed by the ACMD's 3 reports on HIV.[18,19,20] The first of these, *AIDS and drug misuse. Part 1* (1988), was also a very innovative document concerned with the prevention of HIV spread, and the enactment of its recommendations have enabled the UK to move ahead of almost all its European neighbours in effectively tackling the prevention of HIV spread amongst drug users and heterosexuals. In *AIDS and drug misuse. Part 1* it was concluded that 'The spread of HIV is a greater danger to individual public health than drug misuse. Accordingly, we believe that services which aim to minimise HIV risk behaviour by all available means should take precedence in development plans.' It became important to develop outreach services to make contact with those drug users who did not wish to seek help for their drug problem and also with recreational drug users, in order to help them move away from sharing injecting equipment and to encourage them to use condoms.

There were other important recommendations, though not all were accepted immediately. It was recommended that syringe exchange schemes should be set up, building on the success of pilot projects; and that all services for drug misusers, including general practitioners, should have the facility to provide free condoms. There were particular recommendations for Scotland and for prisons. Prescribing goals were no longer solely aimed to help the drug user become drug-free. Prescribing was recognised to be a useful tool in the prevention of HIV spread and a hierarchy of goals was proposed:

(a) the cessation of sharing of equipment.
(b) the move from injectable to oral drug use.
(c) decrease in drug misuse.
(d) abstinence.

This concept of harm minimisation, with the use of prescribing by specialists and GPs primarily for public health reasons to prevent the spread of HIV out into their local general heterosexual community, and only secondarily to help drug users address their drug problem, has been the mainstay of treatment policy since that time and there is some evidence of its efficacy.[21] While impressive in the control of the transmission of HIV, harm minimisation strategies have been less successful in preventing the epidemics of hepatitis, with estimates of between 50 and 80% of injecting drug users infected with hepatitis B and as many as 60% with hepatitis C.

Thus HIV has provoked a move to a much broader public health approach, with *all* injectors and potential injectors now being the target population, not just those seeking treatment. Anyone who was in danger of becoming infected with the virus needed to be reached and persuaded to take steps to protect themselves. Anyone who already might have been infected with HIV needed to be persuaded to take measures to protect others. For both parties the message needed to be "don't share injecting equipment (including needles, syringes, spoons, filters, and water) and take precautions for safer sex". Since that time there is evidence that efforts to reduce the sharing of injecting equipment have met with some success, but much less has been achieved in reducing unsafe sex among drug injectors.[22] With a rapidly growing pool of drug injectors, this is a cause for serious concern. Also, although there has been a fairly rapid development of outreach services, most have worked via multiple contacts with established patients, rather than acting in a front-line role maximising brief contacts with drug users who are out of touch with services. As a result there has been a perceived need for outreach services to redefine their goals and objectives, and a new structure for outreach services has been proposed.[23]

For more than two and a half decades drug use has continued to expand in the UK as it has throughout the western world. As it has grown, so the UK's response has adapted and expanded. The ACMD has addressed education[24,25] and the issue of community safety.[26] However, recommendations have not always been acted on.

In 1995 a major new initiative was launched under the white paper '*Tackling drugs together*'[27] with the setting up of multi-agency Drug Action Teams (DATs) in every health district, their membership comprising a small group of senior representatives from health, local authorities, and the criminal justice agencies, and their stated remit being to reduce the harm associated with drug use by:

(a) increasing the safety of communities from drug related crime.
(b) helping young people to resist drugs.
(c) reducing the health risk of drug misuse.

The emphasis of this being on a co-ordinated approach at community level, maintaining the two-pronged approach of both supply and demand reduction. Scotland and Wales have also published similar important local strategies.[28,29] Northern Ireland has not formulated a corresponding strategy but is pursuing an anti-drugs campaign, the *Northern Ireland Drugs Campaign* launched in 1996 and has produced a policy statement.[30]

In the UK and in America there is a growing belief that the drugs problem is more likely to be contained if there is a shift of resources from supply reduction to demand reduction. At present, throughout the country, health services for drug misusers are becoming increasingly overstretched and less able to cope with the increasing demands being placed upon them. With fixed budgets at local level there are limits to the extent to which changes can be made. The extent to which new resources can be found to provide adequate and effective ways of both preventing and coping with what is, in many parts of the country, an expanding problem of major proportions, will challenge those who are given the task of implementing the new local strategies.

Overview of drug misuse in the United Kingdom

In spite of the level of concern which surrounds drug misuse, we have a far from adequate picture of the extent and pattern of illicit use in Britain. Population statistics are readily to hand for alcohol, tobacco and prescribed medicines. However, no regular, reliable national surveys record drug misuse in the way that the nation's drinking and smoking are monitored by the General Household Survey. With no 'official' national drugs survey one of the most basic questions about drug misuse — how much of it is there? — is left unanswered. As an illegal activity, people rarely speak openly about their drug misuse, and with the limited information available, such behaviour can be subject to stereotyping and misrepresentation. In order to make effective policies and plan appropriate services, it is necessary to gain as accurate a picture as possible of the drug using population and their patterns of misuse.

Who takes drugs?

From recent surveys we can estimate that:[31,32,33,34,35,36,37,38,39,40,41]

- Around 1 in 4 (25%) of the population aged 16 and over has taken an illegal drug at some point in their life. This is around 10 million people. However, the vast majority of these will have only taken cannabis and perhaps on only a couple of occasions.

- In any year, at least 10% of the population aged 16 and over will take an illegal drug — 4 million people. Again, cannabis is the drug most likely to be used.

From these data, it is clear that the word 'drug', when applied to 'real-world' situations, effectively means 'cannabis'. Over 80% of all drug use relates to cannabis and this should be borne in mind when reading this report. However, many people who have used (or are currently using) cannabis also take other drugs: a recent national survey found that about 40% of people who had used cannabis in the last year had also taken another drug type.[42] The same survey found that over 40% of those who had used any drug at some point in their life had also used another drug.

The phrase 'at some point in their life' means precisely that: someone has taken the drug at some point in their life. There is no indication as to whether they were given the drug once at a party 30 years earlier or are currently addicted to it. 'Use in the last month' can be more generally taken to indicate that an individual is currently misusing a substance.

Age

Most drug users are young people (under the age of 35), but their drug use is by no means spread uniformly across the years. Studies agree that the use of drugs is considerably less common during the years of compulsory schooling than in the young adult years.[43] Very low rates of experimentation with drugs at the beginning of the teenage years peak by the end of them to an estimated 1 in 3 20 year olds who may have taken drugs. The pattern for volatile substance misuse differs, with use peaking in the mid-teens and then decreasing.

No survey, however, has provided the definitive answer to the sensitive issue of the extent of school age drug use. Some surveys have small samples, some large but not representative of the UK school population, and, when carried out in school, all may suffer from the probability that drug users are less likely than non-users to be in school on the day when the survey is carried out — some studies have shown that drug users are twice as likely as non-users to play truant.[44]

In 1994, however, nearly 50,000 schoolchildren were surveyed in Exeter University's annual poll.[45] Although this yearly survey is far from perfect, its size and regularity make it a valuable source of data. A quarter of 14-15 year olds and a third of 15-16 year olds said that they had taken drugs. This result is very similar to those in 1993 and 1992. The Exeter University surveys stretch back a decade and can be used to gain an idea of trends in young people's drug use. Interestingly enough, the most significant trend has been in the use of cannabis — in 1988, 3% of 14-15 year olds said they had tried it; by 1993 this was 16% and by 1994, 23%. The Health Education Authority undertook a survey of 5020 11-35 year olds by interview throughout England in 1995. Of these, 4932 answered questions on personal drug use on an anonymous self-completion questionnaire. It found that 45% had taken at least one drug, with use most likely among 20-22 year olds. Cannabis was confirmed as by far the most commonly taken drug.

Perhaps the results arousing most concern in 1995 were those reported in *Drugs Futures*, the account of a 3 year study of young people in the North West of England.[46] Seven hundred and seventy six 14-15 year olds were studied in the first year, 752 15-16 year olds in the second, and 523 16-17 year olds in the third. By this last year, 51% said they had taken drugs.

Another major survey was carried out in 1992, referred to as the 'Four City' study. Five thousand people aged 16 and over, in 4 urban centres, were questioned by researchers from Sheffield University.[47] Not only did each location provide a main sample of 1,000 people, but also a 'booster' group of 250 young people who, because they were of low socio-economic status and lived in deprived inner-city areas, were felt to be most 'at risk' of drug use. The results show, however, that levels of use were similar in the main sample and the socially deprived 'booster' group. In the main sample, 36% of 16-19 year olds and 41% of 20-24 year olds had taken drugs, while in the 'booster group' 42% of 16-19 year olds and 44% of 20-24 year olds had taken drugs. The booster group figures suggest that 1 in 4 of those living in Britain's deprived areas have used a drug in the last year, 1 in 3 have taken cannabis at some time, and as many as 1 in 2 will have used drugs at least once in their lives.

In 1995 a national survey was undertaken of 7722 pupils aged 15 and 16 in 70 secondary schools throughout the UK. This revealed that 42.3% had taken an illicit drug, mainly cannabis, at some time, with 43% of boys and 38% of girls having tried cannabis. Levels of drug use were higher in Scotland than in England, Wales or Northern Ireland. The results confirm a large rise in drug experimentation among this age group since 1989.[48]

Gender

In 1994 over 10,000 people in England and Wales aged 16 to 59 were interviewed about their experience of and attitudes towards crime in the British Crime Survey.[49] Three quarters of respondents completed an anonymous questionnaire about drug misuse in which half of the men (50%) between 16 and 29 said they had tried a drug in the past while over a third of women (36%) in the same age range had tried a drug. Results were similar for the 11-35 age group surveyed by the Health Education Authority in 1995, which found that 49% of men had ever taken a drug compared with 39% of women.[50] While the use of most drugs is commonest among young men, women seem to be equally likely to have used volatile substances compared with men.[51]

Socio-economic status

The British Crime Survey found at all ages that drug use was reported by a greater proportion of those in households where the head was employed in a non-manual occupation than in those where the head was in a manual occupation. At no age and for no particular drug was drug use more prevalent in households headed by someone in a manual occupation than by someone in a non-manual one. The Four City survey found that overall the most likely user would be in the AB or C1 socio-economic groups (professional and skilled workers). ABs from the main sample were twice as likely to have ever used a drug than C2s (semi-skilled workers), and were more likely to have recently used any drug including heroin. Among 11-35 year olds, the Health Education Authority found that socio-economic groups AB, C1 and E (unskilled workers) appear slightly more likely than other groups to have come into contact with drugs.

As already mentioned, there is however a difference between someone who may use drugs rarely and someone who uses them regularly. Socio-economic status may play a part in this (though it cannot be said to be a causal relationship). When examining 'patterns of use,' the Four City survey found that of those C2s and DEs (unskilled workers) who did use drugs, they did so more frequently and were more likely to inject than ABs and C1s. Thus — as a socio-economic group — professional and skilled workers were most likely to take drugs, but the drug use of unskilled workers was more frequent, using more dangerous methods of administration.

Ethnicity

Detailed information on drug misuse by different ethnic groups is difficult to obtain and the current literature therefore provides a rather limited picture. The Four City study traced ethnicity, and found that over half the white respondents in one location's booster group had taken drugs while only a third of black respondents had. This result is supported by the British Crime Survey, which was also able to recruit a valid ethnic mix (a rarity amongst drug surveys). There was hardly any difference between white and African-Caribbean drug use, with around 30% of each saying that they had ever taken a drug. This compares with 15% (1 in 7) of Pakistani and Bangladeshi respondents. White people were more likely than African-Caribbeans to take amphetamine, LSD or magic mushrooms, and there was little difference between the proportions saying they had used cannabis, ecstasy or cocaine. Only 1 in 10 Indian respondents had taken a drug, but none had used heroin, contrasted with 1% of whites and African-Caribbeans, and 4% of Pakistanis and Bangladeshis.

Drugs categorised by pharmacological action

Table 1: Drugs that depress the nervous system

Drug group	Principal drugs		Legal status	Recommended medical uses
	Scientific names	Trade names		
Benzodiazepines	Minor Tranquillisers: diazepam chlordiazepoxide lorazepam oxazepam nitrazepam flurazepam triazolam temazepam flunitrazepam	Valium Librium Ativan Serenid Mogadon Dalmane Halcion Normison Rohypnol	Prescription Only Medicines. Controlled drugs but legal to possess without a prescription, (except temazepam).	Relieve anxiety. Promote sleep in insomnia. Detoxification from alcohol dependency.
Solvents and gases	toluene petrol butane trichloroethylene trichloroethane	glue lighter fuel aerosols cleaning fluid cleaning fluid	In UK illegal to sell knowingly for inhalation. In Scotland misusers may be taken into care.	None
Alcoholic beverages	ethyl alcohol or ethanol	beers wines spirits liqueurs alcopops	Can be bought by adults (18+) and drunk outside a pub bar by children (5+). Need a licence to sell.	

Table 2: Drugs that alter perceptual function

Drug group	Principal drugs		Legal status	Recommended medical uses
	Scientific names	Trade names		
LSD	lysergic acid diethylamide and lysergide		Controlled drugs; LSD not available for medical use.	None
Hallucinogenic mushrooms ('magic' mushrooms)	psilocybe semilanceata (contains psilocybin and psilocin)		If prepared for use may be a controlled drug. Otherwise unrestricted.	None
	amanita muscaria (Fly Agaric)		Unrestricted	
Cannabis	cannabis sativa (contains tetrahydro-cannabinol) herbal cannabis cannabis resin cannabis oil		Controlled drugs; not available for medical use except synthetic form (Nabilone) available for medical use. Dronabinal (cannabis derivative) can be prescribed but not yet licensed. Illegal to allow premises to be used for smoking cannabis.	None, although synthetic form and cannabis derivative may be prescribed as anti-nausea drugs.
Khat	catha edulis (contains cathinone and cathine — norpseudo-ephedrine)		Khat itself is not a controlled drug but its active ingredients cathinone and cathine are Class C drugs. Cathinone may not be lawfully possessed, supplied, etc except under a licence for research.	No licensed use in the UK.
Mescaline	mescaline (found in the peyote and SanPedro cacti)		Mescaline is a Class A drug. The cacti are unrestricted unless prepared for use in which case they could be regarded as Class A by the courts.	None

Table 3: Drugs that reduce pain

Drug group	Principal drugs		Legal status	Recommended medical uses
	Scientific names	Trade names		
Opiates, opioids, narcotic analgesics	diacetylmorphine, diamorphine or heroin		Prescription Only Medicines. Controlled drugs.	Pain relief, cough suppression, anti-diarrhoea agents. Treatment of opiate dependence (methadone).
	dipipanone	Diconal		
	methadone	Physeptone		
	buprenorphine	Temgesic		
	pethidine	Pamergan, Pethilorfan		
	dextromoramide	Palfium		
	dextroprop-oxyphene	Distalgesic (Includes paracetamol)		
	pentazocine	Fortagesic, Fortral		
	phenazocine	Narphen		
	opium	Gee's Linctus*, Cyclimorph,	Prescription Only Medicines, except in the form of some very dilute mixtures (*) available without prescription from pharmacies.	
	morphine	Oramorph, Sevredol, kaolin & morphine*		
	codeine	Codafen*, Durogesic	Controlled drugs, but (*) legal to possess without a prescription.	

Table 4: Drugs that affect the endocrine system

Drug group	Principal drugs		Legal status	Recommended medical uses
	Scientific names	Trade names		
Steroids	anabolic steroids	Nadrolone Stanozolol Dianabol Durabolin Deca-durabolin	Prescription only medicines. Class C under the Misuse of Drugs Act	Persistent anaemia. Protein build-up.

Table 5: Drugs that stimulate the nervous system

Drug group	Principal drugs		Legal status	Recommended medical uses
	Scientific names	Trade names		
Amphetamines and amphetamine-like drugs	Amphetamines: amphetamine sulphate dexamphetamine (combination of the above)		Prescription Only Medicines. Controlled drugs.	Treatment of narcolepsy and hyperkinesea.
	Amphetamine-like drugs: methylphenidate phentermine pemoline fenfluramine dexfenfluramine	Ritalin Ionamin, Duromine Volital Ponderax Adifax		Short term treatment of obesity, and attention deficit disorder in children (Ritalin).
Cocaine	cocaine hydrochloride		Prescription Only Medicines.	Rarely prescribed. Local anaesthetic.
	cocaine freebase		Controlled drugs.	
Alkyl nitrites	amyl nitrite		Prescription only medicine.	None
	butyl nitrite isobutyl nitrite		Unrestricted.	None
Hallucinogenic amphetamines	methylenedioxyam-phetamine - MDA 3,4-methylene-dioxymethylam-phetamine, MDMA also known as Ecstasy MDEA		Controlled drugs; not available for medical use.	None
Tobacco	tobacco nicotiana tabacum nicotiana rustica nicotiana persica	Tobacco Cigarettes Snuff	Illegal to sell to children under 16.	None

What drugs are taken

Cannabis

As already stated, cannabis is undoubtedly the most widely misused drug in the UK. The 1994 British Crime Survey[52] found that of the 16-59 year olds questioned in England and Wales:

- 21% admitted to having ever used cannabis.

- 8% said that they had used cannabis the previous year (only 2% a decade earlier).

The Four City study found that:

- 15% of the main sample had used cannabis, i.e. 1 in 7 of the general population aged 16 and over – at least 7 million people.

- 7% of the main sample had taken cannabis in the last year, again broadly in line with the British Crime Survey findings.

In the British Crime Survey, current use of cannabis was primarily limited to the under-30s. Thirty-four per cent of 16-29 year olds said they had taken cannabis at some time, while 29% of 16-19 year olds and 23% of 20-24 year olds said they had used the drug in the last year. The corresponding figure for recent use by those in their 30s was nearer 3% and for those over 40, under 2%. The Health Education Authority survey found that of the 11-35 year olds in England questioned 37% had ever taken cannabis, and 11% had used cannabis in the last month.

A regular cannabis user might smoke 1 or 2 'joints' (cannabis cigarettes) several times a week shared among a small group of friends. In total this might use up about a sixteenth of an ounce of cannabis resin,[53] at a cost of about £7.50.[54]

Heroin, cocaine and crack cocaine

These drugs have been taken by perhaps 1 or 2% of the population. This minimal level of use, when compared to that of cannabis, should not imply minimal concern — 1% of 20-50 year olds is still a quarter of a million people.[55] Furthermore, although the British Crime Survey did find that about 1% of the population said they had taken heroin at least once in their lives, 4% of 25-29 year olds claimed to have taken cocaine.

The Four City survey found that heroin, cocaine and crack (a different form of cocaine which is purer and can be smoked) had been used by 1% or less of the main sample. As for the booster group of young people 'at risk', crack was used by 1%, but heroin and cocaine use had risen to 2% and 4% respectively.

A dependent heroin user might inject or smoke a quarter to a third of a gram a day, at a cost of about £30, while a heavy cocaine user may take a gram a day costing about £100.[56] Recent anecdotal evidence suggests that these prices may have dropped to £20 and £50 respectively. A regular crack user could consume far higher quantities – perhaps 10 grams or more over a weekend – at a cost of well over £1000.[57]

The 1994 British Crime Survey, however, did find that 3% of African-Caribbean women (as opposed to only 1% of white women) had taken crack, observing that 'The use of crack runs at fairly low levels among both whites and Afro-Caribbeans, although it is just slightly more common for the latter group'.[58]

Regarding numbers of injectors, all surveys indicate that fewer than 1% of people have ever injected a drug. By way of example, a household survey of nearly 19,000 people conducted in the early 1990s found that 0.8 % of men and 0.4 % of women had ever injected a non-prescribed drug.[59] The Four City study, however, did find a variable related to injecting: only 0.2 % of those who were employed (7 respondents out of 3,700) had ever injected but 5% of the sample who were presently unemployed had injected at some time in their lives.

Temazepam

A recent trend in illicit drug use has been the non-medical use of the benzodiazepine temazepam. In particular, the drug has acquired a reputation for easy injection rather than oral use. This type of use began in Scotland in the mid-80s, as individuals looked for a more easily available and cheaper injectable heroin substitute. In 1989, the manufacturers changed the formulation of temazepam capsules from liquid to gel, to prevent users injecting the drug, but the practice continued with the potential for even worse damage as molten jelly cools and solidifies in blood vessels.[60]

Since the mid 1980s, temazepam has spread from the small population of injectors into oral use among the wider population of young people attending nightclubs and 'raves', but only as one among many cheap and legal alternatives to ecstasy and LSD. In 1992, the Advisory Council on the Misuse of Drugs called for a tightening up on the prescription of temazepam, and after nearly 3 years which have witnessed temazepam virtually taking over as 'the street drug of Glasgow', the government has rescheduled the drug so that it is now illegal to possess it without a prescription. They have also banned the gel-filled capsule formulation of the drug from prescription on the NHS, effectively outlawing its legal use. Misuse of benzodiazepines generally seems to be commonest among the socially disadvantaged with less formal education, some experience of criminality or imprisonment, and with polydrug use. Misuse is patchy across Britain, but in Edinburgh, benzodiazepines have taken over from heroin as the most commonly misused drug,[61] at an average cost ranging from 50 pence to £2.00 per tablet.[62]

Volatile substances

The misuse of volatile substances seems to become common in very localised areas, perhaps confined to an estate or a school, and sometimes disappearing as quickly as it arose. Recent studies suggest that typically 4-8% of secondary school pupils have tried solvents, and that sniffing peaks around the third and fourth years of secondary schooling.[63,64] Volatile substance misuse can be extremely dangerous and from 1985 to 1991, over 100 people died every year from it. Since then, partly due to a television campaign by the Department of Health, the annual number of deaths has fallen below that figure. In 1994, 57 people died, over half of whom were aged 14-17 years.[65]

Amphetamine, LSD and ecstasy

The most significant increase in drug use in the last decade is in the use of so-called 'dance drugs' — amphetamine, LSD and ecstasy (methylenedioxy-methamphetamine-MDMA) — which have become the most popular drugs after cannabis[66] since their use at all-night raves and warehouse parties in the late 1980s, although this is not the only context within which they are taken.[67]

In 1988, Exeter University asked 34,000 school children about their drug use.[68] Only 1% of 15-16 year olds had taken either amphetamine or LSD; by the 1994 survey, this had increased ten-fold to over 10% for each drug, while ecstasy use stood at about 4%.

Certainly, amphetamine and hallucinogens (LSD and 'magic' mushrooms) were revealed to be the next most popular drugs after cannabis in the Four City study. The British Crime Survey found 11% of 16-19 year olds trying amphetamine, 9% ecstasy, and 8% LSD.

The Four City survey also explored the associations between drug types. Certain drugs were found to be 'mutually used' — when one of these drugs is taken, the user will invariably use another as well. Chief among these were LSD, amphetamine and ecstasy, each of which is likely to be used with 1 of the other 2.

Ecstasy is taken in tablet form and a typical user may take 1 or 2 when at a dance club, at a cost of about £30. Amphetamine is normally sold in powder form, and a heavy user might consume up to 8 grams a day, costing about £80. LSD is marketed in single dose units (usually absorbed on paper squares) selling for a few pounds each.[69]

Performance enhancing drugs

Unlike most other illicit drugs anabolic steroids are misused for their physical rather than psychoactive effects in order to build up muscle tissue. Use is common among those devoted to building muscular strength[70] and has recently become evident among young people who simply want to 'look good'. Steroids also have a 'functional' role in occupations where strength is a desirable asset. Anabolic steroid use appears to be spread through many parts of the UK. Since 1st September 1996 steroids have been classified under Class C of the Misuse of Drugs Act. It is now an offence to supply or possess steroids with intent to supply, but unlike other drugs in schedule 3 it is not illegal to possess them for personal use. A wide range of steroids are available via illicit manufacture, or diversion of pharmaceuticals, some of which may have been intended for veterinary use only. Although there are few available statistics on the use of steroids, a UK survey of 21 gymnasia found steroid use reported in all but 3. The average age of first use was 21.

The average cost of a course of steroids (about 16 weeks) is £140. Data relating to a Scottish college of technology showed 4.4% of the men and 1% of the women had used steroids.[71] Most are distributed through public gymnasia, bodybuilding clubs and the like. These drugs can be taken orally or injected. Many steroid users inject; one needle exchange in a town where bodybuilding is particularly popular, records that over a quarter of its clients are steroid users[72] and in the same town 81% of steroid users contacted through gyms and sporting clubs had injected.[73] This figure was confirmed in a study undertaken in the North West of England between 1995 and 1996.[74] The same study found AS easily available to all those wishing to use them. It confirmed steroid use as a predominantly male activity, with a majority in full time employment.

There are also reports of abuse of nalbuphine hydrochloride among anabolic steroid users to allow them to continue training despite musculoskeletal pain either from training or from sports injuries. Nalbuphine is an opioid licensed for the treatment of moderate to severe pain, and is only available in injectable form.[75]

Nitrites ('poppers')

Amyl nitrite is classified as a prescription only medicine under the Medicines Act 1968 (until 1997 it was a pharmacy medicine). In the past it was used in the treatment of angina. Its partner among the alkyl nitrites is butyl nitrite. This variant is not classified as a medicine and is not subject to Medicines Act restrictions as long as it is not sold as a medicine. Neither substance is controlled under the Misuse of Drugs Act.

Butyl nitrite is sold in sex shops, pubs, clubs, and bars at about £2-£3 a bottle under such brand names as 'Rush', 'Ram' and 'Thrust'. Some outlets have advertised 'English poppers', believed to be amyl nitrite, possibly from pharmaceutical sources.[76]

The vapours of these drugs are inhaled to give a short-lived 'rush'. Nitrites' muscle relaxant properties are also used by some gay men to enhance sexual activity. A study of 102 male prostitutes in Edinburgh in 1988 found that 22% used amyl or butyl nitrite monthly.[77]

Nitrites are also used as a 'dance drug'.[78,79] Perhaps 5-10% of older teenagers have tried these drugs,[80] more in some areas.[81]

Other drugs

Barbiturate use in Britain has largely fallen away from the levels of concern experienced in the 1970s and early 1980s. Between October and March 1994, only 9 people who used barbiturates as their main drug started 'new episodes' with English drug agencies (out of a total of 17,864), and only 60 reported using barbiturates at all.[82] Up-to-date figures are not available for the street prices of barbiturates. However barbiturates are still found as adulterants (cutting agents) in heroin. There are many other drugs — both legal and illegal — which are misused by small numbers of people. They include cyclizine, ketamine, Khat, 'GHB' (gammahydroxybutyrate) and '2CB' (4-Bromo-2,5-dimethoxy-phenethylamine). While their use may cause users difficulties, they are not sufficiently established as major drugs to have received much attention from researchers and policy-makers alike.

Over-the-counter medicines

Over-the-counter (OTC) medicines can be bought by the public without a doctor's prescription. In Britain and Ireland there are two categories of over-the-counter drugs: those on the general sales list which can be sold in any shop, and those which may only be sold by registered pharmacists. Most self medication is designed for common problems of the skin, colds, coughs, sore throats and for pain relief.

Misuse of over-the-counter preparations is likely to be for any opiate-like, sedative or stimulant effects. Tincture of opium is included as a cough suppressant in some preparations while the morphine in kaolin and morphine is intended to combat diarrhoea. Codeine is similar to morphine, but much less potent and is used as a cough suppressant and analgesic, as well as for diarrhoea. Medicines with stimulant-like effects include nasal decongestants or cough syrups containing ephedrine. Cough suppressant tablets containing ephedrine, caffeine and theophylline, are misused for their amphetamine like effect.

Virtually all OTC medicines liable to misuse are not on the general sales list and are only available from pharmacists, who may refuse to sell them if they suspect misuse. An up-to-date list of products known to be abused nationally appears in the Royal Pharmaceutical Society's Guide for pharmacists — *Medicines, ethics and practice* in which its code of ethics states that 'Every pharmacist must be aware of any problems in his area, whether or not they are general, or known to the Society. He or she should be aware of any products which are sold in excessive quantities or with abnormal frequency. Almost any product can be misused and the guidance given [below] is not exhaustive.'[83]

Misusers of illicit drugs may turn to OTC preparations when they are unable to obtain their usual drugs — three bottles of codeine linctus are roughly equivalent to a quarter gram of street heroin. They may also be used to enhance or mitigate the effects of other drugs they are using.[84] However some individuals restrict their misuse to OTC medicines, dependence on which may have developed through prolonged use for a legitimate medical purpose. It has been estimated that 20,000 people in the UK could be dependent on OTC medicines.[85]

A survey of injecting drug users attending an NHS drug treatment facility, many of whom were polydrug users, showed that 66% had misused OTC medication at some point. A high proportion had misused OTC preparations in the previous twelve months. Fifty three per cent had misused OTC medication containing a stimulant and 38% had misused those containing opiates. It is interesting to note that of those who misused stimulant containing preparations 46% did so for their own sake irrespective of the availability of street drugs.[86]

A recently established independent drugs agency in Dumfries, Scotland, specifically for those with OTC drug problems, found that women aged 25-45 and men aged 40-50 were particularly represented among its clients. This is older than those using illicit drugs. The main concentrations of clients were found in London and central Scotland especially the Strathclyde and Lothian regions.[87]

Increasing availability

In a move towards greater self-prescribing, Britain's drug licensing body, the Medicines Control Agency, has deregulated 27 prescription only drugs since 1992 for sale by pharmacists. Among the reasons behind this move are greater convenience for patients and government's desire to reduce the NHS drugs budget by transferring the cost direct to the consumers.[88] In the process of converting prescription-only medicines to OTC preparations, there has been a move to reduce the quantity of active drug, eg. in Paramol the codeine content was reduced from 10mg to 7.5mg. If this is intended to reduce misuse, it is questionable whether it is effective and may serve to increase the likelihood of paracetamol overdose among misusers.

Current national activity

Tackling drugs together

The British Government's strategy addressing drug misuse has been in place since the mid-1980s. The UK-wide plan was first outlined in 1985's *Tackling drug misuse: A summary of the government's strategy*,[89] but in 1994/5 each of the countries in the UK developed their own strategies for the next 3 years.

In 1995, after an extensive consultation period, the Government published the White Paper *Tackling drugs together*, outlining the strategy for England for 1995-1998.[90] Although much of it is specific to England, the general thrust of the strategy applies to the rest of Britain. Scotland's strategy has already been implemented,[91] and a Welsh strategy is currently being implemented.

The strategy is built on the following Statement of Purpose, focusing on crime, young people and public health:

"To take effective action by vigorous law enforcement, accessible treatment and a new emphasis on education and prevention to:

- increase the safety of communities from drug-related crime;

- reduce the acceptability and availability of drugs to young people; and

- reduce the health risks and other damage related to drug misuse."

To realise the above goals, there is a new emphasis on multi-agency co-ordination and demand minimisation. At the national level, this will be achieved by the Ministerial Sub-Committee of the Cabinet on the Misuse of Drugs (which co-ordinates the government's policies), the Central Drugs Co-ordination Unit (which acts as a liaison body between government departments) and the Advisory Council on the Misuse of Drugs. Over a hundred new Drug Action Teams (DATs) are being established to carry out the strategy at the local level. These will be made up of senior representatives from the police, probation and prison services, local authorities (including education and social services) and health authorities, with co-option of voluntary sector representation encouraged. In Wales there are 5 drug and alcohol action teams. Perhaps the best medical example of local multi-agency co-ordination is the emphasis given by the strategy to 'shared care', a partnership approach between drug agencies, doctors and pharmacists to provide appropriate levels of care to drug misusers.

Policing and enforcement activities

Police

Currently police enforcement arrangements are based on the model recommended in the 1985 report by the Working Party on Drug Related Crime, commissioned by the Association of Chief Police Officers (ACPO) Crime Committee (The 'Broome' Report).[92] This model bases police operational strategy on a three-tiered approach with divisional personnel responding to small scale and local drug offences and drug related crime; Force Drugs Squads operating against medium level dealers and co-ordinating force information on drugs and a third tier of regional/national level action through Regional Crime Squads and HM Customs and Excise, operating against national and international dealers, supported by the National Criminal Intelligence Service.

Preventing drug related crime is one of the Home Secretary's 5 key objectives for policing.[93] *Tackling drugs together* defines drug related crime as any criminal activity which is committed either to fund or as a consequence of drug misuse. This includes:

* all offences under the Misuse of Drugs Act 1971;

* criminal acts by persons acting as a consequence of drug misuse;

* acquisitive crime (such as theft, burglary and fraud) to finance drug misuse;

* the laundering of the profits of drug trafficking, either to fund further smuggling attempts or to allow unrestricted use of the assets; and

* violent crime carried out in the course of drug distribution and trafficking (for example, violence between dealers or against innocent parties).

This therefore includes the crimes of manufacture/cultivation, supply and possession of drugs, which are not usually (or elsewhere in this report) included in the definition of drug related crime.

The Government's national drugs strategy is intended to influence local policing strategies, with an emphasis on multi-agency partnership, and each police force has published its own formal drugs strategy in response to *Tackling drugs together*. These strategies have been examined by HM Inspectorate of Constabulary to ensure consistency with key policing objectives and the inclusion of the elements required by the White Paper. The Inspectorate highlighted examples of good practice and recommended that police forces' drugs strategies should be re-examined on a regular basis. It also considered that the three-tier model recommended by the 'Broome' Report should be reviewed to assess whether it is still relevant.[94]

There has been an increase in the use of cautioning for drug offences rising from 2,000 to 44,000, from 1984 to 1994 compared with an increase in convictions over the same period from 18,700 to 34,600.[95] The Task Force supported the use of cautioning as effective against re-offending in the case of some drug misusers, but recommended that it should be used consistently. In Scotland, cautioning is not available.

Customs and Excise

HM Customs and Excise and the police services have responsibility for enforcing drugs legislation. There is a degree of overlap in their work, but guidelines specify that Customs have the primary responsibility for dealing with the illegal import and export of drugs, while the police have responsibility for dealing with offences of manufacture, supply and possession.

Following the 1994 Customs and Excise fundamental expenditure review, the total force of 5000 customs staff concerned with drugs (including investigation and intelligence staff) has been reduced by 292 front line anti-smuggling staff. As a result a new strategy has been introduced involving flexible intelligence-led response teams, the efficacy of which has been monitored and the results will determine whether a further 300 front-line drugs staff will be lost.

National Criminal Intelligence Service

The National Criminal Intelligence Service (NCIS) brings together staff from both police and customs. It collects and collates information relating to current drugs operations and distributes intelligence to both services. NCIS is staffed by police, Customs and civilian personnel and has 5 regional offices and a dedicated Drugs Division comprising over 100 staff.

Arrest Referral Schemes

It has been estimated that one fifth of those on probation are problem drug misusers, 11% of convicted male prisoners and 23% of convicted female prisoners have been assessed as drug dependent on admission to prison.[96] The use of this contact with the authorities for getting problem drug misusers into treatment has been encouraged by the Task Force and the NHS Executive in its draft guidance on purchasing effective treatment and care for drug misusers.[97]

Most police forces operate some form of Arrest Referral Scheme, but the extent of this varies with some only providing contact numbers for drug treatment services and others providing a structured response with contactable drug workers.[98] Results reported are promising and the Task Force has recommended that Arrest Referral Schemes should be provided at each police station and that Drug Action Teams should consider whether there are cost benefits to provision of support from specialist drug workers.

The Scottish Ministerial Task Force's report considers 'diversion schemes' where treatment can provide an alternative to prosecution, and recommends that this may be appropriate in particular cases. While continuing to emphasise the need to punish those involved in major dealing/supply, it recommends that decisions on diversion from prosecution should be made on the basis of the circumstances of the individual drug misuser and the alleged offence.[99]

Prison Service

The reduction of drug use in prisons is 1 of 10 strategic priorities identified by the Prison Service in England and Wales in the 1994-97 Corporate Plan. The Scottish Prison Service has also issued guidance on managing prisoners who misuse drugs.[100] As of April 1996, mandatory drug testing has been introduced in all Britain's prisons — every month, 10% of each penal establishment's population is randomly tested, and if the results are positive, inmates can be penalised with administrative sanctions (such as the loss of remission or the curtailing of visits). During the pilot programme of testing from January to May 1995, drugs tested for were opiates, amphetamines, cannabinoids, methadone, benzodiazepines, barbituates and LSD.

Probation Service

The Association of Chief Officers of Probation stated, "the Probation Service's roots lie in Victorian attempts to break the link between alcohol and crime".[101] The Service therefore has a role to play in dealing with drug-using offenders, a role which was explicitly recognised by the White Paper, *Tackling Drugs Together*.

In 1991, the ACMD published a report which examined the role of the Probation Service in dealing with drug misusers and which made several recommendations as to community sentencing.[102] Last year, the Probation Service published its response to the report which also acted as a response to *Tackling drugs together*.[103]

The response was in the form of guidelines which advised that local policies and strategies should be put in place to address the problem of drug use amongst offenders on probation. Among the key issues of good practice which the guidelines highlighted were the provision of appropriate services for offenders, the involvement of probation services in the community care planning process, involvement of drug specialists in the preparation of pre-sentence reports and also the potential use of probation orders with conditions of treatment as sentencing options.

Education and prevention in schools

Requirements for drug education can be found both in the mandatory National Curriculum in England and Wales and in the wider curriculum offered by schools. In 1995 the Government issued guidance to schools, directing them towards teaching about the risks associated with drug use and also advising how to develop school drug policies and deal with drug incidents.[104] The implementation of this guidance will be monitored by Ofsted. Drug education in schools was addressed by the Advisory Council on the Misuse of Drugs in 1993.[105] The issue of drug education is a highly controversial one, as — despite attempts by groups who believe in it and by groups who oppose it — little rigorous long-term evaluation has been undertaken to date.

In Scotland, drug education is taught as one element of health education which is offered in all schools. The school curriculum is not laid down by Parliament, and responsibility lies with education authorities and head teachers to decide the broad scope and detailed content of study programmes. In Northern Ireland issues relating to drugs are taught as part of health education which is a theme integrated into subjects across the curriculum. Health education is mandatory and schools are required to keep a written, up-to-date statement of curriculum policy including health education.

Education and prevention in the community

The Home Office Drugs Prevention Initiative was set up in 1990 to encourage local communities to undertake drug prevention activities. In some areas Drugs Prevention Teams work with local residents, businesses, religious organisations, the voluntary sector and local press and radio. Through their work, they aim to raise drug awareness, educate and train people, provide alternative activities to drug use and support community and environmental development. Since its launch, the Drugs Prevention Initiative has financially supported over 1,500 specific projects, as well as contributing to the development and co-ordination of local drug prevention strategies. Between 1990 and 1995, each of the 20 Drug Prevention Teams had £75,000 per year to grant aid to local prevention work.[106] *Tackling drugs together* recast the teams into 12 larger teams to cover expanded areas and to be funded until 1999.

National Drugs Helpline

The UK Health Departments jointly fund the National Drugs Helpline which provides a free, confidential 24-hour advice and information service for drug misusers, their family and friends and others. For limited hours each week a number of ethnic language lines are also available, including Welsh, Bengali, Punjabi, Gujarati, Urdu, Hindi, Cantonese, Italian, Portuguese and Spanish. It also provides free, printed literature and has been widely advertised. Following evaluation the National Drugs Helpline's funding has been confirmed until March 1998.

Social care

The NHS and Community Care Act 1990 changed fundamentally the organisational and funding arrangements in the NHS and local authorities, introducing purchaser-provider divisions within the NHS and giving lead responsibility to local authorities to provide care for a range of patient groups. Under the legislation, each local authority is responsible for assessing the needs of its population for social care and must define a level of need for which it accepts responsibility to make provision, which includes the needs of drug and alcohol users.[107] Thus instead of always providing these services themselves, local authorities are responsible for managing care which they purchase from a range of providers which, in relation to drug services, often includes the voluntary sector. Since 1991 there has also been a specific grant for which local authorities in England can apply for providing services to drug (and alcohol) misusers from voluntary sector organisations. Priority has been given to developing community based alternatives to residential care.[108]

Health authorities are also involved in the provision of services to drug misusers, and the Advisory Council on the Misuse of Drugs has recommended that health and local authorities work together in identifying and meeting health and social care needs of their drug misusing populations.[109]

Many aspects of the operation of community care in alcohol and drug services have received criticism. A study undertaken of its workings was completed after its first year and its findings included a lack of collaboration between local and health authorities in purchasing services; inadequate budgets for local authorities to purchase services (meeting only 70% of the cost of residential care in 1993-94); excessive paperwork for providers and a market where competition fragmented provision and discouraged co-operation between providers.[110] Although some good practice was noted, problems were still found in SCODA's later survey (1995-96) which showed that the implementation of community care assessment and funding procedures varied largely between local authorities. Funding allocations were under-prioritised and insufficient, and the majority of drug service providers reported that they considered access to residential services had been reduced as a result of community care. The Social Service Inspectorate's own inspection report in 1995 found community care assessments to be resource rather than needs led, and only conducted in response to requests for residential care. Furthermore, no patient or carer was involved in the planning process of services.[111] The Task Force endorsed the recommendations of the Social Services Inspectorate and proposed that priority be given to services for drug misusers, with particular attention on young people.[112]

Public health

Health Authorities are responsible for ensuring that their local populations receive appropriate health education and promotion information, and part of their work is necessarily drug-related. Allied to this general health promotion is work specifically targeted at both drug misusers in touch with services and at those hard-to-reach populations which are not known to drug agencies. Health services not only aim to provide a comprehensive range of local services to help drug misusers give up drugs, but also seek to reduce the harm that drug users can do to themselves. A central element to this 'harm minimisation' programme has been the provision of clean needles and syringes to drug injectors. This was advised by the ACMD as a means of containing the spread of HIV.[113] More than 300 needle and syringe exchange schemes have been set up since the mid-1980s. Since April 1991, there has also been a specific grant payable to local authorities in England which enables them to support voluntary organisations providing services to drug and alcohol misusers. A total of £8.2 million has so far been provided.

Treatment

In April 1994, the Department of Health commissioned a wide-ranging review of English drug treatment services, The Task Force to Review Services for Drug Misusers (commonly known as the 'Effectiveness Review'). This aims to determine how effective different treatment modalities are, and the National Treatment Outcome Research Study yet to be published (which specifically looks at methadone treatment) is its core project. The Task Force's findings were published in April 1996. It endorsed the Government's multi-agency approach[114] and found positive benefits to both the drug user and the community from a range of interventions. Reaching drug misusers not in contact with services was therefore felt to be important. The Task Force recommended that all treatment be monitored and available quickly to those seeking it. No single form of service delivery or medical treatment was preferred as the wide range of individual needs were seen to require tailored care. Purchasers were therefore advised to gain access to the full range of services, and particular benefits were observed from specialists in drug dependence units (DDUs) and residential rehabilitation programmes, and through methadone reduction and oral methadone maintenance programmes. Although abstinence was the ultimate aim of treatment, small gains were encouraged where this was not achievable. According to the Task Force, the provision of 'shared care' between GPs and specialist services, approved in the Government's *Tackling drugs together* should be made as widely available as possible. There were many other recommendations regarding, amongst other issues, the provision of care in prisons, hepatitis B vaccination, and syringe exchange schemes (see Appendix III for a summary of the Task Force's recommendations).

European activities

At a European level, the EU has developed a broad framework for action in its plan to combat drugs.[115] It recommends action to be taken by Member States in 3 main areas: demand reduction, criminal justice and international aspects of drug misuse. Demand reduction covers prevention, social reintegration and action with high risk groups. Among their goals, EU action plans and programmes aim to provide a context within which doctors can exchange information and experience with colleagues elsewhere in Europe.

Following Article 129 of the Maastricht Treaty which gave the EU a remit in public health, the European Monitoring Centre for Drugs and Drug Addiction (EMCDDA), a European Community information centre, was established in 1994.

Its aims, to provide 'objective, reliable and comparable information at European level concerning drugs and drug addiction and their consequences', are described in more detail in its Annual Report on the State of the Drugs Problem in the European Union 1995.[116] Further information about the EMCDDA's activities can be obtained from its operational focus in the UK, the Institute for the Study of Drug Dependence.

2

Defining the problem

Concepts and definitions

The use of drugs (including alcohol and tobacco) for non-medical purposes is a little understood aspect of human behaviour. The most extensive and solid scientific work on drugs relates to their chemical composition and effects on laboratory animals. We also know something about the characteristics of people whose use of drugs has caused them medical, social or legal problems (they are the users most likely to come to the attention of doctors, drug services or the police). However, information derived from these sources does not particularly contribute to our understanding of drug use, nor how social and psychological processes can influence the outcome of drug-taking behaviour.

The psychological and physiological effects of drug-taking are most strongly influenced by the amount taken and the chemical make-up of the drug, and secondly whether the drug is new to the individual, what the user wants and expects to happen (their 'set'), the surroundings in which it is taken (the 'setting'), and the reactions of other people.[1] All these influences are themselves tied up with social and cultural beliefs about drugs, as well as the individual drug user's psychological profile and more general social conditions. The same person will react differently at different times. It is therefore often misleading to make simple cause and effect statements about drugs, such as 'drug X always causes condition Y'.

Drug terminology

Although throughout this report we will refer to 'drug misuse', some people prefer to use the terms 'drug use' or 'drug abuse'. Theoretically, the 3 terms may be used to indicate a spectrum of harm which an individual may be doing to themselves: 'use' being fairly controlled, 'misuse' being less so encompassing use that is harmful, dependent or use of substances as part of a wider spectrum of problematic or harmful behaviour[2] and finally, 'abuse' being chaotic. However, the term 'abuse' has acquired somewhat judgmental overtones and is therefore best avoided; misuse is used here.

'Addiction' is another word which, while a distinct clinical concept, has become associated with society's reaction to dependency, so medical experts now sometimes avoid the term as carrying too many non-medical connotations of censure. 'Dependence' describes a compulsion to continue taking a drug as a result of its repeated administration. Insofar as this is to avoid the physical discomfort of withdrawal, we speak of physical dependence; insofar as the compulsion has a psychological basis — the need for stimulation or pleasure, the need for a chemical 'crutch', or the desire to obliterate reality — then it is referred to as psychological dependence. Research has shown, however, that the 2 may be interlinked: the mental anticipation of the user about to take a drug to which he is accustomed may prompt physical changes which reduce the effects of the drug and lead to 'tolerance'.[3] There is also a socio-cultural dimension to dependence.

'Tolerance' describes the body's habituation to the repeated presence of a drug, meaning that higher doses are needed to maintain the same effect. Tolerance develops at a different rate for different actions of the same drug. For instance the respiratory depression caused by opioids reduces faster than the euphoric actions and therefore the heavily dependent can use doses of heroin that would be lethal to less frequent users.[4]

Detrimental consequences may also be experienced by drug users who are not dependent as well as those who are hence the term 'problem drug use' has been coined to refer to drug use resulting in social, psychological, physical or legal problems associated with dependence, intoxication or regular consumption.

Alongside 'dependent use' and 'problem drug use' can be set the terms 'experimental use' and 'recreational use'. The period of initiation into drug use is known as experimental use. Recreational use, as its name suggests, is the use of drugs for pleasure or leisure purposes. Again, while some people prefer to see these terms as part of a spectrum — with 'experimental use' at one end and 'dependent use' at the other — this can be misleading, as it implies a spectrum of harm. Many people will cease drug use after experimenting for a time, while others may experience severe social, legal or medical problems in this phase. Some recreational drug users will be able to control their use while others could be said to be 'problem drug users' and dependent users may have 'chaotic' lifestyles or live relatively 'normal' lives.

Describing these patterns of drugs use as a 'spectrum' also implies a progression from one end to the other — the 'escalation hypothesis' with the use of cannabis and the so-called 'soft drugs' leading onto the use of heroin and the so-called 'hard drugs'. There is no conclusive proof that this is so — people can be dependent on cannabis or may use heroin recreationally; they could experiment with many different drug types, exposing themselves to obvious health dangers, or rapidly become dependent on a particular drug. In fact a 1993 Government study could find no relationship between the use of cannabis and the use of opiates such as heroin, putting pay to the theory of cannabis as a 'gateway' drug. While 96% of opiate users had taken cannabis in the previous year, only 7% of cannabis users had taken heroin.[5] While this 7% represents a higher number than the heroin use among the general population (estimated at 1%), it nevertheless does not constitute a causal link. However, a recent survey of school children found that the use of cannabis was particularly high among cigarette smokers. Only 6.9% of the non-smoking 15 and 16 year olds had ever tried cannabis, while 89% of smokers had.[6] A drug-centered explanation of patterns of drug misuse may however be misleading; the relationship between the use of one licit or illicit drug and another may be determined more by attitudes to risk taking than the experience of a particular drug or the resulting contact with other drug misusers.

Differing perceptions of drug use

One of the greatest difficulties medical professionals face when dealing with drug users is the differing perceptions they have of drug use and drugs. Doctors tend to view the user as a 'patient', and bring a medical perspective to their drug use — with 'cure' (ie abstinence) as the final goal. Many drug users who come into contact with doctors will not have such a view of their drug use.

Doctors' experience with dependent patients may influence their prescription practices to 'non-drug users'. Many doctors will avoid the use of drugs like morphine in pain relief, because they believe that their patients will become addicted. An American study found that the majority of physicians (including GPs, surgeons and cancer specialists) believed that if morphine was used in the management of cancer pain an increased need for morphine indicated that the patient had become tolerant to the pain relief.[7] In fact, it generally indicates an increase in pain. Tolerance, if present, only plays a minor part and there is little chance of morphine dependence.[8] Morphine may also be stigmatised as its use can be seen by some patients as a signal that death is imminent. Such misconceptions are based on traditional attitudes towards opiate use, and require that the attitudes and beliefs of doctors who treat severe pain are challenged. The treatment of pain relief in opiate misusers is discussed in Chapter 3.

Factors which influence drug use

There is little agreement on the causes of drug dependence, let alone the causes of drug use. It is generally assumed that both dependence and misuse are prompted by a number of inter-dependent factors, however a recent review of the literature found several unicausal theories still being proposed including failure of personal development, personality defects, unresolved family deaths, and a desire to seek new experiences.[9] The same study also identified no less than 8 factors which were seen as contributing to multicausal theories, including personality, society, peer pressure, genetics, family and pleasure. These can be split into 2 broad categories — individual influences (personality, genetics, etc) and environmental influences (family, peer pressure, society, etc).[10] One of the major difficulties in identifying the causes of and motives for drug use is that much of the research into influences on drug use has to be — by its very nature — descriptive. Certain personality types, socio-economic situations and family structures are also coexistent with drug use. Whether one can be said to encourage or cause the other, however, remains unresolved.

Personality and mental illness

One of the longest running debates in the drugs field is whether there is a relationship between an individual's mental state and drug-taking, and whether the former can be said to cause the latter, the former is the result of the latter, or whether they are simply strongly associated. A recent Dutch study found that 9 in 10 polydrug users undergoing treatment could be 'dual diagnosed' for at least 1 personality disorder[11] ('dual diagnosis' refers to the coexistence of substance use and 1 or more separate psychiatric disorder).[12] Very little research, however, has been undertaken in the UK on this relationship. One of the few studies carried out, found that 55% of patients admitted to a psychiatric unit in the South-West of England had a history of drug or alcohol dependence and that serious violence was particularly associated with such dependence.[13]

Studies have found that schizophrenic patients using drugs have an earlier onset of psychosis[14] and their functioning is better than non-drug using schizophrenics prior to their illness. This has been interpreted as suggesting that drug use may have precipitated their psychotic illness but it could alternatively be the case that those in the acute stages of illness may have had a milder disorder which had been exacerbated by the substance misuse.[15]

Among the severely mentally ill, those most at risk of co-morbidity are young men with chronic psychotic illness; in the general population it is also young men who are most frequently drug misusers. A number of reasons have been suggested for which psychotic patients might take drugs. The most commonly used drugs taken by schizophrenics are hallucinogens and stimulants, both of which can reproduce psychotic symptoms.[16,17] Perhaps the knowledge that these symptoms can be reproduced by a drug gives users a sense of control, despite recognition of the adverse effects on their condition.[18] Reasons given by psychotic patients for their drug misuse are similar to other drug misusers: relief of boredom, decrease in anxiety and improved socialisation.[19] Drugs, (particularly cannabis) may also be used to 'self-medicate' symptoms or the side-effects of psychotropic medications. In one US in-patient survey, 15% of patients gave this as their reason for drug misuse.[20]

Psychotic symptoms such as paranoid psychoses can be produced by stimulants (amphetamine and cocaine) or cannabis but usually resolve with discontinuation of the drug within a few days or weeks and should not be confused with psychotic illness. A causal link between cannabis and schizophrenia has not been established but there is clearer evidence of a detrimental effect on pre-existing illness.

In addition to the dual diagnosis debate is the concept of the 'addictive personality'. This has at its core the view that there are some well-defined personality patterns (ranging from anxiety to violent tendencies) resulting from both genetic and environmental influences which are specific to drug users.[21] The 'addictive personality' concept is broadly confirmed by the Minnesota Multiphasic Personality Inventory (MMPI), an index designed to measure people's psychological state. When measured on the MMPI and associated scales, dependent drug users consistently score highly, appearing to be susceptible to neuroticism, depression and low self-esteem.

However, such results on the MMPI are by no means unique to drug users and well-controlled studies on the 'addictive personality' are rare. Many of the scales which have been developed from the MMPI have not been proved reliable[22] and the concept of the 'addictive personality' continues to be controversial. A recent Scottish study, for example, suggests that drug use may actually be a facet of delinquency, and consequently the user usually grows out of it.[23]

There are a number of studies, particularly from the US, which suggest that for some users, 'addiction' has been to the drug using lifestyle rather than the drug *per se*. For instance one such study found that purity levels of heroin on the New York streets were so low as to make clinically-defined addiction virtually impossible; what drove users was their commitment to the street life.[24]

Another problem is that what may simply be associations are often interpreted as causations, for example low self-esteem causes drug use.[25] It is interesting to note that British research which found a link between high self-esteem and smoking amongst schoolboys was still interpreted within the low self-esteem paradigm — smoking boosted low self-confidence rather than high self-confidence causing smoking.[26]

Genetics

Although a number of large-scale studies on the genetic and hereditary bases of alcoholism have been undertaken, little work has been carried out on humans with regard to use of illicit drugs.[27] However, alcoholism can provide a model for studying a genetic vulnerability to drug use.[28] Most research focuses on twins and adoptees (the best studies being of twins who have been split up) and have found that biological sons (though not always daughters) of alcoholics even when adopted by non-alcoholics have higher rates of alcoholism than control subjects.[29,30] Evidence has also been found that an adopted child with an alcoholic biological parent faces a higher risk of drug use than a control.[31]

Family

While genetics is a field which has been left unexplored, the family as an influence on drug use has been heavily studied.[32] Family disruption, conflict between parents, divorce, lack of emotional closeness and ineffective supervision have all been shown to be factors in the initiation of drug use and delinquency.[33,34] The issue of lone parenting, however, remains unresolved, as many studies have failed to demonstrate that coming from a one-parent family predicts drug use.[35] In fact, it appears that family structure may not be as important as the processes which occur within that structure — in other words, the quality of the relationships.[36]

Perhaps the most important process within the family (and the one which affects the parents as much as the children) is that of parenting skills. Research has found respectively that both authoritarian and too permissive parents exhibited poor parenting skills being 'high on discipline but low on warmth' and 'low on discipline but high on warmth'[37] and that these traits can dispose children to progress beyond experimental drug use. This view is not just held by the researchers: when compared to a control group, drug users themselves have categorised their fathers as lacking in emotional warmth and their mothers as overprotective.[38] Interestingly, young people who only experiment with drugs have been found to have the most stable backgrounds, while abstainers have similar parental difficulties as frequent users.[39]

The influence of family problems in childhood may also carry through into adulthood. In terms of drug misuse, this could mean that childhood problems move beyond merely influencing initial take-up of drugs and become entrenched as factors which affect prolonged drug use. An American study has found that about a third of dependent drug users experienced considerable family disruption when they were children before their initiation into drug use.[40] Another American piece of research listed 9 'types' of young people who should be deemed at risk of drug use — children of drug users, victims of sexual, emotional or physical abuse, those with poor school records, pregnant teenagers, children in families of low socio-economic status, delinquents, those with mental health problems, those with suicidal tendencies and those with physical or mental disabilities,[41] although British research does not show those of low socio-economic status to be at increased risk.[42,43] Some people will clearly use drugs to ease the trauma and pain of unsatisfactory relationships and the physical and emotional abuse arising from unhappy home lives.[44]

The study of such factors — known as 'life events' — has developed its own measurement devices, such as the LEDS (Life Events and Difficulties Schedule).[45] While there is little research on the effects of life events on illegal drug use, studies have shown that traumatic life events (such as bereavement or divorce) can act as triggers for alcoholism and that positive life events (such as the development of new relationships) can push people towards recovery from heroin dependence. For instance, over three-quarters of alcohol-dependent subjects in 1 recent study reported severe life events in the year preceding their dependence,[46] while nearly two-thirds of ex-heroin addicts in another piece of research cited new relationships as a major factor in their abstinence.[47] It is also apparent that some people are more vulnerable to traumatic events ('event prone') than others, an issue which links life events to the discussion of personality.

Peer pressure/preference

By the teenage years, the influence of friends rather than family is perhaps the factor which directly affects young people's take-up of drugs the most.[48] As such, peer pressure is widely believed to be one of the best predictors of drug use[49] although it has been found that young people regularly move from one peer group to another[50] and that it is almost impossible to predict whether someone is liable to take drugs from an examination of their peer group 2 or 3 years previously.[51] Among young people who are involved in criminal offences in addition to their drug misuse, moving away from delinquent peers may be a factor in giving up both activities. It is unclear, however, which comes first — whether the young person wishes to give up delinquent behaviour and drug misuse and therefore disassociates himself from peers who commit offences, or whether the move itself influences the drug misuse and criminal activity.[52]

While the importance of peer groups must be recognised, whether peers have an impact on continued rather than initial use is another matter. Studies show that parental influence remains strong on long-term decisions (such as career and education) while peer influence is more short-term in its importance.[53] Research has also found that early drug use within peer groups is not associated with later problematic use.[54] Another matter is whether 'peer pressure' is actually the right term, as it suggests a one-way action where the individual submits any free will to 'pressure' from the group. It has therefore been suggested that 'peer preference' may be a more appropriate phrase, and this raises the unaddressed question as to how people choose their peer groups. Consciously or unconsciously drug use — and the choosing of drug-using peer groups — may act as a means of defiance against the values of adults and parents in a wider context of adolescent rebellion.

Socio-economic factors

As was shown in the previous chapter, socio-economic factors have some part to play in whether people take drugs. In Britain, official statistics of drug users who have sought help from doctors and drug agencies consistently show that around three-quarters are unemployed although the relationship may be one of association, rather than cause and effect.[55,56,57] It has been suggested that any relationship between unemployment and dependent drug use may actually be based on a psychological search for a routine to replace that of work.[58] However this perhaps tells us more about people whose drug use has become so problematic that they either seek help or come to the attention of drug researchers, than drug users in general.[59] Household surveys, such as the British Crime Survey,[60] and representative prevalence studies, such as the Four City survey,[61] repeatedly challenge the stereotype of the deprived drug user.

Relatively little work has been carried out to examine the link between socio-economic factors and drug misuse, the main reason being that the relationship is perhaps the most complex of all in the drug field. Although experience of drug misuse appears to be more likely among those of higher socio-economic status,[62,63] research points to low socio-economic status, poor housing, inner city and criminal environments as among the best predictors of heavy drug use.[64] Heavy drug use may be a response to poverty-related stress or alternatively income gained from drug dealing may be an alternative means of gaining status in a community where work and legitimate income are hard to come by.

Pleasure

This is all too often ignored as a motive for drug use. The majority of drug use is recreational rather than dependent and most people take drugs because they find the effects enjoyable. Not much research has asked about the hedonistic reasons to take drugs, but an English survey carried out in 1990 amongst nearly 4,500 16-19 year olds found that around a third of these young adults felt that people took drugs 'to relax'.[65] Only a quarter of the whole sample said that they had taken drugs, so it is unclear whether the view of drug-taking as an aid to relaxation is one held by the drug users, or those who have not tried drugs.

Availability and advertising

There is considerable pressure to use legal substances — alcohol and pain relieving drugs are regularly advertised on television. Although the advertising of tobacco products is banned on TV, research carried out by Strathclyde University concluded that other forms of cigarette advertising encourage young people to start smoking and reinforce the habit amongst existing smokers.[66]

Obviously, the illicit market is more discreet, but references to drugs are common in the media and the fashion and music industries. As far as 'advertising' the availability of drugs goes, in the most vulnerable group of potential users — schoolchildren — at any given school where drugs are available, the identities of peers who have already taken drugs are often badly kept secrets. The Health Education Authority carried out a survey of over 11,000 9-15 year olds in 1989, and found that by the time they were 15 years old, over 40% of boys and nearly 50% of girls knew people of their own age who took drugs.[67] The Four City Survey also measured people's contact with drug users. The 'booster' group, made up largely of 16 to 25 year olds, of low socio-economic status from inner city areas showed that nearly 70% knew someone who had taken a drug and over 50% knew someone who regularly took drugs.[68]

Price

Heroin and cocaine are expensive when compared to cannabis and LSD. Street prices indicate that in 1995 a gram of heroin cost between £70 and £100 in

Glasgow and London, while a gram of cocaine cost £50 to £80. A dependent heroin user may take a quarter of a gram a day,[69] and a dependent cocaine user, between 1 and 2 grams.[70]

The so-called 'soft' drugs are considerably cheaper. Cannabis tends to be sold in fractions of an ounce and costs between £50 and £100 per ounce. A regular user may use about a quarter ounce each week, enough for perhaps 20 'joints'.[71] However, LSD is probably the most 'cost effective' illegal drug (benzodiazepines which have been diverted from legitimate sources will be cheaper still). It is usually marketed in single dose units (absorbed onto small paper squares) costing under £5 each. Dependent LSD users are hard to find, as after a few days of increasing the dosage, the drug becomes ineffective.[72] A regular user, however, may take a few 'trips' (an episode of a hallucinogenic drug experience) each week lasting about 10 hours each. It is unclear what role, if any, price plays in the consumption of illicit drugs.

Prescription

Dependence on mood-altering drugs is not restricted to the illegal market. Among those receiving prescriptions for benzodiazepine tranquillisers, it has been estimated that more than a million people use the drugs 'chronically'.[73]

The dependence potential of benzodiazepines is clear, but whether the medical use of opiates in the relief of chronic pain may lead to addiction is less certain. Many medical professionals are reluctant to use morphine, for example, because they believe that tolerance will quickly develop and the drug will therefore become useless. However, the oral administration of 'slow release' morphine has been shown to reduce the likelihood of tolerance developing amongst patients with severe pain.[74] The question of whether dependence upon prescription drugs leads individuals to experiment with illegal drugs has not been satisfactorily answered.

Youth culture

Alongside the above influences, an understanding of the cultural role of drug use is important to comprehending the motivations of those taking drugs. The changes observed in 'youth culture' since the 1960s may help us to develop an understanding of the role of drugs among the main users — those under 30 years.

'Youth culture' has evolved around the increasing independence, leisure time and spending power of young people.[75] Distinctive 'subcultures', displaying visible style and attitude, have emerged at particular historical moments each with distinctive patterns of drug misuse. The Teddy Boys of the 1950s, Mods, Rockers and Hippies of the 1960s, skinheads and punks of the 1970s all grew and faded, although they are maintained in contemporary society in a defused and nominal way through nostalgia, fashion and music.

Use of drugs increased among youthful groups in the 1960s, particularly cannabis, heroin and amphetamines, at a time of artistic and political protest and expression of mistrust of establishment values and enforced conformity.[76] Types of drug use and youth cultures continued to develop and change and in the late 1980s the dance and music trend known as the 'rave' scene emerged with the growth in the use of drugs such as ecstasy and amphetamine, which became associated with the need to stay awake to dance all night. Although this functional use of drugs for dancing had its parallels with the use of amphetamine by Mods in the 1960s, current use of 'dance drugs' amongst young people is significantly more widespread.

While subcultural theorists have focused their attention on some of the more notorious and colourful youth subcultures of the past 40 years, there is also a far greater mass of 'ordinary' young people whose essential routine concerns are school, home and employment. They may adopt the demeanour, fashion and slang of a particular subculture including the occasional or experimental use of illegal drugs without necessarily adopting the lifestyle or any serious commitment to drug use. However, the majority of young people's drug use is still restricted to the use of tobacco and alcohol — for many the pub is the centre of social life.

Problems arising from drug misuse

Problems for society

Costs

It is extremely difficult to quantify the social costs of drug use, for the same reason as it is difficult to quantify the number of drug users in the UK — drug use is an illegal act. One of the few estimates that is available relates to the economic cost of drug use; drug and alcohol-related absenteeism is calculated to cost British industry between £600 and £800 million per annum.[77] Added to this is the cost of government activity, information campaigns and health education, treatment and rehabilitation services, social services and the criminal justice system including the police, HM Customs and Excise, the courts, the prison service and the probation service.

The only reliable costing of the supply of drugs relates to those prescribed by doctors — in 1994 benzodiazepines worth nearly £13.4 million were issued in England, £7.7 million of which covered temazepam. The vast majority of people in receipt of prescriptions retain them for their personal use, but the fact remains despite the precautions taken, that some of these drugs do leak onto the illicit market.[78] The British Crime Survey found that 1% of those questioned had used temazepam in the last year,[79] while a study of drug users found that 16% had taken benzodiazepines in the last month, with 18% of the sample reporting benzodiazepines as their main drug of choice.[80] There is no illegal manufacture of benzodiazepines — they are commonly obtained from pharmacy or factory break-ins.

Families

There is often a great deal of secondary damage caused to families of long-term drug users.[81] However, because this appears to be such a common-sensical assumption, the consequences of drug use on the family (as opposed to the family as a factor in initiation into drug use) is an under-researched area. It is clear, however, that dependent drug users are usually triggered into seeking help by traumas in the family — marriage break-up, the loss of a child, their own violence — and more generally, by the stress which their drug use places on their relationships with partners and children.[82] Despite the lack of research on the effects of drug-using parents on the family and their children, the information that is available points to a positive correlation between parental drug use and the drug use of children,[83] and there is anecdotal evidence to suggest that children of drug-using parents may experience behavioural and psychological difficulties.

Crime

Perhaps the drug-related social issue which most concerns the British public is that of drug-related crime. The relationship between drugs and crime (other than that of breaking the law by possessing or supplying drugs) has been much debated, and it has been claimed by some politicians that as much as 50% of all crime is committed by drug users to finance their drug use.[84]

The main argument for a causal relationship between drugs and crime is that dependent drug users resort to crime to pay for their habits — it has been estimated that every year up to £864 million is raised from acquisitive crime by dependent heroin users in England and Wales in order to purchase heroin.[85] However, the same study also pointed out that dependent drug users could actually be responsible for as little as 1% of acquisitive crime by value, largely because they have many other sources of income. This argument largely rests on one's definition of crime — possession of drugs itself is, of course, a crime, as is their supply, while much of the 'clean' money earned by drug users may be accumulated dubiously (through prostitution, doing favours such as storing drugs for friends, or benefit fraud). However it is generally accepted, that crime in this context means robbery, theft and burglary. This estimate relies on a number of assumptions which cannot be accurately calculated — the price of heroin, the quantity of heroin consumed daily, the number of heroin users and the proportion of the cost of heroin which is financed by crime. All that can be said is that it is highly unlikely that 50% of acquisitive crime is due to drug users. Interestingly, the Scottish Office's Ministerial Task Force were highly doubtful as to whether an accurate mechanism could be devised for recording drug-related crime, as recommended by the Scottish Affairs Committee.[86]

Scottish research has found that amongst moderate and heavy opiate users, under a third of income is raised through non-drug related criminal activity, with the majority of earnings coming through dealing drugs (60%).[87] A Dutch study in the late 1980s found that opiate users derived around a fifth of their income from crime, a fifth from prostitution (a legal income source in the Netherlands), a fifth from the drugs market, just under 30% from welfare and the rest from 'odd jobs' and legal employment.[88] American researchers have perhaps examined drug users' income patterns most thoroughly, and identified another source of income.[89] This is best described as deferred or avoided expenditure — support 'in kind' from family and friends which may range from travel money through to free rental of rooms, and which amounted to over 20% of dependent heroin users' total income.

On the other hand, there is evidence that drug users commit crimes for reasons unrelated to their dependence. Countering the 'economic necessity' argument are the facts that many drug users are involved in crime before becoming dependent[90] while others continue committing crime even when they have access to 'free drugs' (ie on prescription), while still others commit no crime whatsoever.[91] Until more research is conducted on the 'drugs-crime' connection, all that can be said is that drugs and crime are associated in some way for some individuals. But whether that association allows one to categorise people as drug-using criminals or criminal drug users is another matter.

Problems for the individual

There are serious risks for the individual using drugs and some of the most significant of these apply to most of the drugs commonly misused. Adverse health effects may result from the direct action of the drug itself on the body; the route of administration, such as injecting; or by indirect effects such as an accident caused while under its influence or the chaotic lifestyle which may result from severe dependence. It should not be assumed that the extent to which a drug is legally restricted is an accurate guide to how harmful it can be.

Routes of administration

Many of the risks to health presented by illicit drug use can result not from the active ingredient itself, for instance heroin, but from the route of administration, such as injection or smoking. These risks may be compounded by taking substances of impure or inconsistent quality, or those not intended for a particular method of delivery such as crushed tablets which are injected.

The route of administration may also influence the risk of dependency on a drug. Intravenous use of heroin has been associated with a higher severity of dependence than heroin smoking, while injectors and smokers of cocaine have been found to be more dependent than those taking cocaine intranasally ('snorting').[92]

Injection

In relation to other methods of administering illicit drugs, injection is not a widespread route of delivery — in 1992 less than 0.5% of the general population said that they had ever injected.[93] When injected into a vein, the drug directly enters the bloodstream and is carried straight to the brain, producing a noticeable effect within seconds. For this reason the onset of the drug's effects (the 'rush') is quicker and more striking after injection than after, for example, swallowing a drug, where the drug has first to pass through the liver. In general, the short-term effects are similar though more intense when a drug is injected.

In medical terms, injecting is the most important problem of drug misuse and therefore, despite its low prevalence, this practice has received a great deal of attention in recent years, particularly because of the risk of contracting HIV from the use of contaminated injecting equipment. Policy makers have seen drug injectors as the bridge between HIV and non-drug using heterosexuals, and the success of controlling HIV infection in the general population as being dependent on the containment of HIV within the injecting community.[94] In the early 1990s, it was found that 6% of male drug users and 6.5% of women drug users who attended clinics in London were infected with HIV.[95] The true prevalence of injection-related HIV is hard to gauge, because of the possibility of sexual transmission. In addition, sexual transmission may be more likely between drug users as drug use can affect people's perception of sexual risk.[96,97]

One of the main questions which has preoccupied researchers is why, given the well-known HIV risk, people continue to share injecting equipment. The most recent studies tend to show that injectors have a hierarchy of risks with other risks such as overdosing and welfare risks (housing, money, employment) often being prioritised above HIV.[98] Injectors seem to perform sophisticated cost-benefit analyses when it comes to the risk of contracting HIV. That said, it also appears that injectors have taken HIV-related harm minimisation messages to heart and currently the greatest HIV risk which injectors may face is through sexual contact.[99,100]

Apart from the risk of HIV infection, the injection of drugs carries a wide range of other risks. It is estimated that between 50 and 80% of injecting drug users have been infected with hepatitis B, although only between 1-10% of those who are infected, presuming they were health adults, will become carriers. Of these carriers, 90% will develop antibodies to the virus, but the remaining proportion may develop chronic active hepatitis or liver cancer.[101] Recent research has calculated that in the UK as many as 60% of drug injectors in the UK are infected with hepatitis C, while in London and Scotland 70% are infected with the virus.[102] With hepatitis B, between 1-10% of those infected develop chronic hepatitis; with hepatitis C, the infection becomes chronic in 80% of infected people. With hepatitis C it is currently anticipated that, after a latent phase of 20-40 years, approximately 10-20% will develop cirrhosis, and some of these will go on to develop liver cancer.[103] However, as the date of infection among those currently developing cirrhosis is often unknown, due to diagnostic tests only recently becoming available, the length of the latent phase may be revised. Hepatitis C is notable in the degree to which it is greatly restricted to injecting drug users. Unlike hepatitis B and HIV, it is infrequently transmitted sexually,[104] or from mother to infant (although both occur), but is easily transmitted by blood to blood contact. To date, the health risks presented by hepatitis C have attracted limited publicity, but in view of the enormous resource implications for future treatment, comparable with those anticipated to be needed for HIV, considerable forward planning is now required. Furthermore, diseases affecting injecting drug misusers continue to emerge, such as the reported infections of hepatitis G in Germany.[105]

Infective endocarditis is a condition where the membrane lining the heart becomes inflamed, leading to damage to the heart valves. It is believed to occur in 2 out of every 1000 injecting drug users each year and should be suspected in anyone with a fever and a changing heart murmur. The inflammation can be found on normal heart valves in drug injectors, unlike in non-injectors, and may result in valve damage and heart failure. Early treatment has a good recovery rate, though if injecting is resumed, recurrence is likely.[106]

While overdose is not specific to injecting drug users, it is a risk, especially when injectors have remained abstinent for a time, or combine more than 1 drug, including alcohol.[107] A drug user returning to his or her usual levels of drug use is in danger of overdose as the body will have acclimatised itself to a lower level of the drug or absence. Overdose may also be caused by injecting purer drugs than those usually taken, as the effect is a higher dose than that intended or through the use of adulterated drugs. Anecdotal evidence suggests that these are both particular risks for ex-prisoners which may arise either when drug misuse restarts on the outside following abstinence in prison or following a change from using illicit prison drugs to purer drugs on the outside. A study of heroin users showed that 31% of the injecting users had overdosed at least once (this compared with only 2% of non-injecting heroin users).[108]

The other main problem experienced by injecting drug users occurs at the injection site. If they have a long history of injecting, access to healthy veins may be difficult, and abscesses and gangrene can occur when the needle misses a vein. The lymphatic system is often damaged — resulting in the puffy hands regularly seen in long-term injectors — and thrombosis and clots to the lung have also been reported.[109] Injection into an artery can cause gangrene, particularly when a substance is injected which has not been formulated for the purpose (such as temazepam gel). Sometimes the drug itself will have this effect. This is particularly the case with barbiturates which can cause severe prolonged spasm of arterial walls, leading to gangrene of the distal tissues.

Herbal cannabis may be smoked on its own or with tobacco. The resin or oil is smoked in a cigarette (joint) with tobacco or on its own through a pipe. Although cannabis may be eaten in foods or taken as an infusion, the most common route of administration is smoking. There is evidence that the smoking of cannabis may contribute to bronchitis and cancer, and that cannabis smokers may be at greater risk of these diseases than tobacco smokers.[110] The reasoning behind this is that cannabis smokers inhale more deeply and keep the smoke in their lungs longer than tobacco smokers. This physical damage is associated with the route of administration, however, and there is little evidence at present that cannabis *per se* causes lasting damage.

The smoking of crack has been linked to many respiratory complications.[111] Crack users may also experience a condition which is termed 'crack lung' in America. They present to doctors with the symptoms of pneumonia — breathing problems, high temperature, severe chest pains — but do not respond to standard treatments for the illness.

Heroin may also be smoked when the fumes of the heated heroin are inhaled ('chasing the dragon'). This is a very effective and the commonest route of heroin administration, with similar effects to intravenous use.[112] Respiratory infections are particularly common among those taking heroin, but this may be due to the suppression of the protective cough reflex caused by the heroin itself, rather than the smoking.[113]

Intranasal administration (snorting)
Cocaine may be taken intranasally (snorted) in 'lines', which tend to consist of approx 20-30mg. Cocaine snorting contracts the blood vessels in the nose, and when the drug use is halted, the blood flow resumes with swelling of the nasal lining and the user experiences a 'coke cold' (rhinitis and general nasal irritation).[114] Perforation of the nasal septum has been reported, but its incidence is rare.[115] Amphetamine is often snorted, but while cocaine is rapidly absorbed through the mucous membranes, to achieve the same effect, amphetamine must be injected.

Inhalation
For most people inhaling volatile substances causes no harm, but it is still a high risk activity, with individuals dying from the direct effects of the substance after first use. Deaths have also occurred as a result of suffocation, when plastic bags used to contain the substance have been found blocking the entrance to the nose and mouth passageways.[116] The method of inhaling certain volatile compounds may significantly affect the acute risk. Clenching the nozzle of cigarette lighter refills between the teeth and spraying the cold (-60°C) fluid directly into the mouth carries the additional risk of frostbite of the mouth[117] and death from stimulation of the vagus nerve which can slow or stop the heart.[118]

Short-term and long-term effects

Even in low doses most drugs (stimulants, such as amphetamine or cocaine, excepted) impair motor control, reaction time, and the ability to maintain attention. No matter how people feel, they are not as capable as before, and such activities as driving, operating machinery and crossing roads become more hazardous both to themselves and to others. Stimulants may impair delicate skills and the learning of new skills, and in high doses or after prolonged use will impair performance of tasks which they enhanced at a low dose or in earlier use. Higher doses bring risks associated with intoxication, such as accidents, as well as over-dosing. Judgement about risks may also be impaired. Furthermore, the withdrawal effects of stimulants on psychomotor function may be even more important in causing accidents than the direct pharmaceutical effects of the drug. Further research is needed regarding the effects of drugs on driving — both illegal and prescription and on their role in road traffic accidents. The BMA statement *Driving impairment through alcohol and other drugs* (1996) advises that current advice should remain that individuals should not drive whilst under the influence of drugs either legal or illegal and that the Department of Transport should consider current and future use of drugs testing of those involved in road traffic accidents and 'due cause' situations.[119] When doctors prescribe or pharmacists dispense drugs which could impair driving ability, it is their responsibility to inform patients about these effects. Compared with short-term effects of drug use the long-term effects are much more drug specific; both the short-term and long-term effects of the major drugs are described below.

Heroin

In the 1970s, it was discovered that opiates bind to specific sites (receptors) throughout the body, and that the brain contains opiate-like substances, the endorphins.[120] It has since been found that morphine and codeine themselves actually exist in the animal central nervous system.[121] There is still much to be learned about the body's endogenous opioids, but these findings suggest that heroin and other opioid drugs trigger a number of the body's physiological systems including the pain-relieving system and amplify their effects via endorphin receptor sites.

Heroin and other opioids have analgesic properties; they depress the nervous system affecting such reflex functions as coughing; they also depress breathing; slow the heart rate;[122] dilate blood vessels and depress bowel activity. Low doses produce euphoria, while high doses induce sedation. The speed with which these effects are reached depends largely on the method of administration; injection and smoking will have near immediate effects, while oral administration will take perhaps an hour.

Physical dependence is clearly a factor as opiates can and do alter the body's endogenous opioid system. Single doses have induced a degree of physical dependence in non-dependent volunteers.[123] After several weeks on high doses, withdrawal will result in a flu-like syndrome, including tremors, yawning, sweating and muscular spasms. These symptoms generally fade in about 1-2 weeks.[124] Injecting heroin poses important health risks which include overdose, damage to veins, and where equipment is shared, bloodborne diseases such as HIV and hepatitis.

Psychological dependence on opiates is a very real danger when the prospect of withdrawal is taken into account — the so-called withdrawal avoidance theory, where the fear of heroin withdrawal may itself become greater than the symptoms deserve.[125] However, apart from this, the psychological bases for addiction to heroin and other opiates are similar to those for other drugs, ie habit formation, confidence boosting and the maintenance of a social circle established among other users and dealers.

Benzodiazepines

Benzodiazepines, of which temazepam is the most commonly misused, provide relief from anxiety and tension and can give pleasurable feelings. They are also often used to enhance the effects of other drugs, such as opiates or to counteract the effects of stimulants such as cocaine, amphetamine or ecstasy.

The adverse effects of benzodiazepines in prescribed doses have been well studied, but the pharmacological and pathological effects of misuse in large quantities are poorly understood. In the short-term symptoms may include tiredness, depression of respiration, and sometimes dizziness and unsteady movement. Overdose is common but is rarely fatal unless combined with other sedating drugs such as alcohol or heroin, where it is believed to be responsible for a high number of deaths.

Over the long-term, normal medical doses seem to impair visuospatial function, attention, judgment and memory. For the large doses of misuse, little is known, but brain damage cannot be ruled out.[126] If injected, there are the usual risks associated with intravenous administration.

Physiological dependence can develop and withdrawal may produce short-lived rebound anxiety and insomnia which in more pronounced forms can include insomnia, anxiety, tension, trembling seizures, confusion, paranoia, hyperthermia and occasionally grand mal epileptic fits. Personality factors may be important predictors of withdrawal patterns. Some people dependent even on low doses show evidence of a specific benzodiazepine withdrawal syndrome.[127] Key symptoms result from heightened sensory perception and include hyperacusis (excessive acuteness of hearing), photophobia (over-sensitivity to light), paraesthesiae (numbness and tingling), hyperosmia (abnormal acuteness of smell), headaches, muscle spasms, vertigo and sleep problems.

LSD

LSD is taken orally, and therefore the drug's effects occur about an hour after it is taken, peaking after two to six hours, and fading out after about 12 hours. Physical effects (dilation of pupils, slight rise in body temperature) are relatively insignificant in comparison with the psychological and behavioural ones[128] These can be divided into somatic (dizziness, disorientation), perceptual (altered visual and aural senses, dissociation from the body) and psychic (heightened self-awareness, mood changes).[129] Although unpleasant reactions are often reported (a 'bad trip'), they usually result from the individual's 'mindset' or a stressful external event rather than the drug alone, and the anxiety and paranoia associated with such an experience will pass as the drug leaves the body.

The reliving of the visual experience ('flashbacks') is uncommon and the view that LSD can trigger a psychotic reaction in the user has serious shortcomings[130] with no recorded cases of the drug producing psychosis in previously well-balanced individuals.[131] Reports of flashbacks and psychosis were more prevalent in the 1960s when the average LSD dose was commonly 300 micrograms as opposed to the average of 60 micrograms today. However, it has been shown that LSD may adversely effect people who are genetically predisposed to schizophrenia.[132] The lethal dose in humans has not been determined, although the experimental dose of 300,000 micrograms of LSD proved to be fatal in an elephant.[133] This is around 6000 times the average dose taken by humans.[134] However accidental deaths have been recorded as the secondary results of perceptual distortions, such as from attempts to 'fly' from rooftops although it is not clear how common such events are.[135] Evidence does not support claims of genetic disorders arising from hallucinogens.[136]

Cannabis

As cannabis is usually smoked, the effects start a few minutes after use has begun, and may last for a few hours depending on the dose.[137] The most common effect is that of a relaxed and mildly euphoric state, and when taken in high doses, hallucinogenic effects similar to those of LSD may be experienced.[138] As with LSD, users may also experience nausea, anxiety and panic. Distortions of space and time estimation, reduced vigilance and impaired co-ordination are likely to render heavy cannabis users liable to accidents.

Long-term effects are a matter of controversy. Perhaps the best known effects which have been attributed to prolonged cannabis use are 'cannabis psychosis' and the 'amotivational syndrome'. However, research into 'cannabis psychosis' is inconclusive, as it has not been demonstrated to occur more frequently in cannabis users than non-cannabis users.[139] The amotivational syndrome, under which the user sinks into apathy, is equally unproven. Most of the research which supports this theory is based on studies of highly motivated, middle class college students; when more representative samples are studied, the amotivational syndrome disappears.[140] It must be accepted, however, that some cannabis users do appear demotivated, but this is little different from what might be expected from people dependent on alcohol or other depressant drugs.[141] There is no evidence that their state of mind is specific to cannabis use. With regard to long-term physical effects, there is some evidence that cardiovascular effects include appreciable tachycardia (rapid heart beat), hypotension (low blood pressure) and hypertension (high blood pressure); these changes may precipitate angina or even death in predisposed individuals.[142] Smoking cannabis, regardless of the strength of the main active ingredient tetrahydrocannabinol, results in substantially greater levels of carbon monoxide and tar than smoking a similar quantity of tobacco,[143] and is therefore likely to pose a significant health risk.

Death from the direct short-term effects of cannabis is extremely unlikely: it has been calculated that it would take at least a pound and a half of cannabis to kill a human.[144] However, like alcohol, its indirect effects may be fatal. In one study between 3.7% and 37% of drivers killed in road accidents had significant levels of cannabis in their blood.[145] Experimental research has found that even small doses of cannabis impair driving ability, although it is not known to what extent this might be modified by the age and experience of the driver.[146]

Cannabis has been shown to adversely affect the performance of pilots even 24 hours after smoking,[147,148] and consequently may be expected to have an impact on safety and work performance in other industries.

Amphetamine

Amphetamine (an acronym for **a**lpha-**m**ethyl**phen**ethyl**amine**) has perhaps the most varied routes of administration of all the main drugs. It is usually taken orally or sniffed but it can be smoked and is second to heroin as the most commonly injected drug (45% of people who used amphetamine and sought help from English drug agencies in 1992/3 reported injecting the drug) with the risks to health associated with injecting.[149] When sniffed, the drug takes effect after about 20 minutes, when taken orally, after about an hour, and the intense effects can last for up to 6 hours. The body can take a couple of days to recover from the experience. Injection concentrates the effects, the user experiencing a sudden 'rush' which can only be replicated by repeated injection every few hours.[150] It is a notoriously impure drug, with only about 5% of amphetamine in an average dose (the rest being largely made up of cutting agents or diluents)[151] but the diluents often contain caffeine in pharmacologically active qualities. However, recently there have been reports of higher purity amphetamine, known as amphetamine base, in circulation which is usually found in larger 'wholesale' quantities.

Amphetamine is a stimulant drug, which in the short-term increases the heart rate, raises the blood pressure, reduces appetite and increases urine output. At high doses (up to 20mg of pure drug in 24 hours) peripheral hypothermia may occur (the user's complexion becoming pale and their hands and feet cold) along with insomnia, headaches and sweating.[152] The drug we see is almost exclusively amphetamine, while the drug seen in the US is nearly always methylamphetamine.

In the long-term, amphetamine use is associated with a process known as 'binge/crash'. Tolerance to the drug is rapid — injectors may soon find that doses of 2 or more grams have no effect on them — and so greater and more frequent doses are taken in an attempt to sustain the 'rush' and euphoria.[153] Typically, such binges last 12 to 18 hours, though they may last for up to a week, depending on the user's stamina as sleep is often impossible.[154] Many of those practising 'binge/crash' amphetamine use move on to regular daily use of amphetamine.[155] During this period, the user may develop psychosis, with excessive mood swings, aggression, paranoia, hallucinations and weight loss. Amphetamine psychosis is indistinguishable from acute paranoid schizophrenia apart from the fact that it will eventually disappear after cessation of the drug. Anecdotal evidence suggests that this normally takes about 10 days.[156] Amphetamine use which stops suddenly, known as a 'crash', is characterised by depression, anxiety and extreme fatigue, with the user sleeping for up to 48 hours.[157] This constitutes a pattern of withdrawal, even though it is not as severe as that experienced by heroin users.

Cocaine and crack cocaine
Like amphetamine, cocaine can be snorted, smoked, taken orally or injected. Crack is not a new drug — it is a different physical form of cocaine which can be smoked (a freebase). A side effect of some of the methods of converting cocaine hydrochloride to the freebase is to remove some impurities from what is already usually a relatively pure material. Crack can be up to 3 times as pure as cocaine, although a great deal of the drug is lost when it is heated.[158] When crack is taken its effects last no more than a couple of hours (with the oral route taking the longest and injection and smoking the shortest, perhaps a quarter of an hour).[159]

Although the effects are much more short-lived, both cocaine and crack have essentially the same properties as amphetamine. The most obvious danger is the need to re-administer the drug repeatedly while already under its influence.[160] Psychosis and bingeing/crashing have also been documented. Symptoms and signs specific to cocaine/crack include a lowering of the seizure threshold, and the raising of blood pressure with seizures, strokes and comas being among the most common neurological complications.[161]

Ecstasy
Ecstasy (3,4, methylenedioxymethamphetamine or MDMA for short) is classed as a hallucinogenic stimulant. It is effective at doses of 75-100 mg and is taken orally in tablet form. Although a variety of substances are sold as ecstasy, including amphetamine, LSD, caffeine, ephedrine, ketamine and other MDMA-like drugs such as MDA (3,4 methylenedioxyamphetamine) and MDEA (3,4 methylenedioxyethylamphetamine, known as 'Eve'), reports that rat poison and so-called 'hard' drugs are mixed in the tablets are much exaggerated.[162] In fact, anecdotal reports suggest that most of the tablets currently sold as ecstasy are

MDEA, although both MDEA and MDA may be sold in their own right. The effects of MDMA are experienced after about half an hour and — as with amphetamine — can last for about 6 hours. Pupils dilate, the jaw tightens and nausea, sweating, loss of appetite and rise in blood pressure and heart rate are all symptoms.[163] At moderate levels, the user experiences a mild euphoric 'rush' followed by feelings of serenity and calmness.[164] As with LSD, the use of ecstasy often depends on the mind set of the person using it, and anxiety, paranoia, psychosis and hallucinations have been reported.[165]

There is evidence of associations between ecstasy use and liver damage[166,167] acute hepatitis[168] and jaundice,[169] and doctors have been alerted to the possibility of ecstasy use when a young person presents with unexplained jaundice. Women with a history of genito-urinary tract infection have also been advised not to use the drug as it may activate any latent infections.[170]

There are also concerns about the neurotoxicity of MDMA. In animals it causes a sudden release of serotonin followed by a massive rapid reduction in the serotonin content of the brain;[171,172] the consequences of this for man are unknown.

Estimates vary regarding the number of ecstasy-related deaths. To date, around 50 ecstasy-related deaths have been recorded in otherwise healthy young people, nearly all of which occurred at raves or shortly afterwards[173] but the National Poisons Information Service at Guy's Hospital, which responds to around 1000 ecstasy-related incidents a year, estimates that at least 20 people die each year from ecstasy.[174] Generally, the same symptoms have been reported in these cases: heatstroke (with body temperatures in excess of 39°C) and disseminated intravascular coagulation (DIC). This causes blood to clot where it should not, such as in the lungs.[175] Other conditions found in deaths associated with ecstasy and Eve (MDEA) include necrosis of the liver, the development of fibrous tissues in the heart muscles (myocardial fibrosis), damage to the veins and tissues (perivascular haemorrhagic and hypotoxic changes) and degeneration of neurones in the brain. However, it is unclear whether all these were a direct result of the drugs themselves or from toxic contaminants.[176] Heatstroke occurs because the drug is used to maintain high and sustained levels of dancing for hours on end and the user becomes dehydrated.[177] For this reason, one of the main messages to reduce harm from ecstasy has been to drink plenty of water when using the drug in dancing environments.

However recent deaths from dilutional hyponatremia have called the effectiveness of this message into doubt. This occurs when such quantities of water are drunk that the blood is diluted, and eventually causes a fatal build-up of pressure in the cranium. It also appears that ecstasy may precipitate the release of anti-diuretic hormones (ADH) into the body, which slow down the kidney's fluid-eliminating capacity. This hormone, therefore, may contribute to the hyponatremia.[178] The message to drink plenty of water or isotonic 'sports' drinks still stands but not too much, 1 pint per hour being the recommended amount. It must be re-emphasised that water is not a cure for a 'bad trip' but rather a method of countering the dehydration brought on by dancing for prolonged periods in hot and sweaty nightclubs. The long-term effects of MDMA or the chemically similar hallucinogenic amphetamines such as MDEA and MDA, are unclear. They do not have a long tradition of use like morphine, cocaine and cannabis of which the long-term risks are better understood.

Steroids

Incidence of serious health risks from the use of anabolic steroids (AS) so far reported has been extremely low but systematic evaluation of the long-term effects has not been undertaken.[179]

Anabolic steroids are taken in cycles with an average of about 8 weeks 'on drug' and 8 weeks 'off'. Adverse psychiatric effects have been attributed to AS misuse with hypomania (a lesser form of mania) correlated with use and major depression with discontinuation,[180] as well as mania,[181] and anger.[182]

Evidence also supports the view that AS use increases aggression when they are being taken, and it has been suggested that wives and girlfriends of AS users may be at particular risk while the user is 'on-drug'.[183] Bearing this in mind, it is worth noting that 75% of misusers reported an increase in sex drive when using AS.[184]

Evidence of adverse physical effects include acne, and in men gynaecomastia (breast development),[185] and decreased testicular length.[186] A risk of thrombosis has also been detected.[187] However a major health concern relates to the risks associated with injecting. A recent survey showed that 81% of those using steroids injected, although only 1 user out of 385 admitted to having shared injecting equipment.[188] These risks are also presented by the misuse of the injectable opioid nalbuphine hydrochloride which has been associated with steroid misuse.[189]

Nitrites

Common short-term adverse effects can include dizziness and headaches, and less commonly nausea, weakness and cold sweats. Cases of nitrite dermatitis have been reported affecting the upper lip, nose and cheeks, sometimes accompanied by pain and swelling of the nasal passages resembling sinusitis, clearing spontaneously in approximately 10 days. Inhalation of nitrites increases intraocular pressure, a risk for those with glaucoma and produces hypotension.

Although tolerance develops within 2-3 weeks of continual use, this tolerance is lost following a few days of abstinence. There are no reports of withdrawal symptoms or psychological dependence. The use of alkyl nitrites has been linked to the development of the cancer Kaposi's sarcoma, one of the earliest symptoms of AIDS, though this theory has lost much of its credibility as all study results have been inconclusive.[190]

Until January 1997 it was possible to buy amyl nitrite from a pharmacy without prescription, but it has since been reclassified as a prescription only medicine.[191] As nitrites are not addictive and their use does not appear to constitute a significant social problem, there are no plans to make them controlled drugs under the Misuse of Drugs Act.

Polydrug use

Although most people who use drugs will probably only ever use cannabis, the taking of more than one drug type is common amongst users of other drugs and is an increasing trend. For instance, the Four City Survey found that when amphetamine, LSD or ecstasy is taken by someone, they will invariably take one or both of the other drugs.[192] This does not necessarily mean that different types of drugs are taken at the same time, but it can often mean that different drugs are taken at 'around the same time' — LSD and ecstasy at an all-night 'rave' for example.

The major risk inherent in polydrug use is due to the interactions between the drugs which are being taken (in fact, ecstasy in itself is often a polydrug experience, with amphetamine, LSD and ecstasy's sister drugs MDA and MDEA often being sold as the drug).[193] Alcohol and benzodiazepines when taken together can be fatal because they both depress the nervous system. On the other hand, experienced users may deliberately take different drug types at the same time in order to accentuate the effects. Invariably, the user will take a stimulant and a depressant drug such as heroin and cocaine in the 'speedball', in an attempt to make use of the 'best' effects of each.

Polydrug users tend to be the most emotionally disturbed and the most difficult to treat. Many lead chaotic lifestyles. The high mortality among drug users in Glasgow and Edinburgh since 1990 has been attributed to polydrug use, and particularly the use of heroin with 1 or more of temazepam, diazepam and alcohol. All 4 drugs can cause respiratory depression or vomiting and taking them together may increase the likelihood of these potentially fatal effects.[194] Aside from these dependent drug users, there has also emerged what has been called a "pick 'n' mix culture", where drug misusers cannot be defined by the use of a particular drug, but they will choose from whatever is available at a given time, whether this is cannabis, ecstasy or cocaine.

Over the counter drugs

The misuse of over the counter drugs present a range of risks to health, but because literature on this subject is scarce, it is difficult to determine what proportion of misusers suffer adverse effects. Particular damage can result from the drugs which are combined with the abused drug. For instance, there have been reports of codeine being filtered out of codeine and aspirin tablets, a process which can leave nearly 75% of the aspirin from the tablets remaining after filtration. If injected, the misuser could experience aspirin poisoning.[195]

Paramol (containing paracetamol and dihydrocodeine) carries a particular risk of paracetamol overdose among those misusing it for its codeine content. The preparation contains relatively little codeine in relation to the paracetamol, therefore large quantities of paracetamol are incidentally taken to achieve the intended psychoactive effect from the codeine. Without immediate medical treatment paracetamol overdose can cause irreversible liver damage and death.

As with any other opiate, overdose of OTC codeine, dihydrocodeine, or morphine can cause respiratory depression and unconsciousness. Although death can occur from respiratory failure, it is uncommon.[196] Tolerance to and dependence on OTC opiates can develop from prolonged use.

Medicines with sedative-like effects mostly contain antihistamines which can be dangerous when taken with alcohol. A common such drug is cyclizine, which produces a stimulant and hallucinatory effect when injected in large quantities. Heavy use can cause serious neurological damage. Cyclizine misuse has been particularly common in the North West of England in a pattern of injecting polydrug use.[197]

Pregnancy

There are broadly 2 ways in which drugs — including tobacco and alcohol — may damage a foetus. Firstly, heavy use may affect the mother's health either directly or through self-neglect and poor nutrition. Secondly, alcohol, nicotine and most illegal drugs are able to cross the placenta and reach the foetus directly.[198]

In general, and irrespective of the drug used, there is an increased risk of low birth-weight and premature birth, with the associated risks of perinatal mortality and cot death. Congenital abnormalities are also above average in the babies of drug users.[199] The most dangerous time for the development of such abnormalities is in the first 3 months of pregnancy, when the woman may not actually be aware that she is pregnant.

Drugs like alcohol, heroin and tranquillisers, which depress the adult's respiratory and other bodily functions, will also depress these functions in the foetus and in the newborn. There is also the possibility that babies born to mothers dependent on these drugs will need medical care to avoid withdrawal symptoms.[200] Stimulant drugs, such as amphetamine and cocaine, may cause restrictions in foetal growth which is probably associated with reduced oxygen supply to the baby caused by the constriction of blood vessels which stimulants produce.

The whole area of drug use in pregnancy is under-researched, and such research as there is, is often inconclusive. It should be noted however, that a literature review of research into the effects of cocaine on reproduction found that studies which reported adverse effects were more likely to be published in the scientific press than those which found no adverse effects, irrespective of the validity of the research.[201] Nevertheless, there is a substantial body of research which shows that cocaine and crack are among the most dangerous drugs for pregnant women. The constriction of blood vessels can cause spontaneous abortion at a rate which is higher than that for heroin users,[202] separation of the placenta, which occurs in about 1% of pregnancies in cocaine users,[203] and stillbirth.[204] Much has been made of 'crack babies', who are born 'addicted' to crack or cocaine, but evidence suggests that the baby will recover to full health from any adverse symptoms a week or 2 after birth.[205] It is extremely difficult to attribute any long-term effects on children to illicit maternal drug use during pregnancy, as there are so many interrelated variables in the first few years of life.

One of the largest studies into the effects of cannabis on the foetus found that there were no significant differences in rates of miscarriage, obstetric complications, birth-weight or congenital abnormalities when 700 pregnant users were matched with 700 pregnant non-users.[206] It was shown, however, that the babies of the heaviest users were more easily startled and jittery than those of occasional or non-users, though this passed off after 12 to 24 months.[207]

The limited research evidence for the effects of heroin, methadone and other opiates supports the view that heroin use in pregnancy can lead to low birth-weight, premature birth and increased perinatal mortality.[208] In the third trimester of pregnancy (months 7-9) heroin use can cause episodes of acute placental insufficiency and in 1973 a very high stillbirth rate of 65-70 per 1000 births was reported among pregnant heroin users. The same research showed that if such women were maintained on methadone throughout their pregnancy, the still-birth rate fell to normal levels, but the perinatal mortality increased by a factor of 3.[209] More recent research has been limited because it would be unethical not to treat a pregnant heroin user with methadone since publication of this evidence.

Studies have shown a link between benzodiazepine use in the first few months of pregnancy and cleft palate.[210] There is limited evidence that amphetamine and ecstasy can also cause cleft palate and heart deficiencies.[211] Very little is known about the chronic risks of volatile substance abuse and the 20 or so volatile compounds involved all have different toxicity profiles.[212]   However, chronic heavy exposure to toluene, the principal solvent found in contact adhesives, is known to cause a wide variety of physical pathologies.   There is one report of a foetal solvents syndrome.[213]

Individual differences

Despite some general rules as to how drugs affect people, it must be recognised that different people will be affected in different ways.   As with alcohol, body weight is a factor in the speed of intoxication.   In general, lighter people will experience greater effects and consequently greater dangers for the same drug dose than will heavier people.   Gender differences in response to psychoactive drugs are poorly researched, but it is known, for example, that women alcoholics are more susceptible to liver disease than men, probably because they have less body water.   For this reason they will be more susceptible to the effects of some drugs.

Genetic differences can also account for variations in a drug's effects, as is the case with MDMA.   Differences in MDMA's toxicity have been associated with individuals' ability to metabolise the substance debrisoquine hydroxylase.[214] Chemical tests can reveal whether an individual is a poor metaboliser of debrisoquine hydroxylase and therefore are likely to metabolise MDMA more slowly, but further research is needed into the implications of this.

Deaths associated with drug misuse

The statistical picture of drug deaths in Britain is not clear for a number of reasons.   The Home Office statistics include suicide by overdose as a drug death, even if there is no history of drug misuse, and drug-related road deaths are excluded.   Since 1994 the Home Office no longer collects notified addict death data and solvent deaths are only included where the user was deemed to be dependent on solvents at the time of death.   The Institute for the Study of Drug Dependence (ISDD) have estimated the total numbers of deaths from drug use from 1985 to 1994 excluding suicides and 'undetermined' poisonings. These may be the result of drug dependence, accidental poisoning or overdose or are just drug-related (see table):

Table 6: Deaths from drug misuse

Drug	Deaths 1985-1994
Cocaine	67
Amphetamine	97
Ecstasy	60 approx. (1989 to 1996)
Solvents	1070
Opiates (primarily heroin and methadone)	2395

It is of some concern that it is not possible to make estimates for or to assess trends in drug related mortality after 1994, except in the case of ecstasy for which the ISDD have informally collected its own figures. Were deaths attributable to a new drug, for instance, the lack of data would impede swift information dissemination and preventative action. Other trends might usefully be observed if such data could be gathered and the causes of death investigated.

3

The role of the medical profession

Table 7: Services for drugs misusers

Accident and Emergency departments of hospitals may come into contact with drug misusers when they suffer overdoses, injuries associated with intoxication or other crises. Some also provide needle and syringe exchange facilities.
Community advice and counselling services may offer many of the same services as Community drug teams. They are more likely to focus on non-prescribing services including advice, counselling, groupwork, needle exchange, etc.
Community drug teams (or community substance misuse teams where their remit includes alcohol misuse) provide advice, counselling and information; some run needle and syringe exchanges and undertake or refer for prescribing. They may also refer patients for in-patient detoxification. The roles performed by community drug teams vary susbtantially from area to area.
Community pharmacists: some dispense controlled drugs to drug misusers, and run needle exchange schemes or sell needles and syringes to those who do not want to participate in exchange schemes. Community pharmacists may also come into contact with those misusing over-the-counter drugs.
Complementary therapies are provided for drug misusers by an increasing number of drug services and by complementary therapy specialities. The most common therapies are auricular (ear) acupuncture and herbal medicine. Others include whole body acupuncture, massage, Qi Gong, shiatsu, reflexology and homoeopathy.

Drug Dependence Units (DDUs) are outpatient facilities usually run by a psychiatrist, sometimes with community drug teams attached. Their range of services generally includes prescribing and they are oriented towards the problematic or longer term patients. DDUs are a major provider of methadone maintenance services and the main providers of injectable prescriptions within the NHS, and may also have access to in-patient beds in a local psychiatric or medical ward or designated in-patient units with facilities for detoxification and rehabilitation.

General Practitioners provide general health care for the public including drug misusers and are also able to refer patients for specialist care. With appropriate training, support and remuneration, they may also undertake specialist care themselves or 'shared care' for the treatment of drug misuse. Shared care consists of the GP retaining overall clinical responsibility for the patient and agreeing a treatment plan with a specialist. This may or may not involve the GP prescribing substitute drugs. A 'liaison worker' may be appointed to offer help and support to the GP.

Maternity services are based in hospitals and may have contact with pregnant drug misusers. Staff do not usually have specialist skills in the treatment of drug misuse in pregnancy, but would be able to refer patients to specialist services.

Other criminal justice services make contact with drug users before imprisonment. They may work in police stations with arrested drug users or in courts providing reports and alternatives to custody. Police surgeons may also be called on to provide treatment for drug users in custody.

Outreach services aim to provide advice and harm minimisation interventions to those drug misusers not in touch with services, including prevention of bloodborne and sexually transmitted diseases. They may also provide injecting equipment. Outreach workers visit community settings, such as pubs and homes, or other agencies such as youth clubs and prisons. Some work on the streets with homeless drug misusers or where young people congregate.

Prison based drug services include residential treatment programmes within prisons and advice and counselling services which some community agencies provide for prisoners. Treatment programmes differ in their approach according to the needs of the prison and the agency operating the programme. They may be tied in with voluntary drug testing programmes and drug-free wings.

Probation services make contact with large numbers of drug using offenders. Probation officers may work with drug use as part of their general work on causes of offending while some probation services operate specific services for drug users or fund partnership workers with specialist drug services.

Residential detoxification services provide medically supervised detoxification with counselling and support. They are usually staffed by multi-disciplinary teams including medical specialists, typically treating drug misusers with complex polydrug use problems and physical dependence. These include short stay residential crisis units, based in the voluntary sector and statutory sectors, which stabilise misusers' drug use and also carry out detoxification. Treatment tends to last on average for 4 weeks.

Residential rehabilitation is available through a range of programmes, mainly consisting of therapeutic communities, '12 step' houses using self-help techniques, and general houses including those with a Christian-based philosophy. Some provide detoxification on the premises and others have access to detoxification facilities. Their aim is to help patients return to as normal a life as possible in the community without misusing drugs.

Self-help networks consist of 3 main types: drug users' union and user rights groups (small local groups), family support (Families Anonymous, ADFAM National and some treatment agencies, which aim to support families of drug users) and Narcotics Anonymous 12 Step Groups. There are also some local volunteer support groups for parents of drug misusers. They have a diverse range of goals, activities and settings. Drug misusers often use these groups in conjunction with other treatment.

Social services may come into contact with drug users through their generic work or through specialist work with children, families or mental health issues. They may work with drug issues themselves or, where appropriate, refer to specialist services.

Structured day programmes offer intensive community based support mimicking a working week or college course. They are usually of a finite length either with a rolling programme of fixed activities or individually negotiated timetables. Many take a holistic approach to rehabilitation, including life skills and vocational training.

Syringe exchange schemes aim primarily to reduce the sharing of injecting equipment and thus the risk of transmitting HIV and other bloodborne diseases. Although called 'exchange schemes', the return of old equipment for new is not always required. Syringe exchange schemes are sometimes separate agencies, but may be part of the function of other health care agencies, such as drop-in drug treatment services and community pharmacies.

Young people's services consist of dedicated drug services and generic services with a drugs component. They aim to discourage further experimentation with drugs, encourage safer drug using practises and reduce drug use and can refer young people to other agencies such as needle exchange facilities and medical treatment services.

The multidisciplinary team: roles of medical and other professionals

Social and individual problems associated with drug use

Many people presenting to services for help with drug dependence and drug misuse, untypically of the wider drug misusing population, have major social problems associated with criminality, in particular drug related acquisitive crime. Other social problems include housing, financial and relationship difficulties. Many have been in contact with police, prison or the probation service by the time

Figure 1: Services for drug users

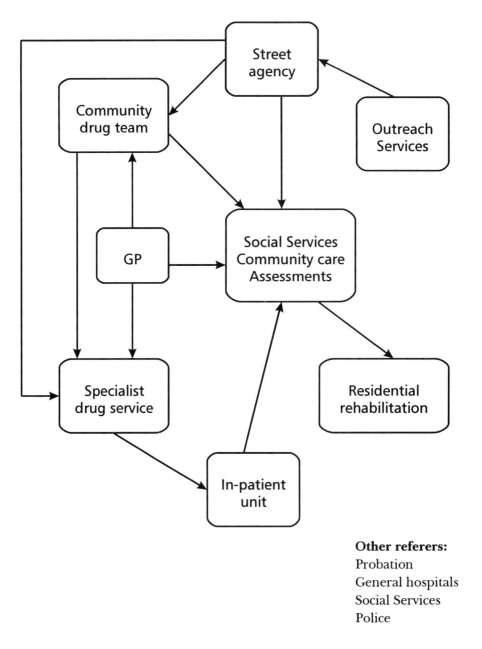

Other referers:
Probation
General hospitals
Social Services
Police

⟶ Represents referral channels
NB: guide only — substantial variation in services in different areas

they contact a drug service. They may have major physical and psychological problems associated with chronic drug misuse.

It is clear that many of the problems facing dependent drug users who present to medical practitioners are associated with high levels of socioeconomic deprivation. The provision of stable housing, job opportunities, education, training and youth and community activities provide important opportunities for dependent drug misusers to become more integrated and to have more meaningful engagement and involvement with many dimensions of social existence. Such activities are far beyond the remit of simple medical interventions.

However, within this wider context of the social and economic problems associated with problem drug misuse, the opportunity for smaller health gains do exist such as reduced or safer use and fall well within the remit of the health service and doctors should be actively encouraged to become comprehensively involved in this more modest task. The complex nature of many drug problems makes it essential that medical practitioners work in partnership with specialists in drug services and other professionals such as social workers within community drug teams. Liaison with social agencies such as the probation service may enable progress to be made with some seemingly intractable problems. This will ensure that as wide ranging an approach as possible is taken in tackling the multiple problems of the individual drug user.

The role of doctors in treating drug misusers

The medical profession has experienced difficulty in defining its role in the management of drug misusers, both at an individual level and at a public health level. ('Management' in this context refers to clinical care which encompasses diagnosis, assessment, preventive care, treatment, referral and liaison with other professionals and services as appropriate.) While the potential role of clinical interventions in responding to large-scale social problems such as drug misuse and poverty should not be overstated, nor should it be assumed that doctors have no potential role in responding to drug misusers. The important role which doctors have to play in the overall provision of services for drug misusers is reflected in many policy documents.[1,2,3,4] Many medical professionals (usually psychiatrists or general practitioners) now work in multi-disciplinary professional teams, both in primary care and in specialist settings, particularly community substance misuse teams.[5] Within these organisational settings doctors need to clarify their roles and their specific responsibilities in the management of drug misusers.

The aims of treatment for drug misusers are diverse. Distinctly medical ones include reduction in injection-related damage, reduction in virus transmission, improvement in physical and mental health and reduction in consumption of illicit substances. Other aims include reduction in crime, increase in employment among drug users and improvement in social functioning, for instance being able to care responsibly for their children.

The role of any health professional in interventions with drug misusers extends beyond the simple issue of drug prescribing and the provision of in-patient care, into ones which contribute towards the achievement of the above diverse intervention aims. The multiple problems experienced by dependent drug users and the possibility of substantial and radical behaviour change is such that all opportunities for change should be facilitated. All health professionals have an important and symbolic role in promoting healthy behaviour. They can facilitate opportunities for behaviour change, using a variety of strategies to encourage motivation to change by understanding the complex and malleable nature of motivation.

Doctors (including specialists, general practitioners and hospital doctors) who have contact with drug misusers (for instance in accident and emergency departments, genitourinary medicine clinics or obstetric services) will have a range of goals which may include health promotion, harm minimisation and treatment or rehabilitation. Interventions may be required for a wide range of reasons.[6] Acute medical activity includes the treatment of acutely intoxicated, overdosed drug users (who may be non-dependent) and those in withdrawal from alcohol, benzodiazepines and opiates. The majority of drug misuse specialists are involved in the management of the long-term drug user, primarily opiate, benzodiazepine or alcohol dependent.

Professionals and services in the drug misuse field

General practitioners

For many drug users general practitioners are a key to early and easy access to care as they are for any other patient, and they remain central to the overall strategy of responding to drug misusers. Substance misuse problems arise in primary care in-patients who are well-known for their drug misuse and in new patients coming into the practice. GPs' circumstances vary and they are not always in a position to offer drug treatment services. For instance GPs based in areas where drug users have been known to act violently may feel vulnerable to attack, or they may wish to avoid the adverse effects on the smooth running of a practice and on other patients which is caused by the disruptive behaviour of some drug users. Some general practitioners manage a small number of drug misusers within their own practice, but some, in practices with particularly high populations of dependent drug misusers have effectively become sub-specialist acquiring substantial expertise to manage a large number of dependent drug users within their practice despite a lack of formal training.[7] Other GPs provide support for clinical and local community substance misuse teams. Some GPs decline to be involved in the management of identified drug misusers although they may be looking after a few whose problems have not emerged. Many GPs express the need for close liaison and support from specialist agencies and non-statutory services.

The recent Task Force report recommends that "shared care" with appropriate support for GPs should be available as widely as possible.[8,9] When working with drug users communication between professionals is important to prevent problems such as double scripting for instance, where the patient could be in receipt of methadone prescriptions from more than one prescriber. In many situations such as the care of a drug user with children a substantial part of the prescribing doctor's workload may be communicating with many different professionals. However, despite a plethora of models and practices in shared care, there is no standardisation of the liaison between primary care and specialist services.

Other generic workers

Health visitors, midwives, community psychiatric nurses, social workers, probation officers and youth workers will inevitably encounter drug misusers in their work, whether knowingly or unknowingly, and the responses and interventions which they make may be crucial in helping drug users move to a less harmful lifestyle. Their training should ensure that they are able to deal with drug misusers constructively.

Specialist drug services

Community drug teams

In the mid-1980s and '90s there was a radical expansion of community based services run by both the statutory and voluntary sector supported in the mid-1980's by a central funding initiative from the Department of Health.[10] These services have continued to grow and evolve since then. In general 'community drug teams', or 'community substance misuse teams' where their remit includes alcohol misuse, have between 3 and 7 staff usually comprising psychiatrists, GPs, community psychiatric nurses, social workers and occasionally psychologists and drug counsellors (from diverse professional backgrounds). The roles performed by community drug teams vary considerably between areas. Their main role is to support GPs treating dependent drug users by offering a shared care arrangement. However in addition most offer some kind of prescribing service either by having their own medical drugs specialist, usually a psychiatrist, or by having general practitioners who will prescribe for them either on a sessional basis or for individual patients. They all offer advice counselling and information services often with a drop in facility. Community drug teams' main task is to act as a specialist resource for GPs and drug users, and in many areas where there is no drug dependency unit, these teams will be the only specialist resource available.

The roles of the different professionals also varies between community drug teams. In most services all professionals will have a caseload, seeing patients for general counselling and help with social and psychological problems — becoming a key worker for the patient. However some professionals will specialise in ways consistent with their particular expertise, for instance a social worker seeing patients with child care problems or a psychologist seeing a patient with an anxiety disorder. Some teams may have members who are only specialist and to whom other team members refer their patients, for instance a housing advice worker. The role of the doctor may also vary. In most teams prescribing decisions will be made jointly between the doctor and the key worker. The doctor is likely to see the patient at the beginning of a prescribing episode, and subsequently if they have specific physical or psychiatric problems. In some teams the doctors will have their own caseload of patients with psychological or physical difficulties.

Drug Dependency Units (DDUs)

Drug Dependency Units tend to be based in large urban areas and consist of outpatient facilities run by a psychiatrist; many have community drug teams attached to them. They provide a range of services, usually prescribing services, and tend to deal with the problematic or longer term patients. They are a major provider of methadone maintenance services and the main providers of injectable prescriptions within the NHS. They may also have access to in-patient beds. These may be beds in a local psychiatric or medical ward but in some cases are designated in-patient units with facilities for detoxification and rehabilitation. Doctors in this setting have a more central role in patient management often seeing a substantial number of patients themselves as well as supervising and training other professionals and junior doctors.

Specialist services receive drug misusers both by patients' self referral and by referral from GPs. The most problematic drug misusers tend to self-refer as they are not always registered with GPs. One of the tasks of these specialist services is then to engage such users with primary care by ensuring registration with a local GP to assist in enhancing and improving their general health and well-being.

Residential Services

The 1970s saw the expansion of residential and nursing home facilities, most in the non-statutory sector with some being entirely private and commercial. The residential sector has been substantially affected by the NHS and Community Care Act 1990 because funding for rehabilitation is allocated by social service departments to individual patients and as social service budgets are limited it is in practice tightly controlled. Access to these services by any individual patient follows either a community care assessment by their local social services department (or its representative) and a subsequent decision as to the patient's suitability and the availability of money or an extra contractual referral with the agreement of the health authority. There may be very little clinical influence on these decisions although a close working relationship with social services can result in cooperation over suitable placements for patients. The treatment provided varies substantially between rehabilitation services but broadly falls into 3 categories: twelve step Minnesota model programmes which call upon the principles of the Narcotics Anonymous and Alcoholics Anonymous fellowships; Christian houses which are Christian in their basic philosophy (although they may not impose this on their patients); and other communities which have a rather looser philosophy, and may for instance encourage rehabilitation into work.[11,12] The different treatment modalities described are appropriate to the wide range and severity of problems associated with drug misuse. Furthermore, any single drug misuser may require different services at different stages in their drug misuse 'career'.

Modalities of treatment

Efficacy of different interventions

Aims of treatment

The main intentions of medical treatment for drug misusers are to generally improve social and physical wellbeing by pursuing a number of goals. These goals may not all necessarily be achieved initially and for some patients progress may only be small:

- Cessation of injecting.

- Initially significant reduction in illicit drug use, leading on to more stable drug use.

- Reduction in high risk behaviour to acquire drugs, progressing to reduced crime.

- Improvement in relationships.

- Ability to gain and maintain employment or education (eg a college course).

- Eventually detoxification and abstinence.

Limitations of UK evidence to date

Much of the evaluation of treatment and service intervention has been conducted in the United States[13] and it is difficult to extrapolate some of the evidence to UK based treatment services due to the different social context of drug taking behaviour and different systems of individual and public health provision. While there is a lack of experimentally designed treatment evaluation in the UK there are a limited number of descriptive reports of treatment evaluations that lend some support to the benefits of these interventions. The Department of Health has completed a major review on the effectiveness of drug treatment which concluded that there is no preferred single treatment but that benefits are conferred by methadone reduction programmes, oral methadone maintenance programmes, residential rehabilitation programmes and specialist in-patient drug dependency units. The review included a large prospective descriptive treatment outcome study — the National Treatment Outcome Research Study (NTORS), which is scheduled to continue until 2001. Evidence published to date is derived from preliminary results, and the study does not include all treatment modalities or services. The findings of the Task Force are discussed below.

Measures of impact and treatment outcome

In discussing treatment it is worth noting the distinctions between treatment settings and treatment modalities. The majority of treatment occurs in the community but a substantial minority occurs in residential and in-patient services. For instance residential therapeutic communities have in common that they are residential but their treatment model may vary substantially from a 12 step Narcotics Anonymous programme to a Christian approach and various counselling approaches differ in their philosophy and whether or not patients are provided with substitute medication as part of the treatment package.

The evaluation of treatment is complex because it involves a multi-dimensional approach, with the need to measure impact of treatment on amount of drug use, physical and psychological health, social wellbeing, reduction in criminal behaviour and improvement in general employment and social functioning.[14] The international evidence to date suggests that both residential and community-based interventions impact positively on all these dimensions of behaviour and well-being and that the majority of drug treatment interventions are cost-effective due to the reduction in problematic social and criminal behaviour that occurs when individuals are in contact with treatment services.[15]

The key variation across these modalities or services however, is the capacity to retain individuals in contact with services. The residential therapeutic communities which provide long-term intensive, usually group, psychotherapy, have the lowest retention of drug users and the highest turnover rates; the outpatient drug-free day programmes and drug-free counselling services also have low retention rates. However, such reduction in retention also frees up these services for briefer, more intensive interventions, potentially increasing the number of patients treated.

Assessing the drug user

Assessments are important, though time-consuming. A good assessment is essential to highlight which packages of care are needed to ensure the best chance of progress with a drug dependency problem. Yet, outside of the information required to make a decision about prescribing for the dependent drug user, obtaining the detail required to enable decisions to be made for a tailor-made treatment programme is such a lengthy process that it is generally impractical for a general practitioner to do.

When drug misusers in need of help attend a GP, there are a number of options. Either these patients can be referred on to a specialist drug service with a request that the service take over completely the treatment of their drug dependency, or they can be treated jointly by the GP and a specialist drug worker on a shared care basis. It is not recommended that GPs handle the treatment of drug dependence entirely on their own. In a shared care situation there are a number of different ways in which the specialist services handle the initial stage. In Edinburgh, for example, it is the practice of the Community Drug Problem Service to assess the drug user and instigate substitution therapy before handing back to the GP. In other places the drug user is assessed by a community drug team worker, who after discussion with the team, will outline a detoxification plan and offer a tripartite contract to be signed by the drug user, the GP, and the Community Drug Team. Some GPs have themselves become skilled enough to decide whether substitution therapy is needed and the dose and regime that is appropriate. Where GPs have referred the drug user to a community drug team for assessment before embarking on prescribing, it is important that the drug service is able to respond quickly so that the patient does not lose motivaton to address his problems. The GP and drug user cannot be left for several days or weeks waiting for a response. For the drug user to be seen within 2 working days would be reasonable and would be consistent with the Patients' Charter, but in view of the heavy pressure on services, this may not be realistic.

Due to the constraints of time an assessment is sometimes best done in 2 phases. The first phase being an initial assessment to determine whether the person presenting for help is dependent on drugs, whether any prescribing should be undertaken, and if so what prescribing programme should be agreed. Where appropriate other doctors should be telephoned to ensure that prescribing is not already being undertaken. A urine specimen should be taken for drug screening at an early stage, preferably by the GP at the time when the drug user is first seen. It is important to prevent the patient from substituting a drug free specimen so he should be asked to provide a fresh specimen (if it is warm, it is more likely to be their own!) A physical examination should be undertaken, looking for injection sites in the arms, legs and groins. Evidence of abscesses, sinuses, and superficial vein thromboses are all helpful confirmatory pointers to the length of history of injecting drug use. It is important during this first stage of assessment to determine the risk of transmission of HIV and hepatitis, and to counsel the drug user about reducing the spread of these bloodborne viral diseases, both through contaminated injecting equipment and by unsafe sexual practice. At this stage pre-test counselling for HIV and hepatitis B and C may be given, and the necessity for hepatitis B immunisation should be determined.

The second stage of assessment is more complicated. It entails an assessment for the rest of the treatment package. Here treatment should be regarded in the widest possible terms as any intervention which helps to reduce the harm that is occurring to both the individual and the local population. For example, where the drug misusers are unemployed, employment may be of great benefit in helping them to overcome their drug problems and therefore part of the assessment process should be to look at what are the opportunities for employment and whether an employment training programme would be helpful. Both doctors and drug workers should be aware of the need to ensure that the assessment is relevant and useful for treatment. It is easy to spend a great deal of time asking questions, the answers to which will have no bearing at all on the treatment given. It is important to assess the amount of motivation of a patient, and the social situation — how can the social support from family and friends who are non-drug users be maximised? Are there opportunities to improve accommodation difficulties? etc. The current criminality of the patient is more important to ascertain than the number of arrests, which really only focuses on the unsuccessful criminals. Nevertheless the threat of an outstanding court case with the possibility of a prison sentence may have important implications for treatment and is often a great spur which motivates people to tackle their drug problem. Those deeply entrenched in the twin subcultures of criminality and drug use are often very resistant to change, although interestingly there are some interventions, such as successful help to find employment and some cognitive-behavioural interventions, which help to move people on from both problems. For all its faults self-reported crime occurring over the past 30 days is the most reliable indication of current criminality.

The way in which people use drugs psychologically often highlights a deficit in their own ability to cope with difficult emotions such as anxiety, depression, anger or boredom and the use of drugs to help them cope over a long period of time may deskill them further disabling them completely from being able to cope with these feelings themselves. Such people would benefit from appropriate skills training. Others use drugs to stop them thinking about difficult past life events, such as sexual abuse or an unhappy childhood, and would be helped by psychotherapy. Sometimes it is the social side of drug use which is most difficult to overcome. One of the most helpful assessment tools is a device which was developed from a technique used in cognitive psychology. It is known as 'the advantages/disadvantages 4 cell matrix' (see table 8). Patients are asked to list the advantages and disadvantages of taking drugs and the advantages and disadvantages of stopping. This gives information not only as to the motivation, and stage of change of the drug user, but also it highlights which are the most important psychological cues to work on to prevent relapse.

With regard to treatment history, previous experience of what was and what was not helpful in the past is often a useful indicator as to what will be helpful in the future. This applies to any drug-free periods that have occurred, whether or not treatment was undertaken. What were the circumstances that enabled a drug-free period to occur and what led to subsequent relapse. In some instances a drug user will have had several attempts to become drug free by repeated detoxifications both as an out-patient and in-patient. Sometimes there will have been more than 1 attempt at rehabilitation in 1 of the rehabilitation houses. Assessment for rehabilitation must be done by a social services named assessor as a separate venture.

There is no clear demarcation between assessment and treatment. The assessment process itself may at times be highly therapeutic and some people believe that the therapeutic process begins with assessment

General medical care

Health benefit opportunities

Prevention of bloodborne infections

The introduction of needle exchange schemes and the opportunity to have health advice and health promotion in this context has also, along with HIV prevention, offered other benefits of reducing the transmission of at least some of the bloodborne viruses. Despite the availability of an effective vaccination against hepatitis B infection, the majority of injecting drug users, those at risk of moving to injecting drug use and those in sexual contact with injecting drug users have not been vaccinated against hepatitis B.[16]

The prevention of the spread of hepatitis C, which is now endemic in the injecting population, is a major challenge for the medical community. Hepatitis B vaccination is particularly important for those drug users with chronic hepatitis C infection, as the combination of the two viruses considerably worsens the prognosis. It is therefore important to encourage drug misusers at risk from bloodborne pathogens to be tested and in view of the high prevalence of chronic hepatitis C infection, it is also wise to include liver function tests which can provide an early warning of liver damage before further investigation is undertaken. Patients should be counselled regarding the implications of a negative or positive result before testing which is an essential prerequisite to HIV testing.[17] The Department of Health recommends that the discussion before and after testing, and testing itself, should be part of mainstream clinical care. Specialist counsellors would not be required unless further discussion was needed where an individual's circumstances were complex and time consuming. It has produced guidance which spell out areas for discussion entitled *Guidelines for pre-test discussion on HIV testing*.[18] Early diagnosis of HIV, bringing infected individuals under the care of suitable specialists, is associated with significant individual health benefits. Its effectiveness in aiding primary prevention of HIV transmission is more debatable.

However the efforts in the UK to contain the spread of HIV among injecting drug users has been resoundingly successful and is clear evidence that health promotion can work within the drug using community to achieve behavioural change. An important 'spin-off' of the HIV prevention campaign has been the evidence that drug users and drug injectors are receptive to some extent to messages and advice about health protection and harm reduction. However the high incidence of hepatitis C among this group raises questions as to the efficacy of such measures in the prevention of hepatitis C. Hepatitis C is more infectious than HIV, and less than hepatitis B, but the actual mechanisms of transmission among injecting drug users are not known. It is possible that the sharing of injecting paraphenalia such as filters which are used to exclude insolubles from the injected drug and spoons used for preparing drug solutions are the route of transmission. In addition, the Task Force report suggested that injecting drug users may vary in their definitions of the term 'sharing' of equipment, for instance not considering the use of a regular sexual partner's injecting equipment as sharing, which may complicate the picture.[19] It is also unclear whether those who have contracted hepatitis C are using needle exchange schemes.

When warning injecting drug users of the risks associated with sharing needles and works (the syringe minus the needle), health care workers can also provide information on how to clean injecting equipment effectively, and how to access local needle exchange facilities. In relation to HIV, the benefits of harm minimisation and health promotion among drug users and drug injectors need to be fully acknowledged and awareness by doctors of their potential to confer benefit is to be further heightened.

Needle and syringe provision

The provision of sterile injecting equipment has been a large part of the UK response to the HIV epidemic and will be of continuing importance also to prevent further spread of the hepatitis C epidemic. Syringe exchange refers to the provision of sterile needles and syringes, antiseptic swabs and containers for safe disposal of used injecting equipment. Syringe exchange occurs in a variety of settings. These include NHS community drug teams, non-statutory drug agencies, outreach workers attached to both statutory and non-statutory agencies, a few mobile clinics, a few accident and emergency departments and an expanding number of retail pharmacies. Drug misusers have reduced their needle sharing behaviour, most reduction probably having occurred between 1986 and 1990.[20] Syringe exchanges have been demonstrated to help drug users achieve this change towards lower risk behaviour.[21] Community pharmacists are increasingly playing a role in the supply, collection and disposal of injecting equipment.

Psychological care

Psychological care for drug misusers is needed not only to help in reducing drug misuse or achieving abstinence, but also in dealing with the psychological problems which may have pre-existed or contributed to the drug misuse.

Assertiveness training may help patients to resist drugs when offered, and relaxation techniques may help to combat the anxiety resulting from withdrawal from some drugs. Identifying circumstances which prompt anxiety and drug-taking may also help in developing coping strategies for difficult situations. Alternatively, where anxiety results from problems such as debts or housing difficulties, patients should be referred to agencies or individuals such as housing workers who can provide practical help.

Motivational interviewing is a technique used within specialist drug services which aims to develop patients' motivation to change their drug misusing behaviour. The notion of ambivalence is recognised to be central and almost universal in those considering behaviour change. The therapist will employ several strategies including reflective listening, to tip the patient's decision making process in the direction of healthy change, which depends upon the awakening of a sense of personal commitment in the patient. The ambivalence of drug misusers to their drug use can be seen more clearly when broken down into the 'advantages' and 'disadvantages' 4 cell matrix (see table 8).

Table 8: Example: 32 year old female heroin user with a 14 year history of regular substance use

Advantages of using	Disadvantages of using
helps depression helps me relax helps to blot things out stops boredom stops withdrawals sharing drug experiences with friends	financial problems poor health (hepatitis C positive) legal problems
Advantages of stopping	**Disadvantages of stopping**
financial	boredom would lose friends

The patient's boyfriend, who was also a drug user, went to jail 2 weeks before she sought help. The 4 cell matrix shows her to be poorly motivated. The main reason she is seeking help is that she herself has an outstanding court case and may go to prison. The matrix gives us considerable information about the way in which she uses drugs. She is taking drugs to try to stop herself thinking about unpleasant past events (by 'blotting things out'). In this case it was sexual abuse in childhood. She uses heroin to help control difficult emotions and will benefit from coping skills training to find other non-chemical ways to cope with anxiety and depression. In addition she will need psychotherapy to help her come to terms with her past. All her friends are drug users. She has no family or non-drug using friends to support her in the community. The only realistic way forward with a reasonable chance of success would be residential rehabilitation if she did decide to try to become drug-free.

Relapse prevention is another psychological technique. It derives theoretically from the "Stages of Change" model describing people as moving naturally through a series of more or less well defined stages from pre-contemplation through contemplation, action, maintenance, relapse and eventually to sustained change (see figure 2). This has provided an important conceptual framework in which it is recognised that effective strategies are likely to be different for individuals at different stages in the cycle. Individuals may 'go round' the cycle several times before finally exiting it. Strategies to prevent relapse have become more important and are based on models using cognitive behavioural strategies. Likely situations and mood states for relapse are identified, and methods to avoid or deal with such situations worked out in a collaborative way. Such a model also encourages people not to see a relapse as a catastrophe, but

Figure 2: Stages of change model

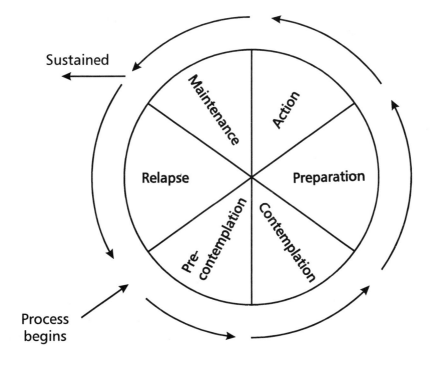

realistically as part of an overall process. Such therapy may be delivered individually or in relapse prevention groups.

Counselling

Basic individual counselling is probably the most common form of psychotherapy provided for drug users. This may be in the form of giving support and advice or as more formal structured counselling with agencies providing structured programmes with clear objectives. The Department of Health's Task Force found that the majority of drug agencies who offered counselling did so without fulfilling the British Association For Counselling criteria, mainly by not having fully trained counsellors although they comment that this did not necessarily imply poor competence. The Task Force also found that where good evidence existed, it suggests that focused structured counselling carried out by well trained and supervised staff in a structured programme helps to reduce drug misuse and criminal activity and increases employment status and social stability.[22]

Group therapy is used frequently especially within the context of residential rehabilitation programmes and groups may also use different models such as relapse prevention. Family therapy is a form of group psychotherapy commonly used in the United States, which involves treatment of more than 1 member of the family simultaneously in the same session. Although anecdotal evidence suggests it is a useful form of treatment, practical issues surrounding the realities of working with drug using families, such as the disintegration of families and the frequent alienation of the family from their drug using member make it difficult. As a formal treatment modality family therapy is rarely used in the UK, but partners and relatives are commonly involved in future management plans for patients, and in this way can play a part in their therapy.

Rehabilitation

The aim of rehabilitation is to return the patient to as normal a life as possible within the community. Some residential rehabilitation facilities undertake detoxification themselves, but most receive patients when they are already drug free. The majority are in the voluntary sector, with some private facilities, and provide a structured programme of psychological, educational and social therapy. The international literature shows that only 15-20% of residents will complete their course, but for those who do, there are significant improvements compared to receiving no treatment.[23] The Task Force recommended that purchasers should ensure access to residential care for those likely to benefit, with prompt access a priority.

Complications relating to injecting drug misuse

HIV

HIV and AIDS are best managed by HIV specialists who in most areas of the country will probably be experienced in the management of intravenous drug users. GPs need to be aware of the need for regular monitoring of immune status and regular prophylaxis against opportunistic infections, providing a prompt response when such infections occur. Good liaison with a specialist is essential. In some areas a multidisciplinary clinic may be available where drug problems can be monitored and treated at the same time as HIV. Given appropriate clinical care, HIV progression does not appear to be more rapid in drug misusers than other patient groups, and is similar in presentation. However, the needs of drug misusers who may have other physical, mental, social or economic problems may be more complex than those of other patients. Specific help may be needed to enable drug users with more chaotic lifestyles to cope with medical regimes, especially combination antiviral therapies where incomplete compliance could encourage the development of viral resistance. These multiple difficulties mean that it is especially important for care to be integrated between high-level specialist centres, local acute, community primary care, social and voluntary services.

Hepatitis B

Acute hepatitis B infection may need specialist management. Drug users may have evidence of past infection, with hepatitis B surface antigen on blood screening, or evidence of possible carrier status and chronic liver disease, with hepatitis 'e' antigen. In the latter case specialist intervention and advice is again needed. Patients who have not been infected with hepatitis B should be vaccinated.

Hepatitis C

Acute hepatitis C rarely needs medical intervention and indeed the initial illness may go undetected. In the carrier state the patient is still infectious and prevalence rates in intravenous drug users in some parts of the UK have been reported to be as high as 85%.[24] Liver function tests do not always reveal significant liver pathology when present in hepatitis C positive patients,[25] but if carried out at the time of the initial serological test it can alert GPs and drug services to impending liver failure among patients who may have symptomless advanced liver disease. Although specialist referral is indicated for hepatitis C positive patients, performing liver function tests early helps prevent these problems being missed among injecting drug misusers, who often default from appointments. Specialist care may involve liver biopsy to gain an accurate indication of the extent of progression of chronic hepatitis C. Treatment with interferon is available although only 1 in 4 have a long-term response.[26]

Side effects of interferon treatments include serious haematological problems and severe depression, the latter of which may be a contraindication for treatment in injecting drug users with existing mental health problems.[27] Harm reduction advice is important and includes ceasing alcohol use and stabilising or stopping drug use.

Deep vein thrombosis

Deep vein thromboses may arise secondary to injection of illicit drugs into the femoral vein. Management usually involves urgent referral to a specialist for anticoagulant therapy.

Septicaemia

This also occurs secondary to injecting and requires urgent hospitalisation. The condition should be considered in any injecting drug user who has a raised temperature. Those who have a cardiac lesion are at particular risk of developing infective endocarditis.[28]

Overdose

While overdoses can follow most forms of drug misuse, they most commonly involve injecting.[29] Overdoses are generally managed in accident and emergency departments. Opiate overdose is managed with naloxone and stimulant overdose by treatment complications such as cardiac arrhythmias as they arise. Many overdoses occur when using more than one drug. The authors of a study of non-fatal heroin overdoses recommend that heroin misusers should receive more information about how to avoid unintentional overdoses, particularly those associated with loss of tolerance or when taking alcohol or other drugs at the same time.[30]

Dealing with violent patients

The reluctance of some doctors to work with drug using patients is sometimes rooted in a fear of violence. A survey by *Doctor* magazine of over 1000 GP respondents carried out in 1992 showed that 13% had experienced actual physical attack, some requiring hospital treatment. Over 70% had been threatened or verbally abused or attacked on a home visit. A year later *Family Practice* reported a survey of around 1000 GPs in the West Midlands, and reported that 63% had suffered abuse of some kind. Drug users are only one of a number of different groups of patients which include occasional individuals who may be violent — the majority are peaceable and polite. Nevertheless, doctors may feel intimidated into meeting the demands of a patient for a prescription, which can be particularly threatening for small or single-handed general practices, or those in isolated rural areas. However, a firm policy for dealing with known trouble-makers can help to control violence while enabling the team to continue to help the patient and prevent the problem from merely being shifted onto another doorstep. A clear and consistent policy adhered to by all doctors and staff can prevent aggression and manipulative behaviour which may lead to violence.

This policy might stipulate that patients:

- will only be seen by appointment, and should be asked to leave if they arrive without an appointment.

- are only seen at appointment if not intoxicated. Otherwise they will be asked to leave without being seen further.

- if they refuse to leave when asked or threaten to or act violently, emergency help should be called (if in a hospital, through the hospital's emergency system) and the police should be alerted. No individual staff member should attempt to argue with such patients.

- should be warned that if they commit a chargeable offence, the hospital, agency or practice will press charges.

These rules should be explained to known problem patients so that on going treatment is possible.

Further guidance on preventing and dealing with patient threats or violence is provided in *Combating violence in General Practice, guidance for GPs*, produced by the BMA General Medical Services Committee, and *Handling aggression and violence in health services* by Willie More and Janet Maguire.[31,32]

Specific treatments of drug misuse

Determining the most appropriate treatment for drug misuse will depend on a number of criteria which should have been considered during the assessment. The patient's degree of personal motivation, psychological and physical wellbeing, social support and the severity of dependence will determine whether he or she should undergo detoxification, long or short-term, and the extent to which substitute prescribing will be necessary. In the prescribing of substitute drugs, there are a number of considerations which need to be taken into account, such as the prescribed drug's cross tolerance with other drugs of misuse, patient preference, overall cost, the likelihood of diversion to the black market, and the mode of administration. Achieving patient compliance will be a primary goal in determining the appropriate treatment.

To date the studies and strategies used to achieve, maintain and enhance compliance in the field of substance abuse have been limited. When prescribing substitute drugs, there is a balance between strategies using relatively expensive daily dispensing (supervised or unsupervised) with a gradual evolution to a less frequent dispensing when there is reasonable evidence of stability. This high level of control and supervision does not occur with any other form of medication and is linked to the potential for abuse and diversion of the prescribed substances. When prescribing these substances, practitioners should exercise appropriate safeguards to ensure a good degree of compliance and to minimise diversion, while maximising an individual's autonomy and independence. This requires considerable organisation and resources. These safeguards should be considered and reviewed in assessment, at initiation of treatment and in on-going assessment. Doctors need to be clear and consistent about what their rules are and about what outcomes they expect a drug user to achieve. In many settings one of the most frequent monitoring tools used to this end is that of urine testing to ensure that the drugs prescribed are being consumed and to monitor use of other drugs on top of prescribed drugs. More recently hair analysis has been introduced, but to date has had limited application in routine clinical settings for reasons of cost. It is performed commercially in the US, but is still treated with caution by many toxicologists. Drug detection using sweat collected by a 'patch' appears to be a promising technique.[33,34] Overall laboratory supervision is costly and needs to be used judiciously with the information gained being fed into clinical decision making processes.

Treatment for opiate misuse

When reducing dependent drug use withdrawal symptoms are likely to occur. To mitigate the effects of this withdrawal, a range of drugs may be prescribed. This process, where the drug of dependence is eliminated from the patient's system, is known as 'detoxification.' If the aim is to achieve detoxification from opiates, opiate or non-opiate detoxification may be chosen. Where polydrug use occurs it may be difficult to distinguish between symptoms of opiate and benzodiazepine withdrawals: both can involve insomnia and sweating. The most reliable and objective sign of opiate withdrawal is dilated pupils.

Short-term detoxification

Clonidine and lofexidine are centrally acting alpha adrenergic agonists which inhibit the release of noradrenaline. Opiate withdrawal is associated with central noradrenergic hyperactivity and therefore both drugs abolish or substantially reduce these symptoms. Clonidine causes hypotension and sometimes rebound hypertension on withdrawal and is therefore less useful as an agent to assist in detoxification from opiates, but although lofexidine can occasionally cause profound hypotension in a few susceptible individuals, it has many fewer side effects and now has a product licence for opiate detoxification (as Britlofex).

Lofexidine may be used as an in-patient or outpatient treatment. The drug is given in an increasing dose over the first 3 days of opiate withdrawal, then maintained at a maximum tolerated dose — judged by the level of postural hypotension — for another 5 days and then decreased to nothing over a final 3 days. Lofexidine is unlikely to completely eliminate withdrawal symptoms (although the extent to which it does varies), it does not affect the insomnia of opiate withdrawal, and it does not eliminate craving. It is however very useful in well motivated patients who want to withdraw quickly in the community or as an agent to detoxify patients in hospital. It may be necessary to give a limited course of a hypnotic to treat insomnia.

Other drugs can be used to assist in detoxification: anti-diarrhoeals, antispasmodics and antiemetics can provide symptomatic and nondependence inducing relief for patients withdrawing from opiates.

Naltrexone is an opiate antagonist which blocks the effects of opiates with the aim of maintaining abstinence when taken regularly. It is sometimes used in a similar way to disulfiram in alcoholics. It is usually recommended to be taken daily and a patient has to be very compliant to continue to do this but a three-times a week dosing schedule may be used if this is likely to improve compliance. Some drug specialists have found it helpful when used in this way.[35] If a patient is continuing to use opiates, naltrexone will bring on withdrawal symptons which may be severe, requiring treatment. As it can be difficult to verify a patient's claims of being opiate-free, use should be initiated in an in-patient setting where the effects of naltrexone can be monitored. Naltrexone has also been used in combination with clonidine and anaethesia to detoxify opiate addicts within a few hours, but this approach has not been formally evaluated. Doctors should be extremely cautious when prescribing naltrexone to patients who are hepatitis C positive, as naltrexone is potentially hepatotoxic.

Methadone may be prescribed for short-term detoxification with doses decreasing over 1 month or less. This may be used in an in-patient setting or with a well motivated patient with a small opiate-smoking dependence who may be going on to in-patient rehabilitation.

Long-term detoxification

Long-term detoxification using methadone would involve decreasing doses over more than 1 month. This is suitable for a patient who is determined to become drug free but may recognise social or psychological factors which will make that difficult. The patient may need or desire to stop injecting before detoxification.

Methadone maintenance therapy

Maintenance therapy involves prescribing a stable dose of a drug which abolishes withdrawal symptoms. Although the patient remains dependent it allows him or her to improve other social and medical aspects of their lives.

Methadone maintenance is probably the most evaluated form of treatment in the field of drug misuse treatment and continues to arouse professional and political controversy.[36] The possible benefits from methadone prescribing range from reduction in illicit opiate use and injection related risk taking behaviour to reductions in the level of criminal activity and other positive social changes. Its relatively long duration of action allows it to stabilise the symptoms of opiate induced euphoria and withdrawal. In particular substitute prescribing can have a significant impact in reducing criminality although such reductions also need to take account of history of individual criminality that precedes substance abuse or dependence.[37] On the negative side, it has a relatively high potential toxicity. There are deaths every year associated with overdose but inadequate data makes calculating and comparing the proportion of heroin and methadone users dying from accidental poisoning extremely difficult. Children accidentally drinking methadone mixture is also a documented hazard.[38] In addition, use by those not receiving a prescription through resale seems common,[39] which may carry an increased risk of overdose.[40]

It has been debated whether the most important component of treatment is simply the provision in a controlled manner of a strong opiate or whether counselling and programme structures are the key ingredient promoting change.[41] Four randomised controlled trials using a no treatment control and some more recent studies using other treatments as controls have consistently shown positive results. In particular, methadone maintenance has a major impact on illicit opiate use and criminal activity at programme entrance; reduction in opioid use and crime was related to the duration of the treatment; and longer involvement in treatment was associated with on-going continued reduction in both drug use and crime. However, it was also noted that while crime was reduced it was not eliminated. Such prescribing was also associated with a very significant reduction in injecting and sharing behaviour. Most of these studies have been done in specialist or dedicated treatment services, but some more recent observational reports in the primary care setting in the UK have reported substantial change in illicit drug use and injecting behaviour over time.[42]

The efficacy of methadone maintenance in helping patients achieve a range of treatment goals is in part thought to be because it abolishes withdrawal symptoms and 'irons out' the peaks and troughs of withdrawal and intoxication that heroin users experience. Historically it has always been thought that methadone must not produce the euphoria or 'high' of injected opiates if the treatment objectives are going to be achieved. However some patients do experience a modified high on methadone and in a limited number of patients this may help them to achieve stability.

There is a conditioning element to dependence and external cues, such as completing a task, or internal cues (emotions and states of mind) such as anxiety or boredom, form part of a pattern prompting drug use.[43] With methadone, a once-a-day dose is possible, which helps to break the psychological associations and cues for drug use and this is useful for the recovery process.

Short-term methadone maintenance: Methadone maintenance may be undertaken over a period of 6 months or less (short-term maintenance) where a stable prescription is given. This may be appropriate for a patient who is continuing to use opiates following unsuccessful previous short or long-term detoxification. He may need to improve social, psychological or physical conditions before a detoxification can be successfully carried out and support from a specialist drug service has been enlisted.

Long-term methadone maintenance: Long-term maintenance can be appropriate for in-patients who have a long history of injecting drug use, poor social support and considerable psychological and social problems. Again support from a specialist drug service is desirable. Methadone dose may be an important variable in successful maintenance. Various studies have shown that higher doses (50mg daily) are associated with less illicit drug use.[44,45]

Dihydrocodeine maintenance therapy

For those patients who do not like the longer, more even effect of methadone, prescription of dihydrocodeine attracts more users into treatment, which assists in achieving harm minimisation.[46] It has a good safety record and a short half life. This means that it provides quick relief of withdrawal symptoms after ingestion, but these return within 12 hours, providing an 'up and down' effect. However, as dihydrocodeine is taken perhaps 4 times a day, the dependent user may follow a pattern of use matching his cues for drug use, and it therefore lacks the advantage of methadone's once-a-day dose in this respect.

Diamorphine (heroin) maintenance therapy

The debate about the prescribing of diamorphine arouses strong emotions.[47,48] Research evidence on which to base decisions regarding the use of diamorphine is extremely limited. Hartnoll *et al* reported an evaluation of heroin maintenance compared with methadone maintenance in a controlled trial in a London drug dependency unit.[49] Ninety-six heroin addicts who had persistently requested heroin maintenance were randomised between the 2 treatments and followed up for a year. Both groups received treatment from a psychiatrist and 92 were successfully followed up. Information was gathered about prescribed and illicit drug use, including urine samples, frequency of injection, involvement with the drug subculture, employment, health and criminal activity. There was no overall difference in illicit opiate consumption, although those offered heroin tended to continue much as before and those on methadone to polarise into a group who achieved abstinence or near abstinence and a group who had high levels of illicit opiate use. The methadone group were more likely to be arrested during the follow-up period and to drop out of treatment. There was no difference between the 2 groups in terms of employment, health or use of non-opiate drugs. The heroin group were found to be injecting more frequently, as may be predicted by the fact that injection was the predominant mode of prescribed heroin use and by the short half life of the drug. No current evaluation attempts are known of in the UK but there are 2 trials being carried out elsewhere in Europe.[50] In Switzerland the Government has supported an evaluation of a programme of on site use of heroin, methadone and mixed prescriptions. The Dutch authorities are in the process of initiating a new heroin trial. Preliminary data is not yet available from either source.

Formulation of medications

Some consideration also needs to be given to the issue of the formulation of medications. Traditionally methadone has been delivered in a concentrated sugar solution which reduces its injectability and thereby its abuse potential. However, it may contribute to poor dental health because the high sugar content causes the growth of plaque. Recent research however, has indicated that intravenous heroin users not on methadone also have dental problems and it may be that poor general dental health is related to other difficulties such as poor dental hygiene and a high sugar diet.[51] The analgesic effect of opiates on pain from tooth decay and other dental problems may also encourage neglect of dental health. Many community pharmacists will make up sugar free and/or clear (no colouring additives) methadone mixture if specially requested, but since such a mixture is injectable, pharmacists should be wary as to the motives for such a request.

There has been considerable interest in the diversification away from methadone only administration, and a number of evaluation trials have been conducted in the United States on buprenorphine — an opiate partial agonist mainly used as a second line analgesic.[52] These trials show comparability of buprenorphine to methadone among middle range methadone maintenance patients and consumption was generally supervised on site. Unsupervised consumption is not recommended as sublingual buprenorphine tablets are highly soluble and thus easily prepared for injection; alternatively the tablets can be ground up and 'snorted' (sniffed).

Injectable drugs: There is considerable international interest in the prescribing of injectable drugs to injecting drug users in Britain because it is a policy which is, with a few exceptions, restricted to this country. Over 90% of prescriptions are however for oral medication. There is a need to look both at types of substance and the context in which it is delivered. The Swiss studies have delivered their injectable drugs in a highly controlled environment at considerable expense. In addition to their expense such delivery systems reduce access but need to be assessed in the context of cost effectiveness where the costs resulting from not treating or controlling highly problematic individuals are taken into account. The Task Force report has recommended that injectable opiates are only prescribed by doctors with appropriate training working within a multidisciplinary setting and by specialist drug misuse services.[53]

The diversification of drugs used in substitute prescribing offers the potential for emphasising the medical and treatment nature of substitute prescribing. With a range of pharmacotherapies available, the choice of substance can be balanced by patient preference, mode of delivery and overall cost of such treatment. In this context newer long acting maintenance agents such as LAAM (levo alpha acetyl methadol), which has a half-life of over 36 hours and allows for 2-3 times a week administration, is of considerable interest in the context of finding a balance between controlling dispensing and consumption and maximising people's autonomy from such daily routines. The potential gains may be considerable in some treatment populations.

Formulations of methadone: The majority of international evaluations of methadone have been with the use of an oral mixture form in the context of predominantly supervised consumption of methadone on site with take-home privileges contingent upon reduced drug use and general improvement in social and physical wellbeing. This, the safest way of prescribing methadone, involves the provision of an opiate substitution that has a long-acting half life, is taken in an oral form and cannot be readily injected, has cross tolerance with the drug of abuse and is associated with reduced desire for consumption of the stated drug of abuse. Methadone tablets (5 mg) are an alternative to methadone mixture which are most commonly prescribed by private practitioners and GPs and most rarely prescribed by specialists in drug services. Methadone tablets are more expensive, are readily converted to an injectable form and obtain a substantially higher value on the black market. The Task Force report has recommended that methadone tablets are no longer prescribed for the treatment of drug dependence.[54]

A significant minority of clinicians in the UK are also involved in some degree of injectable prescribing. The majority of this injectable prescribing is in the form of methadone ampoules. To date there has been no formal evaluation of this type of prescribing, and in general it is a treatment option chosen for more long-term chronic injectors who fail to abstain from injecting illicit drugs on oral methadone. At present there is one formal evaluation of injectable methadone prescribing being conducted as part of a major Swiss trial on the diversification of medically-prescribed narcotic drugs. This trial was initially designed as a randomised trial comparing injectable methadone with injectable heroin but the randomisation process has collapsed because of the failure to recruit people into the injectable methadone form of the trial.

Prescribing for HIV and hepatitis B and C positive drug users

When the HIV epidemic first became apparent many drug users who were HIV positive received "better" treatment, usually meaning more maintenance prescribing. Since then the availability of this treatment for all drug users has improved so this situation does not really arise. Treatment objectives, for instance the achievement of abstinence, may change in an HIV positive patient but it is important to remember that HIV has a long incubation period and many years may pass before the patient becomes clinically ill. The incubation period may be even longer for hepatitis C. Patients react differently to diagnosis and may for instance want to achieve abstinence for their limited life span. The needs of each patient are individual and they need to be assessed as such. It is also important to remember that patients with AIDS or severe HIV disease may qualify for additional social security benefit and improved access to housing on the basis of medical need. This may help improve the prognosis for their drug use. Doctors need to be aware that, for those patients who have very long-standing chronic hepatitis C infection, particular care should be taken to ensure continuing satisfactory liver function if prescribing is undertaken. There is a risk, particularly with long-acting drugs such as methadone, that slow accumulation may occur in the event of deteriorating liver function, with possibly fatal consequences.

Benzodiazepines

The issue of benzodiazapines is complex. Broadly benzodiazepine use follows 3 patterns. Some drug users use regular small amounts of benzodiazepines for what initially may be or have been a legitimate purpose. This would include the use of small amounts (5-15mg) of diazepam to control anxiety symptoms or temazepam (10-20mg) to aid sleep. The patient may well be dependent but the use may not be particularly problematic. Some polydrug users use benzodiazepines to control withdrawal symptoms when opiates are unavailable. These users may not be dependent. Finally some drug users use large amount of benzodiazepines (50-200mg diazepam equivalents) sometimes in binges for their psychotropic effects but some take regular high doses of benzodiazepines. This is the most problematic group.

Within the drug misusing population, there is a substantial minority of polydrug users who are involved in high dose binge benzodiazepine use and injecting benzodiazepine use.[55] There is high availability of benzodiazapines, in particular temazepam and flunitrazepam which appear to have a high abuse potential. It would appear that the shorter acting benzodiazepines have more abuse liability than the longer acting ones, and thus any prescribing in the context of benzodiazepine abuse or dependence should be cautiously entered into, and should aim for a rapid shift from short acting to long acting benzodiazepine such as diazepam or clorodiazepoxide. Temazepam abuse may be associated with high HIV injecting risk taking behaviour.[56]

Due to the increasing evidence of misuse and the particular problems associated with injection of temazepam gel-filled capsules, in December 1995 the Government announced that temazepam would move from schedule 4 to schedule 3 of the Misuse of Drugs Act. This means that unlawful possession has become an offence, pharmacies will have tighter controls on its storage and there will be more control on import and export. It has not however, become subject to handwritten prescriptions. At the same time the government announced a ban on prescribing the gel-filled capsule formulation of temazepam on the NHS.

While there is general recognition that with substitute prescribing frequent dispensing of the controlled drugs reduces misuse, such practice is relatively uncommon with benzodiazepine prescribing. Infrequent dispensing enhances the opportunity for binge consumption and such users may appear drunk and become involved in violence, polydrug use and risky injecting practices. In any context where there is evidence of poor control over consumption it is probable that considerable benefit can be conferred by shifting to more frequent dispensing arrangements. Regrettably, although there are moves towards this, it is at present not possible to prescribe diazepam on the blue prescription form FP10 (MDA) or the equivalent pink hospital prescription form FP10 (HP)(ad), so that several separate prescriptions are necessary for daily dispensing and, because there are no handwriting requirements for benzodiazepines, considerable care is required of the prescriber to minimise the risk of forgery.

Amphetamines

Amphetamines are a drug of major abuse potential and can be abused in the context of diet and eating disorders where they are used as appetite suppressants as well as for the psychoactive effect in mood enhancement and increased energy. They were once routinely prescribed to treat depression before the advent of effective antidepressants but now there are only 2 indications for them — narcolepsy, and rarely, attention deficit hyperactivity disorder in children. Amphetamine sulphate, which is illegally manufactured in Britain, is the commonest drug abused but some drug users obtain illicit supplies of dexamphetamine sulphate which is still made pharmaceutically. Methamphetamine is no longer available on prescription. Ritalin (methylphenidate), which was originally taken off the market, because of its abuse potential, has now returned as a prescribable drug.

It is probable that the majority of people who have experimented with, or occasionally used amphetamines, suffer minor if any adverse consequences. However, some may develop acute complications such as amphetamine-induced mood disorders, suicidal thoughts and occasionally amphetamine-induced psychosis. Such psychosis, which is a toxic effect of high doses of the drug, occasionally requires acute hospitalisation. Amphetamine dependence may be associated with compulsive binge use and also injecting. Such injecting is associated with high levels of risk-taking behaviour.[57] It is estimated that the severely dependent stimulant users have less contact with specialist drug services than their heroin using counterparts with similar severity problems, which may be related to the lack of substitute prescribing and the resulting orientation of drug services to opiate users.

There are a number of advocates of dexamphetamine prescribing as a form of substitute prescribing for dependent amphetamine users. A significant number of practitioners are involved in dexamphetamine prescribing throughout the UK despite the limited evidence of its benefits. One descriptive study[58] reports on a small cohort of amphetamine injectors who received oral dexamphetamine in a supervised mode in a specialist clinic setting. This group showed improvement in a significant number of domains over time through this treatment regime and there is a need for other more thorough evaluations ideally with experimental design of this type of treatment. There are, however, other issues of consideration in the use of amphetamines in that it is clearly associated with acute psychiatric complications in certain individuals, but such adverse effects need to be balanced against other possible physical, psychological and social gains achieved through substitute prescribing of amphetamines.

Daily dispensing should reduce the risk of acute psychiatric complications, as it limits the potential for 'binge' doses. In general practice in England and Wales it is currently possible to write 1 prescription for up to 14 days of daily prescribing for all schedule 2 drugs (including amphetamine), using the blue FP10(MDA) form. However, this does not apply to the equivalent pink form FP10(HP)(ad) for use by hospital consultants or their medical teams and if they wish to provide daily dispensing they would have to provide a separate handwritten prescription for each day using the standard yellow hospital prescription forms FP10(HP) — a time consuming process.

Cocaine

The limited role of medication in the treatment of cocaine users was highlighted in the recent Task Force report with the finding that many different pharmaceutical agents have been used to assist the craving associated with cocaine withdrawal, none with success.[59] Treatment for dependent cocaine users tends therefore to be psychological using cognitive behavioural techniques and counselling. Alternative therapies are popular with the patients but there is a lack of research evidence for their effectiveness and the quality of research assessing the efficacy of acupuncture for the treatments of addictions has received criticism.[60] In-patient treatment may be useful to deal with the multiple crises cocaine users find themselves in, but indications for such treatment would need to be carefully defined.

Hallucinogens

Hallucinogens such as LSD, magic mushrooms (Psilocybe semilanceate), or mescalin are sometimes associated with temporary psychiatric manifestations. Repeated use of LSD can lead to a prolonged psychosis which resembles schizophrenia and requires treatment.[61] Although this lasts for several weeks or months it will eventually clear completely. Doctors may also be asked to help someone who has taken a hallucinogenic drug and is undergoing an unpleasant, frightening hallucinogenic experience. These 'bad trips' are best dealt with by calm and persistent reassurance.

Hallucinogenic Amphetamines

There have been many case reports of serious and fatal complications of ecstasy use.[62] However serious complications are probably rare and most interventions for young people using these drugs are harm minimisation ones centered around an educational approach. Psychiatric complications also occur but there is little evidence as to their true prevalence.[63] There is no known dependence on hallucinogens or hallucinogenic amphetamines and therefore no need for substitute prescribing of any kind.

Performance Enhancing Drugs

Anabolic steroids (AS) are not physically addictive, and are used in cycles which incorporate periods of non-use. Further evidence is needed as to whether AS misusers experience difficulties in achieving complete abstinence. Medical professionals need to be aware of the possibility of AS misuse when patients present with conditions such as high blood pressure and testicular atrophy. Practical information on the health risks associated with AS misuse and harm minimisation strategies such as needle exchange facilities are likely to be of value. Treatment for opioid dependency may be necessary if nalbuphine is being used.

Polydrug use

The importance of careful initial patient assessment in recognising polydrug misuse should be emphasised as drug misusers may only present for treatment for the use of 1 drug, not considering their misuse of others to be problematic.[64] Several major patterns of polydrug use are found, which may include dependence on 1 or more drug. Some polydrug users take more than one drug simultaneously, for instance cocaine and heroin (a 'speedball') to enhance the effects of 1 or both. Polydrug use may involve prescribed and street drugs, for instance when cocaine and prescribed methadone are taken at the same time,[65] or any of these combinations with alcohol. Others alternate between drugs. A common pattern among heavy drug misusers involves switching between opiates and benzodiazepines, two depressant drugs. Some users alternate between drugs with different pharmacological actions, such as opiates and amphetamines. It may be difficult to determine dependence in such users, who may feel that they cannot do without both drugs, but are able to stop using 1 while using the other. A further pattern of polydrug use occurs among recreational users, particularly with 'dance drugs', including amphetamine, LSD and ecstasy.

Approaches to those misusing 'dance drugs' have generally consisted of health education messages, although if dependence on amphetamines develops, this may require a greater level of intervention. Those at particular risk of overdose, such as heroin misusers, should receive information about how to avoid unintentional overdoses resulting from taking drugs (and also alcohol) at the same time.[66] There is very little published evidence on the treatment of polydrug misusers on which guidance can be based. Anecdotal reports suggest that heavy or dependent users, such as those whose use involves opiates, may need to be stabilised on 1 drug as the first step in treatment, but strategies will depend on the individual profile of misuse.

Over the counter drug misuse

There appears to be little provision specifically to help OTC drug misusers, which may in part be because they rarely present to treatment agencies.[67] Those misusing OTC drugs alone may not wish to associate themselves with the stigma of illicit drug use by seeking help at agencies designed for such users. However it has been reported that where polydrug users who also use OTC drugs are referred to drug treatment units for their illicit drug use they do not reveal OTC misuse unless specifically asked. It is possible that illicit drug misusers do not consider their legal drug misuse to be a significant problem.

Research regarding who misuses OTC drugs and their motives is lacking. Until more information is available, it would be difficult to design effective prevention and treatment for this problem.

Special circumstances

Pain relief in opiate misusers

The provision of pain relief to opiate users is often perceived as problematic and doctors may be concerned, because all the stronger analgesic medications are opiate based, that drug misusing patients simply want prescriptions for opiate drugs. Real problems may arise on the one hand when an individual is left in unacceptable pain, and on the other when an individual who claims to be in pain is given opiates and then, for example, promptly leaves the accident and emergency department.

Patients presenting in emergency settings with urgent requests for opiate analgesia should receive prompt assessment and investigation of the symptoms they present with. Assessment should include a history and signs of drug misuse.

Patients presenting with factitious symptoms should be approached carefully and non-confrontationally and offered information about drug treatment or psychological services.

Patients who have painful conditions in addition to their opiate dependence should be treated in order to achieve effective pain relief. It is not necessary or ethical to withhold opiate medication when it is required and because of their tolerance to opiates they will require more, not less, analgesic medication than other patients. However non-opiate analgesics should not be discounted, as they are often effective. Essentially one should assess the condition and give appropriate pain relief as for any patient. This approach is most easily followed when the patient's opiate intake is stable, for instance when an individual is established on an oral methadone prescription, and when the pain is due to an acute condition.

Chronic pain arising from an established pathological cause can be managed by following a similar strategy. The pain may be controlled after assessment by non-opiate drugs or large doses of opiates may be required. The correct dose will provide freedom from pain with no sedation or euphoria. Over time it can be difficult to know whether requirements for increasing opiate medication are due to tolerance, additional illicit drug use, worsening underlying condition or any combination of the 3. Patients with a chronic painful condition can develop opiate dependence on the prescribed medication. Careful history taking, observation of signs, urine testing and patient self-monitoring are helpful.

Chronic pain with no demonstrable pathological cause and opiate addiction can be a particularly complex problem to manage. These patients may be particularly likely to develop iatrogenic opiate dependence. Long-term psychological support and cognitive behavioural strategies provide the best way of managing or containing the problem.[68]

Management of the pregnant drug user

Pregnant drug users present a particular problem for the general practitioner and the paediatrician. Women using some drugs have a higher incidence of low birth weight babies and obstetric complications although it is difficult to establish what actually causes this. It may be the effects of drugs but it may also be poor antenatal care, general poor nutrition and other poverty related factors. The neonate may also have drug withdrawal problems. It is generally desirable to detoxify women in pregnancy from all drugs but abrupt withdrawal should be avoided in dependent opiate, benzodiazepine or barbiturate users, as this can threaten the wellbeing of both mother and foetus.[69] Stabilization of opiate dependency onto an amount of daily methadone in the first trimester and slow methadone detoxification (decreases in the daily dose of up to a maximum of 5mg at any one time) is generally thought to be safe in the second trimester.[70] Women who cannot or will not detoxify should be maintained on a dose of methadone which will prevent them using illicit drugs as the foetus is more likely to be harmed by illicit drugs than a stable dose of methadone.[71] For instance cocaine use may well be harmful to a foetus.[72] Maintenance on stimulant drugs is not appropriate. Pregnant drug users with a history of injecting (or partners of drug users) should be particularly encouraged to accept HIV testing because AZT treatment during pregnancy can reduce the risk of HIV transmission to the baby. Early diagnosis also allows referral to a paediatrician specialising in HIV/AIDS. Women who decline to be tested themselves may still wish to have their babies tested for this reason. The usual harm minimisation techniques, such as discouraging injecting, or providing advice and sterile injecting equipment for those who persist, are also relevant. Because some drugs depress the appetite, patients' eating habits may require detailed discussion. Good liaison between a GP, obstetrician or midwife and paediatrician is vital and indeed many districts have special teams responsible for this or individual 'drug liaison midwives' who work with drug dependency psychiatrists. In some cases social services may also have to be involved as child protection issues may be important (this is not invariable however). In many areas joint working protocols have been developed between social services and appropriate health professionals in order to co-ordinate the management of the pregnant drug user. After delivery a baby may need specialist care and treatment for any opiate or cocaine withdrawal.

Severe mental illness and drug misuse

Drug misusers who are also severely mentally ill present particular clinical and logistical difficulties for their management, and they typically have poorer outcomes than patients diagnosed with either disorder alone.[73] Their drug misuse may not be evident and self-reported information may be unreliable,[74] so requires careful investigation with further questioning and laboratory screening, although such analysis may fail to detect drug misuse depending on when the drug was taken. Such testing will also be important to distinguish between psychotic symptoms arising from drug use, which usually resolve with discontinuation of the drug within a few days or weeks, and psychotic illness. As in the treatment of all drug misusers, dependence should be determined, a factor which may worsen the prognosis for their mental illness[75]

While drug misusers who develop short-term psychotic illness appear to show an improved outcome at discharge from treatment, the prognosis is poorer for continued drug misuse with established psychotic illness, a diagnosis of which is associated with more frequent hospitalisation,[76] greater use of emergency services, greater likelihood of homelessness, and a greater propensity to violent[77] or suicidal behaviour, with poorer compliance with treatment and medication.[78]

Treating both problems at the same time may be difficult as health care professionals may be specialised and or physically located in general psychiatry or drug misuse but not both. It is important that patients are not passed between drug misuse and general psychiatry services but are managed in an integrated way, particularly in relation to their pharmacological management which should be co-ordinated to avoid interactions of drug therapies for their different conditions. Like other drug misusers, social support is important in the treatment of the severely mentally ill and is likely to help them remain in treatment.[79]

Treatment for drug misuse and the courts

Drug misusers may commit crime which is directly related to their need to raise money to fund their drug habit — so called 'acquisitive crime'. Of course they may also commit other crimes such as crimes of violence while intoxicated and crimes unrelated to their drug use. Arrest referral schemes aim to capitalise on the moment of arrest when a suspect is detained by the police, to offer them education and contact with drug treatment services. Offenders may also be given contact with drug treatment services later in the criminal justice proceedings. Treatment of their drug misuse, usually in residential rehabilitation, may be used as an alternative to a custodial sentence and may be conditional on completing a treatment. A recommendation for this course of action may come from a probation officer or psychiatrist asked to provide a report by the defence. Although this is most likely to be residential, it may involve a community placement, usually for a less serious offence.

Treatment of detainees in police stations[80]

If a detainee is drunk, injured or requires medication, decisions on whether to request a police surgeon are made by the custody officer. When in contact with a prisoner who is known to be using drugs in a dependent way, a police surgeon has a statutory duty to notify the Chief Medical Officer at the Home Office.[81] This overrides all considerations of confidentiality. It is preferable, that anyone suspected of requiring medical attention on arrest, should first be taken to a hospital casualty department, rather than to the police station as delays in assessing and attending to their needs may worsen any condition. The care of drug (usually opiate) misusers with withdrawal symptoms can however, usually be managed within the confines of a police station with appropriate medication but withdrawal from benzodiazepines poses a greater risk as fits may occur and a higher degree of supervision and care are therefore required. Guidance is provided in the UK Health Departments' guidelines for clinical management of substance misuse detainees in policy custody[82] which have received the approval of the Association of Police Surgeons, the Royal College of Psychiatrists and the Royal College of General Practitioners, among others.

The main problems faced by the doctor are:

- the lack of a reliable history on recent drug intake;

- the problem of a verification with the prescribing doctor. Prisoners are often detained when for instance, the drug dependency clinic caring for them is closed;

- mixing of medication. Opiate drugs are often mixed with alcohol, amphetamines, benzodiazepines, cocaine and cannabis.

In such situations, the doctor can usually only prescribe according to clinical findings after an examination and undertake frequent reviews. A decision on fitness to interview is often similarly short-term, with assessments made before and after interview to protect the prisoner's interest. Careful directions are given to the custody officer on regular observation and review, with instructions on the timing and dose of any medication provided.

In the UK, the involvement of nurses (sometimes termed forensic nurses) in custodial medicine is very limited. In the USA, notably California, nurses may take a leading role in co-ordinating the forensic aspects in investigating crime. In Australia, closer co-operation between the police, police surgeons and skilled nursing assistance is being developed. There is scope for expanding the role of nurses into areas such as the supervision of alcohol and drug withdrawal in custody, the treatment of simple injuries, liaison with hospitals and psychiatric services.

Medical treatment of drug misusers in prisons

Medical treatment to prisoners is provided by the Prison Medical Service. Treatment available to an opiate dependent prisoner on entrance to prison has in the past varied with local opinion. Some prisons have offered brief detoxification on entrance using chiefly methadone or benzodiazepines; others have enforced sudden cessation of methadone prescription on entry, which is associated with a tendancy among prisoners to resume or increase the level of illicit injecting drug use and sharing of injecting equipment drug use ('cold turkey' in the case of opiate dependence).[83] Studies show that between 60-80% of those who inject in prison reportedly share needles and syringes at least once.[84] HM Prison Service now has a drug strategy *Drug misuse in prison*,[85] which aims:

- to provide a range of services for drug misusers in prison. Such services should mirror those available in the outside community;

- to provide methadone administration both in the short and in the long-term;

- to achieve random, mandatory drug testing programme of all inmates.

The strategy specifies that when prisoners have been identified as having a drug problem, a key member of staff responsible for case work should be appraised of the prisoner's identified needs. This could be developed further so that following assessment the member of staff remains responsible for the prisoner's care as a 'key worker'.

When mandatory drug testing was introduced in British prisons there were concerns that because cannabis persists much longer in the body than injectable drugs such as heroin and benzodiazepines, prisoners would be tempted to switch to these drugs from cannabis with an associated serious public health risk. Data from the pilot studies in 8 prisons show that the proportion testing positive for opiates or benzodiazepines rose from 4.1% to 7.4% between the first phase (February to May 1995) and second phase (June to December 1995) of random testing. Positive tests results for cannabis fell from 33.2% to 29.1% over the same period.[86] The Prison Service has commissioned an analysis of data resulting from mandatory drug testing which will be carried out by the National Addiction Centre at the Maudsley Hospital/Institute of Psychiatry, but a decision as to whether the results will be published has yet to be taken.

There has been some concern about the standards of care for drug misusers within prisons,[87] with claims of insufficient assessment of patients before the prescription of methadone, and a lack of liaison with medical professionals who have been treating the drug user before entry to prison.[88]

The spread of bloodborne diseases through injecting drug use in prisons has also presented problems to prison authorities. A survey of inmates in a Scottish prison found that between a quarter and a third of prisoners who injected drugs were HIV positive, and concluded that the risk of further transmission of HIV and other bloodborne infections was ongoing and required urgent attention.[89]

Needle exchange facilities are not available in UK prisons. Arguments against their provision include fears that such a move would be interpreted as approving illegal behaviour and also that needles could be used as weapons. Whether these risks outweigh those of the transmission of HIV, hepatitis B and hepatitis C is open to question. Doubts have been raised as to the efficacy of household bleach which is commonly recommended as a disinfecting agent for injecting equipment. However, it can reduce the risk of HIV transmission if used according to guidance set out by the US National Institute on Drug Abuse and the Centre for Research on Drugs and Health Behaviour.[90] A practical solution may be the provision of sterilising tablets for decontaminating injecting equipment with clear guidance on their use, as recommended by the Advisory Council on the Misuse of Drugs, along with encouragement for uptake of hepatitis B vaccination.[91] However, prisoners will need to feel secure that they can clean injecting equipment discreetly without being observed by prison officers and identified as drug users. Otherwise, if disinfectants are provided, they may not be used. HIV can also, of course, be transmitted through sexual activity, and condoms should be available in prisons to prevent this.

In prisons where the population has a fast turnover, preventative measures suitable in the community, such as counselling to reduce risk taking behaviour, do not transfer well, although the need for health education continues to be emphasised by the Advisory Council on the Misuse of Drugs (ACMD).[92] This also means that the detection of new HIV, hepatitis B and C infections may not be possible,[93] particularly as many of those infected are likely to be asymptomatic. Research in Sydney, Australia has suggested that methadone maintenance in prison reduces injecting and syringe sharing. The study noted that inmates needed a daily dose of at least 60mg of methadone for the duration of the sentence if these benefits are to be realised.[94] Further evaluation of this practice would be valuable. However, the ACMD has rejected this idea as unfeasible in the generality of prisons.

Voluntary testing units may provide a useful way forward for reducing drug misuse in prisons. A typical voluntary testing unit will be a separate unit of accommodation within a prison that offers enhanced privileges to those living there in return for voluntary drug testing to prove abstinence from drugs. Prisoners sign an agreement stating that they will not take drugs, and if this is broken, the prisoner returns to normal accommodation and loses the privileges of the unit.[95] In its 1996 report the ACMD recommended that prisons should develop voluntary testing units for prisoners wishing to stop misusing drugs.

Aspects of good practice

The United Kingdom is renowned for its diversity of approaches to the management of drug misuse. The Government's drug strategy *Tackling drugs together 1995-1998*[96] clearly outlines the need for greater involvement of general practitioners in the management of drug misusers and substantial progress has been made in some localities. However, overall the level of involvement of general practitioners remains uneven.

Probably the commonest approach is that of shared care between a community drug team and general practice where the doctor discharges the medical and prescribing side of treatment, conducting the initial assessment and regular reviews but the community drug team worker sees the drug user on a weekly or fortnightly basis to address broader issues such as housing, legal and social problems and to provide counselling. Treatment by the community drug team worker will vary, but could include motivational interviewing, relapse prevention work, coping skills training, facilitating employment or further education, advice over financial, legal, and accommodation difficulties, and, where appropriate, networking with the family and friends to increase effective support for the drug user. General practitioners are sometimes recommended to limit the number of patients with drug problems to approximately 6 per 2000 patients; some GPs feel comfortable treating more than this, others less. Also, due to the clustering of drug problems and the results of housing policies, such limits may not be practical in some areas. Specialists are available to provide back up. Two models in Scotland have differed slightly from this. Firstly the Community Drug Problem Service (CDPS) in Edinburgh provides a service where the prescribing is initiated by the specialist service and after a few weeks is continued by the general practitioner, the counselling continuing to be done by the CDPS. Since 1995 the GPs have been paid for the prescribing and monitoring that they do for individual drug users within a well defined protocol. Dispensing is done via community pharmacies and is unsupervised. By contrast in Glasgow the service is run mainly by general practitioners through Greater Glasgow Health Board's GP Drug Misuse Clinics who work closely with the local community pharmacist where methadone dispensing is done under supervision. The GPs have to work within strict limits and are paid to run clinics where they provide the entire service, including counselling.

A number of localities have adopted yet another model of general practitioner liaison teams whose task is to support the general practitioners in developing their policies in the management of drug users. In one area of south London a team headed by a specialist GP offers consultancy and liaison to other local GPs dealing or wanting to deal with alcohol or drug using patients. Many localities are now in the process of developing protocols and guidelines to ensure clarity of working practice between specialist and primary care services, and several are now paying GPs to provide a prescribing service to individual opiate users along similar lines to the Edinburgh model, assisted by initial and continuing training under well defined protocols.

Despite a plethora of models and practices in shared care, there is no standardisation of the liaison between primary care and specialist services. Nevertheless, certain factors are essential for a shared care relationship to work effectively:

- real communication is one essential component, particularly with this patient group who may find it advantageous to play one party off against each other. Consistent messages need to be given by both community drug team workers and GPs. In some situations, such as a drug misuser with children at risk, there needs to be good communication between several different professionals. It should not be forgotten that communication is a two-way process, and it is sometimes easier for a GP to make contact with the drug worker than it is for a drug worker to contact the GP. A few GPs set aside time on a regular basis in which to telephone the drug team and discuss their patients who are in a shared care relationship.

- jointly agreed protocols need to be developed in order to clarify the roles and responsibilities of both primary care and the specialist services.

- shared care will only work effectively where the drug user keeps appointments to see both the doctor and drug worker. It may be helpful at the outset for the doctor to make it clear to the drug user that his prescription will be rapidly reduced or stopped for repeated failed appointments whether they be with the GP or with the drug worker.

- at regular intervals, perhaps once every 3 months, there should be a formal review of the drug user's progress with the sharing of information between specialist worker and GP, an assessment as to the achievement of stated goals, and the negotiation with the drug misuser of new goals to be achieved. For those people who fail to make progress over a long period, an in-depth assessment should be made to determine what is holding them back.

- in sharing care, GP and specialist drug workers may at times need to modify their approach to ensure that goals are achieved. For instance the achievement of important non-drug goals may sometimes be aided by temporary stabilisation of the prescription. With appropriate training and remuneration, methadone maintenance does have a role in general practice setting, particularly for limited periods of time in order to achieve non-drug goals (e.g. for someone starting employment). However, maintenance prescribing of methadone in general practice should always be with a view to eventual abstinence, although it is recognised that for a few people this may occur.

- specialist workers often advise GPs as to what would be an appropriate substitute prescription, and in most cases this advice is accepted. However, as GPs must accept medical and legal responsibility for anything they prescribe, they must have the final say and this must be accepted by specialist drug workers.

The Task Force report recommends that "shared care" with appropriate support for GPs should be available as widely as possible.[97]

4

Constraints on current practice

Introduction

As the clinical experience of managing drug misusers on a significant scale in the UK moves towards the end of its third decade there is an increasing consensus on the need for a broad range of treatment approaches and the need for such approaches to be guided by ongoing monitoring and evaluation. There is reasonable agreement about the general benefits of treatment, and for the capacity of a wide range of practitioners to make their contribution to such treatments.[1] However it needs also to be borne in mind that a considerable number of the drugs misused are illegal in nature and that where treatment involves prescribing controlled drugs doctors have specific responsibilities.

Legal context of the treatment of drug abusing patients

The availability of certain drugs in our society is controlled by the Misuse of Drugs Act, 1971[2] and by several sets of regulations arising from it. Some legal restraints on the treatment of patients are contained in this legislation. The extent to which legislation and its application are a major day to day feature of treatment of drug misusers is limited. Restraints in which drugs may be prescribed and by whom apply to the minority of cases and substances, the vast majority of opiate dependent patients being treated with the relatively unrestricted and widely available drug methadone. This is in stark contrast to the situation in the USA where the provision of methadone is strictly controlled by federal regulations.[3] These regulations define the way in which methadone is delivered, and to whom, decisions which in this country are subsumed under the activity of clinical judgement. In addition, the practice of those attempting to treat dependent individuals in the UK is informed by the 1991 guidelines issued by the Department of Health.[4,5] These are intended to offer advice on good clinical practice. Informal peer opinion and review is a relatively important mechanism by which the prescribing of controlled substances (see below for definition) is regulated in the UK.

Misuse of Drugs Act (MDA) 1971 and subsequent amendments

This Act defines drugs according to the following classification and restricts their possession, production, supply, importation, exportation and cultivation. In addition there are regulations which prohibit the use of premises for any of these activities in relation to cannabis and opium. Examples of drugs controlled under the Act as listed below.

Class A: cocaine, heroin, morphine, opium, methadone, pethidine, dipipanone, LSD, ecstasy and class B drugs when prepared for injection.

Class B: amphetamines, barbiturates, cannabis, codeine, pentazocine, pholcodine and dexedrine.

Class C: amphetamine type substances including pemoline and chlorphentermine, buprenorphine, benzodiazepines, and under certain circumstances anabolic steroids.

Schedules of drugs

The Act also defines 'schedules', perhaps the part of the Act most relevant to the medical profession. While the classes relate to the criminal justice side of the Act, the schedules relate to the medical side.

- *Schedule 1:* covers drugs which cannot be prescribed by doctors or dispensed by pharmacists (cannabis and LSD, for example). Possession is only legitimate with a Home Office research licence. This schedule is the closest British law comes to absolute prohibition.

- *Schedules 2 and 3:* cover drugs considered to have medical uses, and may be possessed by doctors, pharmacists and other medical professionals. For the general public, possession is only legitimate with a prescription. When Schedule 2 drugs are supplied, the person who supplies them must enter the details in a register; this is not necessary for Schedule 3 drugs. Schedule 2 drugs include the opioids, dexamphetamine and cocaine; Schedule 3, barbituates, temazepam, buprenorphine and pentazocine. Drugs in Schedules 2 and 3 are controlled drugs, with the exception of temazepam, and subject to special prescribing regulations. The prescription must contain the address of the prescriber, it must be dated and written entirely in the doctor's own handwriting, including the form of the preparation strength and total quantity in words and figures. Bound registers must be kept for recording all transactions for Schedule 2 drugs that are held by GPs in drug cabinets or in cases.

- *Schedule 4:* covers most benzodiazepines, such as diazepam (Valium) and lorazepam (Ativan). Although only available on prescription, anyone may possess these drugs as a medicinal product, and import or export them without a licence. Temazepam used to be in this schedule.

- *Schedule 5:* covers compound preparation such as cough mixtures which contain small amounts of controlled drugs like morphine. Some Schedule 5 drugs are sold over the counter and all may be legally possessed without a prescription.

Misuse of Drugs Regulations 1985

Addicts Index

Until April 1997 the Home Office kept records of dependent drug users in a register known as the Addicts Index. Under the Misuse of Drug Regulations 1985[6] doctors were required to notify the Home Office of patients whom they attended and believed to be addicted to any of the following drugs:

cocaine
dextromoramide (Palfium)
diamorphine (heroin)
dipipanone (Diconal)
hydrocodone
hydromorphone
levorphanol

methadone (Physeptone)
morphine (Sevredol, MST Continus, Cyclimorph, Oramorph)
pethidine (Pamergan)
piritramide
phenazocine (Narphen)

Doctors were encouraged to phone the Addicts Index to find out if anyone for whom they were about to prescribe a drug was already receiving a prescription of a controlled drug from another doctor. However, due to the limited range of drugs included, and its accessibility only during office hours, the Addicts Index was not frequently used to provide up to date prescribing information. However, the Index was also designed to gather data on cost and numbers of drug misusers and it provided the only continuous statistics for UK drug misusers and as such was a valuable source of epidemiological data.

A recommendation by the Advisory Council on the Misuse of Drugs in its 1982 report *Treatment and rehabilitation*, led to the establishment of regional Drug Misuse Databases which are maintained by each health service region and provide a more detailed picture of the extent of drug misuse, the route of drug administration and number of drug misusers known to services. Doctors are asked to supply anonymised patient information voluntarily, which includes a wider range of drugs than did the Addicts Index, and details of injecting and sharing behaviour. Information for the regional database is sent in such a form that it cannot be traced to a particular patient. The usual requirements are initials (to prevent double-counting of entries), date of birth and primary post code. These regional data are then compiled by the Department of Health to provide a national picture. There is, however, a further need, for up-to-date prescribing information to be accessible locally to prescribing agencies and practices, so that doctors can find out about the last prescription received by a drug misuser and the location of its issue. Such information would need to be available 24 hours a day as it is often required out-of-hours, for instance by police surgeons dealing with detainees when drugs agencies responsible for their prescribing are closed.

Enforcement

The statutes described above are enforced and monitored by the Home Office Drugs Inspectorate and the police. A 'Chemist Inspecting Officer' appointed within each police force inspects retail pharmacies, ie the point of dispensing prescriptions. The inspection of the pharmacy includes storage, supply and accounting for controlled drugs, and details of regular or unusual supplies are reported to the Home Office Drugs Inspectorate to enable doctors' prescribing to be monitored. A clear violation such as the unauthorised prescribing by a doctor of a drug for which one needs a Home Office licence, and problems of scale, such as the prescribing to a very large number of patients or of high doses, are detected in this way. When that prescribing is deemed to be irresponsible the Home Secretary can refer details to a Misuse of Drugs Tribunal which assesses the evidence. Where irresponsible prescribing is established the Home Secretary has the power the restrict a doctor's right to prescribe controlled drugs.

Mental health legislation

In England and Wales the Mental Health Act 1983[7] allows, in certain defined circumstances, for the compulsory detention and treatment in hospital of those suffering from a mental disorder. Substance misuse is a category which is specifically excluded as a reason for treatment under the powers contained in this legislation. Thus a dependent patient may not be compulsorily detained for assessment or treatment of alcohol or drug dependence itself. However it is possible to detain someone for the assessment or treatment of a co-existing major psychiatric disorder such as depression or psychosis which the doctor considers to represent a serious risk to the health of that individual or when that individual may represent a serious risk of harm to him or herself or to others. The Mental Health (Scotland) Act 1984 allows for detention with similar criteria, although detention for longer than 28 days requires the approval of a (legally qualified) sheriff. A diagnosis of dependence on alcohol or drugs alone does not allow compulsory detention.

Childcare legislation

Under the Children Act (1989)[8] and in common with other health care professionals, doctors in England and Wales treating drug dependent patients have a responsibility to report children whom they suspect to be at risk to the social services. Drug use itself by parents need not constitute a risk but neglect or abuse may be associated with problem drug use and should be addressed appropriately. The legislation in Scotland has recently been amended and is in the process of implementation. Legal issues surrounding care for children and young people are further discussed in the NHS Health Advisory Service's review *Children and young people: substance misuse services*.[9]

Injectable opiates — the legal context

Patients presenting with opiate dependence are prescribed a range of opioid preparations. By far the most common is oral methadone but others include injectable methadone, injectable heroin, Diconal tablets (dipipanone plus cyclizine), dihydrocodeine tablets and buprenorphine tablets. All are Class A drugs under the Misuse of Drugs Act. The legal restraints pertaining to each will now be discussed.

Methadone does not have any additional restrictions other than those arising from being a Class A controlled drug. Thus both oral and injectable methadone may be prescribed by any doctor. The Department of Health *Guidelines* are intended to promote good practice in prescribing. They recommend assessment to confirm the presence of opiate dependence with evidence of tolerance and physical withdrawal, the agreement of a 'treatment contract' between doctor and patient, daily dispensing and checks to prevent the patient obtaining multiple prescriptions. However there are no statutory regulations to control the practice of methadone prescribing.

The guidelines for good practice[10] describe the prescription of injectable methadone as a specialist activity and suggest referral of a patient from primary care to specialist drug services if this form of treatment is being considered. The extent to which injectable methadone is provided varies from service to service and is currently a matter of clinical judgement rather than being informed by formal study results. It is not available at all in some areas. In certain areas it is available from private practitioners. Figures from a 1995 survey of 1 in 4 UK community pharmacies indicate that prescriptions for injectable methadone made up 9.3% of methadone prescribed to drug misusers. For comparison the same survey suggests that 79.6% of methadone prescribed was the oral mixture and 11% the tablet form.[11]

Buprenorphine and, in injectable form, dihydrocodeine, are subject to the same legal status as methadone but are much less often prescribed to opiate dependent patients. Dihydrocodeine in tablet form is not a controlled drug.

The prescription of diamorphine, cocaine, and dipipanone for the treatment of dependence is further restricted by the Misuse of Drugs Act. All may only be prescribed by a doctor with a licence from the Home Office, at defined premises, for a defined length of time. The numbers of patients may be defined also. The doctor will be working in a specialist drug treatment setting, ie. licences are not generally issued to those in general practice or private practice. The provision of this type of prescribing is extremely limited. The survey referred to above[12] indicates prescriptions for injectable heroin (diamorphine) were dispensed to approximately 170 individuals, diamorphine tablets to 50 and other forms of diamorphine to 10 individuals in 1994. The actual numbers will be swelled by dispensing from hospital pharmacies to opiate dependent patients which was not recorded in the above survey. A further survey in England and Wales, this time of those involved in treating dependent patients, indicated 35 specialists currently prescribing diamorphine to dependent patients and 8 prescribing dipipanone.[13]

It should be noted that the prescription of opiates by a doctor which is for the treatment of a condition other than dependence is not subject to the licensing restrictions described above, but only by the general requirements of being a Schedule 2 controlled drug. Thus diamorphine and Diconal can be prescribed by any doctor for pain relief. Diamorphine can be particularly useful in the case of myocardial infarction and for long-term pain relief in terminal care.

Cannabis — the legal context

The prescription or other supply of cannabis is not legal in this country. However, in 1995, the Home Office moved the cannabis derivative dronabinol, (Delta 9 tetrahydrocannabinol) from Schedule 1 to Schedule 2, allowing its prescription for those suffering from nausea resulting from chemotherapy. However, it can only be prescribed on a named patient basis, and as it is not currently available on the UK market, dronabinol has to be specially imported; its international product name is Marinol. Nabilone, a synthetic cannabinoid, is not scheduled and can be prescribed for the same indications as dronabinol. A licence from the Home Office may be obtained in order to possess cannabis for research purposes. Cannabis has some potential therapeutic effects in a range of conditions which are being investigated,[14] but these potential uses are outside the remit of this document. It is not suggested that the prescription of cannabis has any role in treatments for dependence.

Ethical responsibilities and constraints

The approach to treatment based on the concept of 'harm minimisation' accepts that drug users may continue to take drugs and attempts to deal with the harm the drug user may do to himself or society. It is a pragmatic approach and requires careful evaluation of the benefits. For instance the supply of sterile needles to an injecting drug user could be regarded as encouraging injecting. However, if it reduces the chances that the individual will acquire or transmit HIV, the benefit may outweigh the risk. When a doctor substitutes one dependence-forming drug (heroin) with another (methadone), he must attempt to establish that the patient is benefiting overall despite the continued dependence on opiates. There is an ethical responsibility to prescribe such drugs in a responsible manner and to accept appropriate peer support and guidance. A major consequence of inappropriate or excessive prescribing is to increase the availability of street drugs, potentially encouraging drug misuse among others.

Some GPs, while providing general health care for drug misusers decide not to treat their drug-related problems themselves. They should, however, be able to help drug users access treatment where this is appropriate. However, where treatment will benefit the drug user, whether it is in providing general health care or substitute prescribing, a medical practitioner is not ethically justified in refusing such treatment, and should not allow his views about a patient's lifestyle to prejudice the treatment provided or arranged. This equally applies to judgments about drug misuse as 'self-inflicted' harm, regarding which the General Medical Council unequivocally instructs doctors that they must not refuse or delay treatment because they believe that patients' actions have contributed to their condition.[15] The extent to which dependent or problem drug users exercise choice in their drug use is a separate, debatable issue.

Patient confidentiality

Patient confidentiality is an essential requirement for the preservation of trust between patients and health professionals, and is critical to maintaining drug users' wish to access health care. A clear, consistent approach needs to be established by those providing care; users need to be able to approach services confident that their illegal drug use will remain within the confidential domain of the doctor, in spite of the fact that they may be inconsistent in approach themselves. A drug user may at one stage in his drug using history, tell many people about his or her drug dependence, and at another stage be desperate to hide the problem.

The increase in joint work between social and health care agencies and shared care between GPs and specialists has led to more patient information being exchanged, which increases the need for awareness of the importance and limits of confidentiality. A policy on confidentiality should be established by the practice, hospital or agency treating the drug misuser and explained to the patient. Information sharing must be limited to those involved in providing care and treatment who have a clearly demonstrable need to know, unless the patient authorises disclosure to other people.

Although patients should not be discouraged from treatment through fear of breaches of confidentiality, neither should doctors give false reassurance about the degree to which it is accorded to a person involved in a criminal activity. The limitation of confidentiality should be made clear to the patient: drug misusers should not receive special protection above other patients involved in criminal activities. At the same time, because the vast majority of crimes committed will be minor, such as petty theft, consideration should be given to the need to retain trust — and therefore the potential for treating the patient — if such crimes can be regarded as of relatively minor importance.

Agencies treating drug misusers are encouraged to complete and return forms on patients presenting for treatment of problem drug misuse to the Regional Drug Misuse databases, which are designed to maintain confidentiality. Confidentiality within medical note taking can be more difficult as access to patients notes can be obtained. Access to patients notes are requested for an increasing range of purposes; life insurance, health insurance and employment and medical reports will incorporate all such information with considerable implications for individuals who choose to confide information about illicit drug use to their doctor. This information can only be released in these circumstances with the informed consent of the patient. Patients may refuse consent to release information, but must accept that the consequences of so doing may be to be refused employment or insurance. It has been reported that in some areas the Police Inspector of Pharmacies reports the names and addresses of those prescribed controlled drugs to the local drugs squad, thus compromising medical confidentiality.[16]

For reasons of ethics and good practice, young people under the age of majority, when mature enough to understand the implications of decisions, should have the same degree of control over themselves and their treatment as other patients, and are entitled to the same confidentiality. Health professionals should act in young people's interests, which are usually best described by the young people themselves and by their own priorities and wishes. If a patient is very immature, the doctor still has a duty of confidentiality to that patient, but may decide not to provide the treatment requested.

In treating minors for drug misuse, this may involve the prescription of substitute drugs, information on safer injecting, or the provision of clean injecting equipment and condoms. If the patient does not wish their GP, parents, or if in care, the local authority, to be informed, the patient may be counselled regarding voluntary disclosure, but as with adults, without the patient's consent, confidentiality should not be breached unless there are clear public interest grounds to do so.

Breaching confidentiality

Drug misusers are by definition involved in illegal activities, that is the purchase and misuse of illicit substances. Those with expensive habits, commonly opiate and cocaine users, may also be involved in additional crimes. The nature of these crimes includes so called 'victimless crimes' such as shoplifting, crimes causing immediate distress to others, crimes causing financial loss to others and violent crimes. They may be dealing in drugs, potentially recruiting other members of society to dependence. Doctors treating drug users have to maintain an often uncomfortable balance in which they are aware of actions which are commonly judged to be immoral and are unlawful, but maintain patient confidentiality.

For doctors to routinely report drug related crimes to the police would be a disincentive to drug users to present for treatment. However, there are certain exceptional instances where the nature of the crime is such that the principle of confidentiality would be over-ridden by the duty which the doctor had to society and where failure to disclose information could expose others to risk. Doctors will have to make decisions about whether to disclose confidential information in individual cases based on the crimes involved and the gravity of the risk to others. For instance, if a drug misuser were known to be recruiting young children into drug use, it would be the doctor's duty to minimise the chances of this recruitment by reporting it.

On difficult questions such as these, there may be a disparity between a doctor's legal and ethical duties: where there is not a clear legal duty to disclose information, there may be a moral or ethical duty to do so. Although there is no statute requiring doctors to disclose in the public interest, a doctor failing to do so may be found liable by the courts if serious harm results. In most cases it is good practice to inform the individual who is the subject before any disclosure is made, including those in the 'public interest'. Information disclosed without consent should be the minimum necessary to achieve the objective. Health professionals who breach patients' confidentiality without consent must be prepared to justify their actions to their disciplinary bodies. It is therefore recommended that when faced with difficult cases, health professionals seek advice from professional and indemnifying bodies to ensure that their decision accords with professional expectations.

The need to test for bloodborne infectious diseases HIV, hepatitis B or hepatitis C also raises questions of whether to disclose confidential information. The doctor must provide facilities for pre and post test counselling and have his own strict procedures for the storage of that confidential information. If the patient tests positive, the doctor has a duty to discuss fully the implications of the patient's condition, the need to secure the safety of others, and the need for those involved in their care to know about their condition. Information about a patient's infectious state should not be disclosed against a patient's wishes unless failure to do so would put the health of another health professional or identifiable person at serious risk.[17] In any clinical area where drug users are likely to be seen staff need to be protected from infection and adequate procedures and guidelines need to be in place to deal with potential opportunities for infection such as needle stick injuries. Doctors also need some awareness of issues surrounding infected staff.

Legal obligations to provide confidential information

Although ethically a health professional may have a duty to provide confidential information about a crime, it is not an offence to withhold such information under English and Welsh law as set out under section 5(5) of the Criminal Law Act 1967 unless ordered to do so by the courts, whereas in Northern Ireland it is an offence under the Criminal Law Act 1967 not to disclose a criminal offence. Where a court or tribunal orders disclosure, health professionals or bodies must disclose but then strictly within the terms of that order, eg if ordered by a court, the information should be handed only to the court. Formal consent would not need to be obtained from the subject, but prompt notice of the order should be given, so that he can have an opportunity to apply to the court or tribunal to have it set aside if they wish and if circumstances permit. The police have powers to seize records under warrant in connection with the Misuse of Drugs Act 1971.

From 1st April 1994, a person must disclose to a police officer as soon as reasonably practicable if they know or suspect a person is concealing money made through drug trafficking if this information came to them in the course of their profession or employment. Withholding such information is an offence under section 26b of the Drug Trafficking Offences Act. Disclosure is also obligatory in cases of serious fraud being investigated by the Serious Fraud Office.[18]

Patient autonomy and choice

In doctor-patient interactions the patient has a legitimate right to expect to be given clear information to enable him to make informed choices about his or her health care. In a situation where a doctor is prescribing substitute drugs such as methadone for a patient, the principle of patient autonomy may be in conflict with the paternalistic approach of the doctor to do what he judges to be in the best interests of the patient. Thus a patient who requests a larger prescription of methadone may be in conflict with a doctor who believes that a lower dose will suffice to alleviate withdrawal symptoms, that the patient's request arises from a desire to continue to experience euphoric effects, and that an increased dose will impair the patient's ability to perform necessary daily tasks. The doctor needs to satisfy himself that in denying the patient autonomy he is doing what is best for that patient and taking an action which may produce a net health gain. This may mean taking advice from specialists and colleagues, assessing research evidence and established guidelines and being able to demonstrate some health gain from his actions.

The individual and society

Drug use affects both the individual and society. A drug user may harm society as well as himself and therefore treating that individual may well bring benefit to society. Such benefit may potentially occur in HIV prevention, crime reduction and effects on users' families. The treatment offered to a drug user may indirectly affect the expectations of others. For instance if a specialist decides to offer injectable drug substitution then the very presence of that service will influence the expectations and demands of all drug users in the area. The availability of such a service may benefit some. However it may harm others, who would not benefit from it, but for whom its existence distracts them from the oral prescription which would allow benefit.

When giving a drug misuser a substitute prescription the doctor has a duty to establish as far as possible that the drugs prescribed for a patient are taken by that patient, to minimise diversion to the black market. While the doctor cannot accept responsibility for the dishonest behaviour of his patients it is reasonable for him to take appropriate precautions to stop drugs being sold on the black market and therefore being available to other experienced and new drug misusers, such as operating a policy that the drug is taken on the premises. The doctor needs adequate training and information to know what reasonable controls on a prescription are.

As with any other patients, drug users often have children, and a doctor has a duty to cooperate with social services to protect those children where they may be in serious danger. Indeed this may be one of the situations where the confidential doctor-patient relationship may be breached. Particular care must be taken when prescribing methadone to those with children to ensure that the risk of the children accidentally ingesting it does not arise. When treating the pregnant drug user the doctor must provide any reasonable treatment to the mother to ensure the welfare of the unborn child. Again in the case perhaps of a drug user who is unwilling to cooperate with this, it may be necessary to breach confidentiality by communicating with the general practitioner and obstetrician in order to protect that child. Liaison with a sympathetic, supportive and appropriately trained community pharmacist should be encouraged.

Training and information needs

General practitioners

Training in the management of drug misuse should aim to improve the care provided by GPs for drug misusers. Training should first address any negative attitudes and misconceptions held by some doctors and then move on to help the GP acquire the necessary skills to assess and plan treatment. All GPs, whether or not they are involved in the treatment of drug misuse itself need to have a basic knowledge of the problems of drugs misuse and the issues of health education and promotion to help those drug misusers to whom they provide general medical care. Undergraduate medical education would be the ideal environment for providing this basic understanding to enable assessment, diagnosis and referral of patients. In 1990 the Advisory Council on the Misuse of Drugs recommended that such basic training should be part of the core undergraduate curriculum.[19] It is unclear how widely this has been implemented by medical schools, although no specific guidance on this subject was provided by the General Medical Council in its 1993 recommendations for undergraduate medical education.[20] The primary health care team including GPs, practice nurses and health visitors is ideally placed to offer opportunistic advice on harm minimisation to drug users. Training should be given to ensure the team provide appropriate information and education.

If a GP is prepared to offer substitute prescribing, either detoxification or maintenance, to drug users, that doctor will require further training and must expect to use easily accessible support and back up. This can be provided by members of the community drug team or other specialist providers acting on a shared care basis.[21] Members of the community drug team may have a variety of professional backgrounds including general nursing, psychiatric nursing, social work and drug counselling. Methadone maintenance in primary care is feasible[22] but may require substantial and ongoing training and support to succeed.

Medical specialists

Doctors working in hospitals will see many drug misusers as they are frequent attenders to casualty and are often admitted to hospital. Some doctors who are not drug dependence specialists will nevertheless have particular contact with drug users by virtue of their particular speciality, for example those treating patients with HIV. These doctors should be able to deal confidently with drug users. Those in all specialisms need the skills to prescribe safely for drug misusers who are admitted under their care, and should be ready to ask for specialist advice. Particular scenarios include the management of pain in drug misusers, both acute as in post operative care and chronic as in musculo-skeletal problems (see Chapter 3, 'pain relief in drug users'). In addition doctors need to be alert to the risk of causing dependence when prescribing opiates in chronic or frequently relapsing conditions such as sickle cell disease.

A commonly cited training need among people working in drug services found by a study of the Task Force was for counselling skills.[23] Education of all doctors in drug dependence needs to be firmly rooted in the undergraduate curriculum and training in drug misuse awareness should be part of postgraduate education for any doctor likely to come into contact with drug misuse in their work. The ACMD's 1990 review of training recommended that postgraduate medical centres should be assisted by regional drug planning teams and regional drug training units in providing drugs training as part of continuing medical education.[24] However, as implementation of the ACMD's 1990 recommendations so far appears to be patchy, the Task Force proposed it should be reviewed by relevant professional bodies.[25] In addition it is an important area for continuing professional development. Formal training can be supplemented by training on the job by liaison services.

Addiction specialists

Substance misuse training comes under the rubric of psychiatry training. Thus all specialists will complete general professional training in psychiatry and specialist higher training in general adult psychiatry and substance misuse. The Royal College of Psychiatrists specifies requirements on the length of specialist training required by psychiatrists in higher training who wish to become career addiction specialists.

Trusts should be encouraged to only employ psychiatrists who are adequately trained specialists. Such specialists would generally work in a DDU, a hospital or do sessional work with a community drug team. In the Advisory Council's *AIDS and drug misuse update* report (1993) a new type of specialist was envisaged. It was stated "It may also be appropriate for a specialist practitioner, such as a consultant psychiatrist, or a GP, to be employed as a 'community consultant' to encourage GP involvement with drug users within a certain geographical area." This was a recognition that the expertise required to encourage GP involvement, which is seen to be a key element of the national strategy, involved not only an extensive knowledge of drug misuse, but also an in-depth understanding of the workings and problems of general practice. An important aspect of the community consultant's work could be to take the lead in developing, and to accept responsibility for, effective working arrangements between GPs and drug services.

Access to courses for those working in the drugs field can be limited by their uneven geographical distribution. It is hoped that a strategic lead on training will be provided by the Drug Training and Development Forum, established to share ideas and promote and develop training to support national strategy. Its secretariat is based at SCODA. All medical professionals who are in contact with drug misusers, should be required to maintain their skills and knowledge through continuing professional development.

Drugs workers

A survey of drug workers in England showed a wide range of qualifications and training, with many having entered the field unqualified. Nurses were the group least likely to have had any additional training since entering the field, and were also less likely to hold qualifications in counselling and therapy of diploma level and above. Counselling and therapy were, overall, common qualifications but lacked standardisation.[26]

Findings of the Task Force's survey of drug workers were similar, with 22% of case workers having no professional qualifications, and of these, 30% had received no additional training. The Task Force concluded that a number of people employed in drug services do not have the necessary skills[27] and also found that 100% of drug service managers reported a need for further management training.

Nurses

An occupational group which has seen particular growth in the last decade is practice nurses, who are mostly employed by general practices. Their work ranges from specific clinical tasks to health promotion and home visits. Despite their potential for supporting GPs who wish to undertake the management and treatment of drug misusers outside their core general medical services workload, there was no consideration of training for drug misuse care in a national census of practice nurses.[28]

Other professionals

Basic training, as described in the Advisory Council on the Misuse of Drugs' *Review of training*[29] should be provided for all those likely to come into contact with drug misusers professionally, such as probation officers and social workers. Standards of competency for social workers and probation officers undertaking an area of particular practice in substance misuse are laid down by the Central Council for Education and Training in Social Work. These include a working knowledge of philosophies, treatment modalities and referral procedures, and the ability to employ at least one specialised intervention such as motivational interviewing.[30] Where help for drug users is provided to probation services by outside agencies, as is an increasing trend, it is important that standards of competence for staff are understood and met.

Risks from bloodborne diseases

Accidental injury from 'sharps' (penetrating instruments such as blades, needles or pieces of bone) is a risk for many staff working in the health service, which carries with it the risk of bloodborne infections. Sharps must be used and disposed of safely in every circumstance, whatever the risk a patient is thought to present. The BMA's *A code of practice for the safe use and disposal of sharps* provides advice on preventing sharps injuries, and on action following such incidents.[31] Protection against hepatitis B is discussed in *A code of practice for: Implementation of the UK hepatitis B immunisation guidelines for the protection of patients and staff.*[32]

Information technology

Each health service region maintains a database of returns about all individuals seen by drug treatment services. This contains demographic information and information about which drugs are currently misused and what treatment is planned. Annual reports are generated from the databases to aid in service planning and monitoring. Several software packages are available for patient record keeping and for prescription generation. The ability to computer generate large numbers of prescriptions is essential for the management of all community drug teams who undertake prescribing. As with other areas of medicine it is likely that improved information systems may help to improve overall management within drug services and may also facilitate communication between specialists and primary care services in their joint management of such individuals.

Research

The Task Force to Review Services for Drug Misusers[33] concluded that there is a paucity of existing UK research on drug treatment effectiveness. There have been no more than 10 randomised control trials (RCTs) of in-patient treatments and no more than 5 RCTs of out-patient treatments in the UK. Well conducted observational studies are not numerous. Because of the lack of investment, the UK is falling behind in treatment and scientific advances. The lack of a substantial research community in the field has meant that treatment developments which have been well studied in other parts of the world have not been assessed and used to improve treatment options in the UK. Given the sizable costs of such treatment and the controversial nature of much of the treatment it is important that this area be substantially developed.

Problems in drug misuse research

Many drug misusing patients are unwilling to take part in trials, and those who have chaotic life-styles may find compliance with the strict requirements very difficult. Control patients are extremely difficult to find, although out-reach workers can help in contacting drug misusers not undergoing treatment. Where treatment is delivered within the community, and sometimes with in-patient settings too, it may be difficult to ensure that medication is taken and in the correct dosage; urinary analysis does not usually quantify substances taken. Compounding these difficulties, drug misusers may covertly be taking other drugs at the same time as those prescribed, thus affecting results.

Qualitative outcomes such as improvements in social functioning are hard to quantify, and patients may be unwilling to reveal their criminal activities and the reliability of some patients' accounts may also be open to question. Familiarity with the patient and his or her circumstances, as well as a range of checks are required to gain an accurate picture of the efficacy of treatments and compliance of patients. Techniques developed by criminologists for testing the accuracy of anecdotal information might also be helpful.

The Task Force commissioned a number of observational studies including the National Treatment Outcome Study (NTORS), and made recommendations for follow up of the cohorts of subjects in treatment to look at long-term outcome and cost effectiveness. Additionally, several issues were recommended for further study:

- the effectiveness of 'shared care' by GPs;

- the impact which training has on the behaviour of people working with drug misusers;

- the comparative effectiveness of different types of counselling;

- the feasibility of increased on-site dispensing in drug services, and supervised consumption of prescribed drugs;

- ways of enhancing completion rates for detoxification, including the use of a range of drugs to assist in the process;

- whether orally-consumed drugs such as LAAM (levo alpha acetyl methadol) are appropriate alternatives to methadone;

- the role and efficacy of injectable opioid prescribing, and development of criteria to indicate for whom such prescribing might be appropriate;

- the treatment of amphetamine dependence;

- the treatment of cocaine dependence.

Evidence is also lacking on the means of preventing hepatitis C among injecting drug users, in particular what role syringe exchange schemes may have.

In addition the Medical Research Council (MRC) Field Review[34] highlighted several areas of high priority research for strengthening the field. These include:

- improved multi-disciplinary work;

- longitudinal studies of the nature and development of drug dependence;

- neuroadaptations to chronic drug effects;

- differences according to route and schedule of administration;

- molecular mechanisms of acute drug use;

- commonalities and differences between effects of drugs;

- variations in sensitivity to drugs at the cell and individual level;

- subjective phenomena of craving and withdrawal using cognitive theory;

- co-morbidity with psychiatric disorder.

There is a need for structured evaluation of strategies to treat those misusing benzodiazepines alone and in the context of polydrug dependence, including the role of prescribing of benzodiazepines. Research into harm prevention and the prevention of use is also extremely limited.

However, the absence of an infrastructure in drug misuse research makes it unlikely that good research will emerge in the foreseeable future without the appropriate investment. The establishment of career posts is needed to generate adequate research activity which is currently impeded by short-term contracts and temporary projects. Due to the very limited funds available for research and the need for good evidence as the basis for policy and treatment decisions, the sharing of expertise and information between organisations within Britain and Europe and with other parts of the world, is more important than ever.

There is a lack of co-ordination of research across the European Union, and greater scope for collaborative research between UK and European professionals in drug misuse. However, a promising development has been the establishment of the European Monitoring Centre for Drugs and Drug Addiction (EMCDDA), which aims to collate and provide comparable data at a European level on drugs and drug misuse. This was established as part of the EU's remit for public health established by Article 129 of the Maastricht Treaty.

The centre has marked out 5 priority areas for information gathering and dissemination. These are:

- the demand for drugs and policies for reducing this demand

- national and European Community strategies and policies

- international cooperation and the geopolitics of the supply of drugs

- control of trade in narcotic drugs, psychotropic substances and precursor chemicals

- implications of the drugs phenomenon for producer, consumer and transit countries

Funding for research and developing new practice has been made available through the 1996 5 year programme for Prevention of Drug Dependence in the Framework for Action in Public Health which aims to improve the quality of drugs policy.[35] The budget for this programme is 29 million ecu, and is intended to be additional to state funding. Projects involving more than one member state can apply for funding by the European Commission which assesses applications, aided by an expert committee with members from the Member States.

Resourcing drug treatment services

This section deals with resources for services devoted to rehabilitation and treatment only and not community care funding.

Contractual and funding arrangements

As has been shown in Chapter 3, the treatment and rehabilitation of drug misusers is provided under a wide range of arrangements. Although the mechanisms for funding these arrangements are complex the sources of funding are comparatively straightforward.

NHS services for drug misusers are funded for the most part from 2 sources. Additional care is provided in residential settings under local authority funding arrangements using processes common to all services covered by the NHS & Community Care Act 1990. The 2 primary sources are:

- health authority budgets either those for mental health services generally or those provided by special allocation from central funds (where funds are reserved for a particular purpose);

- payments under general medical services (GMS).

In the case of the former, these are provided under contracts negotiated between purchasers (overwhelmingly district health authorities) and NHS or voluntary sector providers. Because the provision of non-statutory services is heavily dependent on special allocation funding this introduces uncertainty about future provision from these sources in many areas. Typically, contracts negotiated between health authorities and NHS trusts or voluntary agencies are block contracts with indicative service levels. An example would be a range of client contacts and/or a target for cases closed during the duration of the contract.

Although there is also a ringfenced budget, NHS services provided to drug misusers by general practitioners under GMS attract no explicit funding and are part of the generality of fees and allowances paid to general practitioners for a largely undefined GMS workload. The recent debate on core and non-core services within primary care and Local Medical Committee (LMC) Conference policy means that funding for services provided to drug misusers other than those which are considered as falling within the scope of GMS (ie are arguably independent of the misuse itself) may have to be found increasingly from other sources. Some general practitioners already pass prescribing arrangements for drug misusers to doctors working for Community Drug Teams. In other cases GPs have negotiated payments with health authorities for services to drug misusers. Humberside LMC for example has secured a capitation payment (£102.80) for its constituent GPs for treating methadone misusers. The Greater Glasgow Health Board has negotiated the provision of services in GP drug misuse clinics with eligible general practitioners. These arrangements provide for payment for a notional clinic session of 10 patient attendances (£63.20 per session in 1994/95). Although there is also a ring-fenced budget for HIV prevention of £51 million for 1996/97, this should only be used for HIV prevention and health promotion work.[36] It has remained approximately stable, but from April 1997 will be targeted more towards districts with higher HIV prevalence. The HIV treatment and care budget was reduced by 7.8% for 1996/7 but has been increased by 7% for 1997-8 (both figures in real terms). There are concerns that pressure on HIV/AIDS treatment budgets for new antiviral combination therapies may lead to money being partially diverted from prevention to treatment. For complex reasons, such diversion can potentially occur even though the budget is ring-fenced.

The present level of resources and demand

Tackling drugs together estimates that in 1993/94, £61 million was spent on the rehabilitation and treatment of drug misusers in the UK. Of this, around £35 million was special allocations to health authorities. For 1996/97 the allocation is an estimated £33.5 million, including an additional £5.9 million made available following publication of the Task Force report intended to develop services for young people and structured methadone programmes. Health authorities can also allocate money from mainstream health care services for drug misusers. Whether this level of resources is sufficient for its purpose depends almost entirely on the level of treatment being offered relative to the demand for it.

Data on drug misusers are hard to obtain. There were 34,000 drug addicts notified to the Home Office in 1994.[37] This figure substantially understates the true level of drug misuse partly because it only includes a limited list of drugs used, and also because it only registers drug misusers who are notified. A report prepared for the Task Force to Review Services for Drug Misusers, estimated that there were 84,000 drug misusers.[38] *The fourth national study of morbidity statistics from general practice* (MSGP4) revealed prevalence rates (per 10,000 persons at risk) of 19 for drug dependence (International Classification of Diseases 304) and 17 for non-dependent misuse of drugs (International Classification of Diseases 305).[39] These data are for 1991/92 and identify only those patients in contact with a general practitioner. They suggest that in England and Wales there might have been 98,000 drug dependent patients in 1994 and a further 88,000 non-dependent misusers. Assuming similar rates for the remainder of the UK, implies equivalent UK estimates of 111,000 and 99,000 respectively. Other surveys, such as the OPCS surveys of psychiatric morbidity,[40] show apparently much higher rates of incidence and prevalence but these figures usually include anyone who uses drugs, whereas this section of this report, as indicated above, is concerned only with those users who have contact with medical services.

Cost of treatment

The Task Force to Review Services for Drug Misusers' *National Treatment Outcome Research Study* (NTORS) has collated estimates of the cost of specific interventions although its work is continuing and the estimates available so far are preliminary and based on small samples. Amongst these are counselling (£467 per course of an average duration of 14 weeks), methadone programmes (£54 per patient week) and in-patient treatment (between £47 and £70 per in-patient day). The net cost of methadone prescriptions dispensed is shown in Table 6. An alternative source of cost data is available from work undertaken by the Yorkshire Addictions Research, Training and Information Consortium (YARTIC).[41] This study implies average costs per patient treated of around £600 after allowance is made for the (lower) costs of treating alcohol misuse with which this report is not concerned. This estimate includes both those patients with in-patient stays and those with outpatient appointments only and is based on the activity of the Leeds Addiction Unit, part of a larger mental health services trust. Variation about the average is considerable and it should be borne in mind that in this study the highest 10% of individual costs accounted for over half of the total annual costs of the unit.

Potential resource use

On a very crude basis we can ascribe the average cost of treatment from the YARTIC study to the varying estimates of drug dependent patients as a proxy for total resources required. A lower cost might be applied to those who are non-dependent but who have nevertheless contacted their general practitioner for treatment for drug misuse. The cost involved in such cases has not been calculated. To the extent that the University of Middlesex estimates for the entire drug misuse population are less than the implied MSGP4 data for drug dependence alone, there will obviously be a wide variation around any estimate of resources required. Using the drug dependent estimate of 111,000 and an average treatment cost of £600 generates a minimum requirement of £67 million

Table 9: Methadone Prescribing[42]
Number of prescriptions for methadone hydrochloride by medicament classification, 1991 to 1995 England

Year	Total	Tablets	Mixtures	Linctuses	Injections	Others
Number of prescriptions (thousands)						
1991	490.5	38.3	403.3	6.8	39.0	3.1
1992	607.0	47.7	495.0	5.3	54.5	4.7
1993	735.1	62.4	598.0	4.2	70.1	0.3
1994	846.0	77.3	682.4	4.0	81.7	0.7
1995	970.9	94.9	787.0	3.5	84.2	1.4
Net ingredient cost (£ thousands)						
1991	3,732.5	177.6	1,912.3	19.6	1,611.8	11.3
1992	5,177.2	257.3	2,659.3	16.5	2,227.3	16.9
1993	6,803.6	358.6	3,626.2	11.7	2,803.1	3.9
1994	7,993.9	469.2	4,444.8	9.2	3,065.1	5.7
1995	9,086.8	594.2	5,328.0	9.1	3,145.5	10.1

1. The data cover all prescription items dispensed by community pharmacists and appliance contractors, dispensing doctors and prescriptions submitted by prescribing doctors for items personally administered.
2. The data cover all prescriptions for methadone hydrochloride and do not identify those solely for drug addicts.
3. The net ingredient is the basic cost of drugs before discount and excludes dispensing costs or fees.
4. The figures may not add up due to rounding.

— close to that currently spent. However the true requirement, bearing in mind the imprecise nature of the prevalence data, could be close to twice this figure.

The capacity of the funding system to generate the necessary level of resources is limited by the resource allocation process. Ring-fenced finance has historically been allocated to regions largely on the basis of the population aged 15 to 34. Subregional allocations have been made on the basis of local needs. With the reorganisation of the Health Service these allocations will be made directly from the centre and will be based on yet to be determined measures of need.[43] As we have seen, however, this finance accounts for only £35 million of total expenditure on the rehabilitation and treatment of drug misusers. The remainder has to be found from general allocations. Health authority allocations are to be based in future on a more sensitive formula incorporating needs indices. These are compiled using a range of criteria, such as the proportion of households with a single parent. A study from North Thames region using Regional Drug

Misuse/Database information as a measure of need established rented accommodation and unemployment as variables associated with problem drugs misuse. Results from the 1994 British Crime Survey identify a number of geographical and personal variables which are associated with drug misuse in a statistically significant fashion but this association may be as much effect as cause.[44] The relationship between these variables and those used to measure high psychiatric or acute and general need is not sufficiently close that we can rely on current needs weighting to redistribute resources to those areas where dependent drug misuse and morbidity are highest. The psychiatric needs index contains much greater variation than the acute part of the resource allocation formula (i.e it would redistribute the same sum of money more radically) and any lack of correlation is thus heightened by the use of this index. It is likely that in a climate of limited resources drug misuse will have to compete still more fiercely for its share of these resources.

Funding problems particular to drug services

Having considered the macro picture of drug service resourcing, what does the experience of health care professionals 'on the ground' tell us? Throughout the country there are numerous instances of services for drug users facing major difficulties through lack of resources and, as a result of fixed budgets, becoming incapable of responding adequately to the rising patient load. Few cash limited NHS trusts have been able to divert funds from other sources to drug services. There are a number of reasons why drug services are having such difficulties and why serious consideration should be given to solving the funding difficulties which almost all of them face.

The difficulties which have arisen are:

- a rising workload. In some areas this has been rapid. All other departments catered for by the NHS can predict their workload for the coming year usually to within a very small margin, and their historically-based budgets are usually adequate to meet their needs. The cash-limiting of NHS Trusts was based on the assumption that the patient workload for any particular area would remain relatively stable.

- there is no primary care backstop because most general practitioners do not consider the treatment of drug dependence to be part of General Medical Services.[45] Other fields, for example mental health, can shut the gate on referrals when they are working at peak capacity and expect the remainder to be cared for by GPs until they are able to be seen. Specialist drug services can, however, be directly accessed by drug users, but, unlike general practice, money does not follow the patient.

- where GPs are involved in the treatment of drug misusers, it is national policy that they should do so in a shared care relationship, again increasing the workload of the specialist drug services. Furthermore the extent of GP involvement is not under the control of the specialist drug services so they have an open-ended commitment to do this work.

- there is a significant disparity of funding of local drug services. There are still some areas of the country where in-patient detoxification is not locally available, where there is no designated local specialist in substance misuse, and where local drug workers have never been able to meet or contain the demands upon them. There are several reasons why this has occurred: the fact that many are only recently introduced services; that because most drugs are illegal the problem often remains hidden and, as the need for services cannot be accurately quantified, it is difficult to define a budget; and that drug users are not usually seen as an attractive funding option when competing for scarce NHS resources.

- the provision of seamless care for drug users is threatened by the artificial division between funding for treatment and for rehabilitation, and the bureaucratic process of applying for funding may hamper patients' progress. A fundholding GP may purchase a patient's detoxification treatment in a drug dependency unit, and the patient's local authority may then purchase the residential rehabilitation. While cooperation between health services and local authorities is excellent in some parts of the country, in others it is less so.

Cost effective resourcing

Early treatment in many fields of medicine saves greater expense later both on an individual and public health level such as in the prevention of bloodborne infections. However, there are wider, non-medical implications of making drug users wait for treatment. Although some drug users waiting for treatment stop on their own, others develop an increasing number of medical, social, psychological, and legal problems related to their drug use. As they deteriorate and their drug use becomes more entrenched they are an increasing threat to community safety both from the spread of HIV and hepatitis and from drug-related crime.

Although at times this link between drug misuse and associated criminal behaviour appears to have been exaggerated,[46] there is a well established connection between drug misuse and crime and it is recognised that treatment often has a dramatic effect in reducing criminal behaviour. The Task Force to Review Services for Drug Misusers commissioned research on 1,100 drug misusers who had committed 70,000 crimes in the 2 years prior to entering treatment, costing their victims an estimated £34 million. The Task Force commented that there was clear evidence that treatment, which embraces social care and support as well as clinical interventions, can be notably effective in reducing such harm.[47]

Local funding arrangements for drug services

Because treatment can result in widespread gains in other areas apart from the health of the individual drug user, such as a reduction in criminal behaviour and improved community safety, it is pertinent to consider whether funding for treatment programmes could be transferred from other sources. The various options are listed below:

- NHS funds should be top-sliced to pay GPs for the specialist services they are undertaking when they become involved in the treatment of drug dependence. This is occurring in an increasing number of areas. However where this is undertaken, funding for NHS trusts will then be reduced at the expense of other service provision. Also there is a requirement to fund the shared care arrangements with local specialist drug services

- emulate the Care Programme Approach which has been nationally adopted in the mental health field. Here there is a joint assessment by named assessors from health and social services, comprising the mental health treatment needs of the individual and a social services needs assessment, with funding implications for both health and social services. For drug users a tripartite assessment by named assessors from health, social services and probation would be more useful. One person could be the named assessor for all 3 services. There would be difficulties to overcome, for example probation officers are at present only allowed to see people who are on probation. If these and other problems were ironed out such an approach might also lead to a closer working relationship between the 3 services which would benefit the patient.

- protected funds for specialist drug services so that they do not have to compete against funds from other NHS resources. In the competition for funds drug services often lose out and top-slicing would protect resources allocated for drug services. If a national formula were found for allocating these funds, top-slicing could also help to even out disparities of funding. A case could be made for a system of budgetary growth, according to need, in line with known statistical increases in drug misuse.

- pooling of resources from police, the health service, probation, prisons, education and social services and reallocation by Drug Action Teams (and in Wales Drug and Alcohol Action Teams), whose membership is made up of chief executives, or their deputies, from each service (police, the health service, probation, prisons and local authorities including education and social services). There would be a question as to which resources should be pooled but potentially this option could result, either in a shift of resources from enforcement (supply reduction) to treatment services for drug users (demand reduction), or vice versa. Even in those instances where demand reduction benefits at the expense of supply reduction, demand reduction services could find themselves involved in fraternal infighting and competition for resources which could be disastrous for service providers. So, although in theory this should ensure a balance of spending which is more sensitive to local needs, allowing supply reduction and demand reduction to vary as the local situation warrants it, any experiments along these lines would need to be closely monitored by an external agency. As membership of DATs is through appointment rather than election, there would be concerns as to their accountability. They would also need a more robust set of performance indicators than is currently available, so that monitoring could be a coherent exercise.

5

Conclusion and recommendations

Conclusion

Few would disagree with Government opinion that "tackling drug misuse is a long-term process",[1] and the use of illegal drugs (those controlled by the Misuse of Drugs Act 1971) has risen steadily in the UK during the past 25 years. Although there are few national sources of data on the prevalence of drug use, the information that is available tends to suggest that levels of drug use are increasing slowly but surely. In the 1990s, 1 in 6 people will have taken a drug — mostly cannabis — at some point in their life and at least 10% of the population will take an illegal drug in any year, while the number of people coming forward for treatment is also rising. Urgent action is needed to reduce drug misuse and the harm it causes.

In the late '80s, the Royal College of Psychiatrists published a comprehensive report on drugs and drug dependence.[2] The authors commented "Society's relationship with drugs is a matter of ebb and flow, of shifting co-existence. New drugs arrive and old drugs go out of fashion". Although the report was intended for a 'general readership', it included a valuable chapter on 'treatment' and 3 treatment recommendations were proposed: on determining treatment efficacy, improving the availability of treatments of proven efficacy and ensuring good practice among doctors under-taking private work with drug misusers.[3]

Within a short time illicit use of drugs in the UK has increased and patterns of use have diversified. Data for 1995 from the Home Office Addicts Index (published in July 1996), showed that the number of notified addicts in the UK had risen to 37,200, an increase of 9% compared with a year earlier. Since the late

1980s a new trend has emerged with an increase in amphetamine, LSD and ecstasy use as part of a 'rave' dance culture. Perhaps 1 in 10 young people may have tried a 'dance drug', most commonly amphetamine, with LSD and ecstasy each being tried by 5-10% of young adults, the long-term consequences of which are unclear.

In May 1995, the Government launched its 3 year anti-drugs strategy *Tackling drugs together*, and complementary strategies were launched for Scotland, *Drugs in Scotland: Meeting the challenge* (1994) and Wales, *Forward together* (1996), focusing on crime, young people and the protection of public health,[4,5,6] encouraging collaboration across agencies through the formation of Drug Action Teams, and their equivalents and the Northern Ireland Office participated with an anti-drugs campaign and a policy statement.[7] These were followed by the report of an independent evaluation of drug treatment services in England — The Task Force to Review Services for Drug Misusers (1996). This important report included a range of recommendations and posed some key questions for future investigations, but as yet there is no national strategy for coordinating the care of drug misusers across the services providing treatment and social support.

Questions evoked in people's minds by drug problems are diverse and include the nature of drug problems and the responsibility certain groups may have for causing or solving them. Drug problems have social, psychological, medical and legal parameters. For police and customs officers, not only drug use but also drug trafficking may be seen in part as social and economic problems (as well as being criminal). Internationally, problems may arise from plant drug cultivation, production and supply, as well as consumption, and have extensive political and developmental implications.

Health workers come into contact with drug problems in many different forms. This does not imply any responsibility for the wider global picture — but doctors have a responsibility to respond to the problems as presented to them, within the limits of their professional competence, in physical and psychological health, and that of colleagues in their teams. They also have a duty to speak out in the interest of public health and against factors likely to exacerbate ill health. Taking account of the excellent work of the Task Force and the Advisory Council on the Misuse of Drugs, this report has focused on the range of interventions to which doctors and their colleagues can usefully contribute their expertise, and the structures and processes necessary to enable the best care to be delivered.

Resources

The treatment of drug misusers can not only benefit patients, but also the wider community. Drug misuse creates 'knock-on' costs in social and criminal problems, and treatment including social care and support can reduce this harm. For this reason, budgets for drug misuse should be given greater priority.

Early treatment in many fields of medicine saves greater expense later both at an individual and public health level both in terms of treatment and human suffering. This is particularly the case with the prevention of diseases such as HIV, hepatitis B and hepatitis C. The aims of the AIDS prevention budget, which presently can be used for HIV prevention or health promotion work, need to be broadened to include the prevention of hepatitis B and C and increased in order to promote safer injecting and sexual practices. The total cost of methadone prescriptions is steadily increasing, and the costs of treatment for populations of injecting drug misusers with HIV, hepatitis B and hepatitis C, will require long-term funding.

At present, a single patient's care may be funded by a range of agencies; the patient's fundholding GP might purchase his detoxification treatment in a drug dependency unit, and his local authority may then purchase his residential rehabilitation. This impedes the provision of seamless care and makes it difficult to calculate total spending

Research and information

Evidence-based medicine is an ideal to which medical professionals and others involved in care aspire, but research into drug misuse and treatments is currently hampered by the lack of an infrastructure, short-term contracts and temporary projects. Unless resources are found to invest in a strong research base, policy and treatment decisions will be impeded by a lack of evidence on their efficacy.

In addition to the immediate problem of research funding, the efficacy of treatments for drug misuse can be difficult to measure. Research involving drug misusing patients can present a range of difficulties for researchers arising from patients' chaotic lifestyles or inability to comply with a strict regime of medication without using additional street drugs. Outcomes, such as an improvement in family relationships, are difficult to quantify and such assessment may be further impeded by the questionable reliability of patients' accounts, as they may not disclose illegal activities. Methodologies which are capable of establishing the outcome of interventions in treating drug misusers is therefore a clear need in this field of drug misuse research.

There are several issues which this report has only been able to touch upon briefly, but which require much more detailed study. For instance the most widely misused illicit drug in the UK is cannabis, yet its long-term psychological and physical effects are insufficiently understood. Its potential as a therapeutic drug also requires further research. Drug testing in the workplace is a further issue likely to be of significance in the future.

Training

Drug misuse is a complicated, multifactorial problem which doctors in almost all specialties will encounter at some time. Consequently all doctors have a responsibility to understand the basics of aetiology, life histories and recognised treatments for this group of patients and how this impinges upon their practice. Drug misuse education and training for medical staff who are not specialists in the field, have long been neglected, and in view of the rising numbers of people misusing drugs and presenting for treatment, this need is greater than ever. Furthermore, if ideals of patient management, such as multidisciplinary care, are to be achieved in practice, medical education needs to lead the way. Education in drug misuse is required during undergraduate and postgraduate education and continuing professional development. Although there are numerous courses in drug misuse, many of these demand a considerable time commitment and are not evenly geographically distributed across Britain. For other professionals working in the care of drug misusers, levels of training and qualifications vary widely, with some drugs workers having no professional qualifications or additional training since entering the field. Further management training is also an identified need among those responsible for running drugs agencies.

Where competencies have been laid down for professional groups, such as probation officers and social workers, employers should ensure these are achieved. Where the roles of professionals in the care of drug misusers are less clear, training requirements should be reviewed. In addition to those whose work is directed to caring for drug users there are many professionals, such as teachers, who incidentally come into contact with drug users in the course of their work. The basic training described by the Advisory Council on the Misuse of Drugs' review of training is likely to be appropriate.

Doctor and patient responsibilities

Doctors and other health care workers have a responsibility to provide medical services for patients with acute and chronic dependence problems. For GPs, this may range from referral to specialist drug services, as part of their provision of general medical services, to taking part in shared care arrangements. The complicated problem of the management of drug misuse is likely to mean that communication across and cooperation between specialities will be necessary and sharing of patient information and responsibility essential.

All patients, whether drug misusers or not, have a right of access to appropriate care, but it is helpful if doctors determine which forms of care are appropriate before discussing them with the patient. When treatment is being discussed, it may be helpful for the health professional and patient to agree on a treatment plan, which might include standards for compliance with treatment and behaviour. Whether such a plan is written as a 'contract' (though not a legal document), or not, it is most important that health professionals be clear and consistent in their expectations of patients and that these, including the consequences of non-compliance, are discussed and agreed with the patient before treatment begins. In return, patients have a responsibility to provide their doctor (and associated health professionals) with accurate information and to comply with jointly agreed treatment plans. When negotiating the terms of a patient contract or a treatment plan, the patient may feel himself to be in a weaker position than the doctor or other health professional and so care should be taken that goals are mutually agreed and set at realistic levels.

Patient care issues

Assessment of patients allows the most urgent needs to be identified, the potential for progress to be determined, and the means to make progress. It is important that this is carried out as soon as practically possible after the first contact with the patient. Many drug misusers presenting to services have a range of problems, some of which are medical, others psychological, and many of which are social, financial or legal. Drug misusers may need assistance in accessing the help they need from different services and health care professionals can help by referral and liaison to the appropriate agency. Improvements in these aspects of life through, for instance, the provision of stable housing or employment, can improve the outcome of medical interventions for drug misuse. This 'total patient care' should be accessible through GPs or specialist services, including those in primary care such as community drug teams, whether or not GPs take on the management of drug problems themselves. Liaison between professionals and different agencies can be time consuming but is important for achieving effective team working.

Drug misusers are a diverse patient group and present with a wide variety of needs. It is these needs which should lead the development of services, so that no single treatment modality or setting dominates where wider choice would be beneficial. As well as the drug misuse itself, patients may suffer from specific problems of mental health, or, for instance, hepatitis C, or the patient may be young and unsuited to services which are designed for adults. In the past, local provision has developed in a somewhat haphazard fashion, with perhaps voluntary services dominating in one area, and statutory services in another. There is a need for an individual, at health authority level, to oversee both the development and coordination of treatment services in the field of drug misuse. In the planning of services it should not be forgotten that treatment also requires the support of laboratories which carry out toxicological tests on drug misusers, both during life, and if they die.

The danger should be avoided of narrowing the focus of services to treatment with methadone maintenance, which although a valuable form of therapy, is not suitable in all cases of opioid dependence.

Prevention of bloodborne diseases

Despite the success of HIV prevention measures, the risks of bloodborne diseases to injecting drug users, their partners and the wider population remain; it is essential therefore that prevention work continues. Although there is an effective vaccine for hepatitis B, coverage of the population of injecting drug users and their sexual partners is far from comprehensive. Health advice and promotion should discourage injecting drug users from injecting; or if they do so, encourage them not to share equipment or injecting paraphernalia; explain how to disinfect equipment; dispose of equipment and access needle and syringe exchanges. Patients should also be advised about practising safer sex. To ensure comprehensive availability of injecting equipment, a wide range of settings, such as pharmacies or community drug teams, should provide injecting equipment. Users of these services are not always required to return used equipment, and in such cases sharps containers produced to British Standard specifications, should be provided. Where this is not possible, advice on safe disposal should be given, so that used equipment does not cause injury, infect others or contaminate the environment.

Prescribing

Substitute prescribing can have beneficial effects on drug misusing patients, including reducing the symptoms of withdrawal, reducing criminal activity (as the need to buy street drugs is reduced or removed), and moving to safer modes of administering the drugs. However, achieving patient compliance when prescribing to drug misusers is often difficult, and doctors need to be aware of the dangers of substitute drugs being diverted to the 'black market'. Drugs with an abuse potential, such as benzodiazepines, also require caution in prescribing, so that they do not become drugs of dependence or misuse.

As a safeguard against forgery, doctors are required under regulation 15 of the Misuse of Drugs Regulations 1985 to handwrite prescriptions for Schedules 2 and 3 controlled drugs (with the exception of temazepam and phenobarbitone). To avoid patients taking more than one day's dose at a time in a 'binge', doctors may write out several prescriptions by hand for a patient. Only doctors working in drug dependence units who prescribe to 10 patients or more can apply to the Home Office for exemption from this time consuming requirement. However, any change in the regulations themselves must be considered by the Home Secretary, who is under statutory obligation to consult the Advisory Council on the Misuse of Drugs.

In general practice in England and Wales it is currently possible to write 1 prescription for up to 14 days of daily prescribing for all Schedule 2 drugs (including amphetamine), using the blue FP10(MDA) form. However, where hospital consultants or their medical teams wish to provide daily dispensing, they would have to provide a separate, handwritten prescription for each day using the yellow FP10(HP). In Scotland, all prescriptions can be written on an FP10.

To prevent drug misusing patients acquiring more than 1 prescription at a time for substitute drugs, doctors need a fail-safe system for checking a patient's last prescription. Until April 1997 the Addicts index had been used for this purpose, which although of limited value due to its inclusion of a relatively small range of drugs and accessibility only during office hours, without a suitable replacement, the scope for double-prescribing is now even greater, and a useful source of epidemiological data has been lost.

Patient confidentiality

Every general practice, hospital or agency should have a policy on patient confidentiality, which should be understood by all staff and patients. This is particularly important for drug misusers as their drug misuse involves illegal activities, and they may be breaking the law in other areas too.

Prisons

There is considerable concern at current standards of health care in many prisons, which generally do not match those of the NHS.[8] The extent to which prisoners with drug problems should receive the same treatment as they would on the outside, such as methadone maintenance, continues to be debated.

The BMA supports equal standards of care for patients inside and outside prison, while recognising that this may not mean that the same treatment is given that would be provided in the community. As the prison environment differs, patients' clinical needs should be met in a way that is compatible with prison life. The trading of drugs in prison, for instance, may affect what is feasible operationally within the prison. Continuity of care may therefore not necessarily mean the same treatment, but a successful treatment should not be stopped merely due to imprisonment.

Recommendations

1   Central government should establish an agreed national strategy for the management of drug misuse which involves a multidisciplinary care approach co-ordinated between the local authorities, health authorities, the prison service, the probation service and the health education authority, to provide the spectrum of care from the community into specialist care and return to the community.

2   All purchasers (GP fundholders, health authorities and local authorities) should ensure access to structured treatment programmes for drug misusers via specialist services, or through GPs in shared care arrangements. This approach should be capable of encompassing:

   • structured counselling;

   • where appropriate, the prescribing of approved medications to manage withdrawal and substitution pharmacotherapies;

   • solving medical, psychiatric, social and legal problems caused by drug misuse;

   • working with families;

   • facilitating employment or further education.

3   Drug Action Teams should ensure that every health authority or health board offers a full range of treatment services and settings corresponding to the widely varying needs of drug misusers, as outlined by The Task Force to

Review Services for Drug Misusers. This includes harm reduction services, such as outreach schemes, geared towards drug users who are not yet willing to contemplate reducing or ceasing their drug use. Treatment programmes, including residential detoxification facilities where appropriate, should be available, preferably locally, for all drug users, whatever their drug of use.

4   Central government should provide increased protected resources for the management of drug misuse, in line with the statistical increase of the problem, to be delivered within an agreed national strategy. Combined local budgets for drug misuse would allow all purchasing bodies (local authorities, health authorities, GP fundholders, and the prison and probation services) jointly to commission care with greater transparency.

5   The AIDS prevention budget needs to be increased and also used to contain the already extensive hepatitis C epidemic among injecting drug users. This budget should, perhaps, be renamed the 'bloodborne virus budget'.

6   Every health authority should ensure that within the services they provide are:

- an individual responsible for overseeing care services relating to drug misuse;

- access to sufficient consultants/specialist medical staff who are trained and assessed as being competent to manage the psychological and physical consequences of drug misuse and who will work closely with fellow professionals from other disciplines, providing care locally that can be accessed by drug misusers within a reasonable time period;

- primary care staff of sufficient competence in drug misuse to assess and refer patients, as necessary.

7   GPs must be made aware of available local services for the treatment of substance misuse.

8   GPs should give appropriate General Medical Services (GMS) care to patients with psychological, psychiatric and/or physical complications of their substance misuse.

9   GPs should be enabled to participate in the management of drug dependence by the provision of adequate accredited training, adequate support from the specialist drug services, and adequate reimbursement for the work which they

undertake, and should consider participating in shared care arrangements. Such work should be subject to clear written protocols and contracts.

10 When prescribing benzodiazepines, to reduce the likelihood of dependence and misuse, doctors should consider the following:

- the favouring of long-acting formulations such as diazepam and chlordiazepoxide, which are less liable to misuse; however the risks of misuse should be balanced against the risks of accident and impaired performance caused by the effects of the hangover;

- regular reviewing and auditing of benzodiazepine prescriptions;

- more frequent dispensing arrangements for benzodiazepines liable to misuse.

11 In England and Wales form FP10(HP) should be brought in line with form FP10(MDA) to enable daily dispensing of any Schedule 2 drug by hospital specialists from a single prescription. Both forms should be adapted to include diazepam. The feasibility of exempting all GPs from the legal handwriting requirements for prescribing methadone should be considered by the Home Secretary.

12 A national, comprehensive, confidential information system is required to provide up-to-date prescribing information on individuals, accessible to general practitioners and other prescribers, and available out-of-hours, including week-ends.

13 Effective strategies for the prevention and treatment of over-the-counter (OTC) drug misuse are needed, and should include:

- a warning label to be added to drugs known to induce physical or psychological dependence, such as the following: *Warning: this medication contains ingredients known to cause a physical or psychological dependence, if misused or taken over a long period. Do not take in excess of 7 days continuously. Consult your pharmacist or doctor for further advice and/or information.*

- the Department of Health to provide information to GPs to raise awareness of OTC drug misuse.

14 Health care workers should be educated in the social and medical issues of drug misuse through multidisciplinary education.

15 Training in drug misuse awareness, which should be available locally, should form part of postgraduate medical education for any doctor likely to come into contact with drug misusers in their work. Where relevant, through a multidisciplinary approach, medical professionals should develop competences which enable them to manage the issues of drug misuse (social and medical) within their everyday practice. These should include:

- knowledge of drug misuse and its impact on health;

- ability to conduct basic assessments of patients' drug misuse and related problems;

- ability to refer appropriately to other agencies;

16 Medical professionals who are involved in the treatment of drug misuse should be able to demonstrate competences which underpins their practice. This should include:

- knowledge of prescribing issues and options;

- theories of dependence;

- policy issues;

- management of drug treatment.

Continuing professional development (CPD) should include the physical, psychiatric and psychological problems of drug misuse.

17 In line with the Advisory Council on the Misuse of Drugs' recommendations on training, all other professionals likely to encounter drug misusers as part of their work should receive basic training about drug misuse. Where particular individuals, eg. some social workers, probation officers, youth workers, teachers and further and higher education staff are likely to come into contact with significant numbers of drug misusers, they should receive additional training to ensure they are competent. In some circumstances it may be appropriate for individual staff to be identified in order to provide more significant levels of service and particularly to collaborate with drug services staff, as initiated by the probation service.

18 The role and training requirement for GP practice nurses, nurse practitioners and community psychiatric nurses in dealing with drug misusers should be reviewed. GPs should encourage individual practice nurses and the primary

health care team as a whole to attend postgraduate courses to develop their clinical skills in dealing with drug misuse where appropriate.

19 Standards of competence of drug services staff should be raised to commonly agreed levels through the use of National Vocational Qualifications (NVQs). Managers of drug services must receive appropriate training to deliver effective services.

20 Local Drug Action Teams (DATs) should facilitate attachments, placements and secondments, to deliver expertise at the appropriate level, as part of an overall DAT training strategy.

21 Health needs assessments of drug misusers should be carried out within the shortest practical time scale from the time of referral or self-referral.

22 Patients at risk of contracting bloodborne infections such as HIV and hepatitis B and C, should be offered pre- and post-test counselling and diagnostic tests, including liver function tests, wherever appropriate. Immunisation against hepatitis B should be provided for all non-immune injecting drug users (including prisoners) and their sexual partners.

23 Sterile injecting equipment should be comprehensively available in the NHS along with health advice and promotion, to reduce the spread of bloodborne diseases and to improve general health among injecting drug users. 'Sharps' containers meeting British Standard specifications, should be available for safe disposal of injecting equipment, and where this is not always possible, eg in the home, advice on safe disposal should be given.

24 Every practice, hospital or agency should ensure that their procedures and safeguards for patient confidentiality are explained to all patients. Information sharing must be limited to those involved in providing care and treatment who have a clearly demonstrable need to know, unless the patient authorises disclosure to other people. Information which for ethical or legal reasons must be disclosed without the consent of the patient should also only be disclosed on a 'need to know' basis. Such policies should consider:

• the limitations of confidentiality, including the possible uses of patients' medical notes, eg. for reports for insurance companies;

- breaching patient confidentiality in the public interest. Health professionals should first consult their professional and indemnifying bodies to ensure that their decision will accord with professional expectations and legal requirements;

- information about a patient's infectious status should not be disclosed against a patient's wishes unless failure to do so would put the health of another health professional or identifiable person at serious risk;

- disclosure of confidential information ordered under law (eg by a court or tribunal). In such cases health professionals or bodies must comply, but then strictly within the terms of that order and should first consult their professional and indemnifying bodies. Prompt notice of the order should be given to the patient.

25 Standards of care in prisons should be as high as for those in the community, and tailored to the particular needs of patients, including the provision, through shared care arrangements, of approved drugs for detoxification such as lofexidine and methadone for opiate addicts with withdrawal symptoms. Prison policies should include the following:

- prisoners identified with a history of drug misuse should be allocated a key worker on entering the prison system;

- cleaning materials, such as sterilizing tablets, and instructions for disinfection and safe disposal of equipment should be provided for injecting drug users;

- mandatory drug testing of individually identified prisoners should be used only with the provision of a full range of treatment services;

- liaison should be improved between prison medical services and those services outside prison treating drug misusers before and after imprisonment.

The Prison Service should publish its current study into drug misuse and mandatory drug testing in prisons when complete, which may necessitate changes to the system of mandatory drug testing. The Prison Service strategy *Drug misuse in prisons* (1995) should be reviewed regularly and appropriate measures taken to reduce the risks to prisoners, staff and the health of the wider community through education and counselling of drug users.

26 Research should contribute to the formulation of policy-making, with centres of excellence being established throughout the UK in all aspects of drug problems and policy. Regular national surveys should be undertaken to provide information on drug misuse in the UK.

27 Research studies should be more closely linked to the coordination of drug information and research facilitated by the European Monitoring Centre, and international partner institutions.

28 Many areas of drugs research need to be funded; as a priority, funding should be provided for the areas identified by the following:

- The Medical Research Council (MRC) Review *The basis of drug dependence*.[9]

- The Task Force to Review Services for Drug Misusers *Report of an independent review of drug treatment services in England*.[10]

- *Tackling drugs together* and its national equivalents *Drugs in Scotland: Meeting the challenge*; *Forward Together: A strategy to combat drug and alcohol misuse in Wales* and *Drug misuse in Northern Ireland*.[11,12,13,14]

- Greater awareness of the European Union programmes and plans should be encouraged among health and allied professions by government and national agencies: The European Plan to Combat Drugs,[15] the 1996 5 year programme for Prevention of Drug Dependence in the Framework for Action in Public Health,[16] and the five priority areas of the European Monitoring Centre for Drugs and Drug Addiction.[17]

Appendix I

The legalisation debate

> The issues discussed in this section are complex, and inevitably rely greatly on supposition, due to the lack of hard evidence on the effects of change to the status quo. Furthermore, value judgements are inevitable in the ranking of different forms of harm, such as criminal or medical. The views expressed do not represent BMA policy but are put forward for discussion.

Definitions

- Decriminalisation is generally taken to mean either the non-enforcement or the abolition of criminal sanctions for the possession of small amounts of illicit drugs for personal use. Although the use of drugs would be tolerated, trafficking (including supply, offer to supply, production, import and export) would remain illegal. Because cannabis accounts for the vast majority (nearly 90%) of all drug offences some debates consider only the decriminalisation of this drug.[1]

- Legalisation of some or all drugs, where all points in the supply and consumption process are legal, is rarely proposed without some restrictions. The proposed degrees of regulating the distribution and consumption of drugs vary and alternatives range from licensing commercial premises for sale and consumption, such as Amsterdam's 'coffee shops' for the use of cannabis, to restrictions similar to those for the sale of alcohol, including a minimum age.

Current laws

In raising the question of whether any illicit drugs should be decriminalised or legalised, we should first consider the purpose of the UK's current laws. The main legislation covering illicit drugs, the Misuse of Drugs Act, states that it aims 'to prevent the unauthorised use ('misuse') of drugs which are being, or appear likely to be misused and of which the misuse is having or appears capable of having harmful effects sufficient to constitute a social problem'.[2] It rests on the principle that curtailing the freedom of the individual may be justified for the greater good of society.

The Act also fulfills the UK's international obligations to control drugs. All the major Western industrialised nations have signed the 1961 UN Single Convention on Narcotic Drugs which obliges its signatories to make possession and other drug related activities 'punishable offences'. It could be assumed that no major relaxation of the drug laws is possible without opting out of the Convention. However, the official commentary to the Convention makes it clear that nations have wide scope in the interpretation of this provision as it applies to possession, where minor penalties could be deemed appropriate. Imprisonment is only necessary for "serious offences".[3] Several legislatures have used this flexibility to mould the Convention's provisions to their own cultures and legal systems.[4] However legalising, rather than decriminalising drugs would require enormous international momentum to change these agreements, which at present looks highly unlikely.

It has been suggested that the Misuse of Drugs Act does not succeed in its aims[5] and also that the Act and associated anti-drugs legislation cause more harm than they prevent.[6] This criticism partly reflects the continuing rise in offences.[7] In 1994, well over 100,000 drug seizures were made, nearly 4 times the number made a decade before; although this may be due to patterns of enforcement, research published in 1995 found that the majority of young people have taken drugs (the proportion had been a third 3 years earlier).[8] Even if the results of this study were found to over-represent the extent of drug misuse it is clear from longitudinal research that has been carried out in the last decade that the numbers of drug users has increased.[9]

Countering the argument that the laws against drug use should be repealed on the grounds that they are widely flouted, the Government makes the point that armed robbery or assault would never be considered for decriminalisation.[10] However, robbery and assault cause direct harm to others, whereas the chief effect of drug misuse is on the individual using the drug.

Drug-related crime, such as robbery, theft and fraud to fund drug use, has also received considerable attention in recent years.[11] It may be suggested that such crime would be significantly reduced if drugs could be bought legally. However, this depends on a number of assumptions: first concerns the proportion of crime which is drug related — estimates vary considerably (see Chapter 2, 'Crime'); second, it is assumed that legislation would significantly reduce the cost of drugs (which is uncertain) and third, were drugs cheaper when legal, that those involved in criminal activities would cease breaking the law. Drug users' motivations for acquisitive crime may be more complex than simply funding their drug use.

Current policy and future direction

Party political debate of legalisation and decriminalisation has so far been limited. The Government viewpoint is uncompromising — both the Green and White Papers, *Tackling drugs together*, rejected any arguments for legalisation or decriminalisation[12,13] on the grounds that "wider use and addiction . . . are very serious risks which no responsible Government should take on behalf of its citizens". The Labour Party also opposes liberalisation of the drugs laws, but the Liberal Democrats passed a resolution in 1994 that a royal commission should be established to look at a range of issues relating to drug misuse, including the possibility of decriminalising the use and possession of cannabis.

The Misuse of Drugs Act sets out the maximum penalties for possession, supply, production, import and export, but there is considerable discretion in how the law is applied. For instance, despite the fact that the maximum fine for the possession of cannabis (and amphetamines and codeine) has risen from £500 to £2000, many police forces only caution those found in possession of small quantities of cannabis. Discussion of anti-drugs legislation has been more open among the police, with some individuals calling for a reconsideration of the law. One police officer commented of the Misuse of Drugs Act, 'Most of us would define a bad law as one which is unenforceable or infringes personal liberty. A law which falls into both of these categories has little to commend it'.[14]

European developments

In the Netherlands, the amended 1976 Opium Act separated some drugs on the basis of risk. Penalties for heroin, cocaine, amphetamines and LSD, which were classified as 'presenting unacceptable risk' were raised in line with other countries, while use, possession and trading of small amounts of cannabis was effectively decriminalised with cannabis being sold from designated premises. Recently the Netherlands has come under intense pressure to revise its policies and is currently doing so. France, concerned about the movement of terrorists across borders and the import of drugs from the Netherlands and Belgium, slowed down the implementation of the *Schengen Convention* creating a 'borderless' region in Europe.

In May 1994, the German Supreme Court removed the obligation for police officers to arrest and for authorities to punish those found in possession of small amounts of cannabis, but with scope for varying local implementation. In Spain personal possession of any drug is not a criminal offence. After a referendum in 1993, Italy chose to respond to the possession of drugs for personal use only with 'administrative' sanctions, such as fines. These countries' experiences in decriminalising some substances provide evidence for debate. However, as there have been no experiments with the legalisation of drugs, much of the evidence is speculative and untested.

Advantages and disadvantages of decriminalisation and legalisation

The decriminalisation of cannabis: The issue of decriminalisation explored here will focus on cannabis, as this is the minimum change to the law generally considered in debates with the other extreme of legalising of all drugs discussed in the next section. It should be remembered that, although considered by many to be a "soft drug", there are a number of health risks associated with the use of cannabis, including those arising from smoking and accidents caused to the user and others (for instance while driving under its influence). While cannabis users do not usually experience severe withdrawal symptoms on discontinuing use, tolerance to a number of the drug's effects does develop.

The main argument in favour of the decriminalisation of cannabis is that it could save considerable resources in the criminal justice system because 4 out of 5 drug offences in 1993 were related to cannabis, and most of these were for possession. However, such a change in the law is seen by some as a first step towards wider reform of the law[15] and would constitute an inconsistency: while it would not be a criminal activity to possess or consume cannabis, the process by which it was provided to the user would involve criminal offences. The problems associated with the illegal market, such as unregulated product quality, would remain, but individuals for whom the use of cannabis is their only criminal activity, would no longer be at risk of prosecution.

The Government has argued that decriminalising cannabis would attract those who experiment with it as 'forbidden fruit' to use more 'dangerous' drugs.[16] The decriminalisation of cannabis in the Netherlands seems to have been followed by a fall in the prevalence of its use from 13% of those aged 17-18 in 1976 to 6% in 1985. The assertion that decriminalisation of cannabis could lead to increased use of 'hard' drugs such as heroin and cocaine has been refuted by a recent Dutch study which found that since cannabis has been tolerated in 'coffee shops', the majority of cannabis smokers have distanced themselves further from heroin, cocaine and also alcohol.[17] Most cannabis smokers in the study saw themselves as participating in socially acceptable behaviour, putting even greater distance between themselves and the users of 'harder' drugs. However, this was a relatively small scale study and further research would be required to confirm these findings.

Decriminalisation and legalisation of all drugs

Social controls: The consumption of legal drugs such as tobacco and alcohol are socialised activities. Accepted norms — for instance that one does not drink in the morning — have developed through a long co-existence with these drugs, moderating consumption. Those found behaving outside these norms may risk, for instance, social embarrassment, or worse, the loss of a job, although this does not entirely prevent misuse. For the majority of the population who have not experienced most illegal drugs, such moderating patterns do not exist and are not necessary. Were all drugs to be decriminalised or legalised at once, casualties of excessive or inappropriate use might therefore occur before the drugs became integrated into social life, although it is uncertain how long it would be before such norms developed. However, social norms vary between groups and do not necessarily correlate with maintaining health or avoiding dependence. This is clearly illustrated by the case of tobacco smoking, where a habit of 10 cigarettes a day may cause dependence and appreciable risk to health but is considered 'moderate' consumption. Among certain groups, the norm for alcohol consumption may easily exceed the recommended daily limit of 3 units per day for men and 2 for women.[18]

Varying potential for harm: The question should also be asked as to whether moderate, controlled consumption is possible with all drugs or whether some drugs have special properties which predispose the user to heavy, problem use. In the case of possession of all drugs being decriminalised, the current problems of quality associated with the black market would continue with their associated hazards for drug misusers. However, were drug quality to be controlled, as it might well be in a legal market, the problem of drug dependence would persist. In reply to a call for legalisation of all drugs,[19] a heroin addict argued that dependence on heroin created a continual cycle of use which made dealing with life problems increasingly difficult. To support his case he cited the widespread addiction to prescribed, legal tranquillisers.[20] However, dependence cannot be attributed solely to the drug taken: while the concept of the 'addictive personality' continues to be controversial, research has shown that of those who experiment with drugs, some groups in society are more likely to become dependent or heavy drug users than others (see Chapter 2).

Would drug use increase: This argument rests on the assertion that the number of users would increase if drugs were decriminalised or legalised. The American experience of the prohibition of alcohol (1920-1933) may shed some light on this issue. Although prohibition was seen as a failure which fostered a lucrative black market and the development of organized crime, it has been shown that heavy drinking did decline in the 1920s and that alcohol related diseases rose again when prohibition was lifted.[21] However it is highly doubtful whether the case of prohibition over 60 years ago, is comparable in either cultural or political terms, or with regard to the substance involved.

It is unknown whether newly legal/decriminalised drugs would replace the use of currently legal ones, or be used in addition. However, many drugs are not simply taken for their capacity to intoxicate, but for their specific functions, whether stimulants, hallucinogens, etc, and their patterns of use also differ. For instance nicotine is generally taken throughout a working day with minimal interference to other normal activities, whereas alcohol is usually limited to leisure time. Although difficult to predict, with a wider range of drugs and effects available, it seems probable that there would be some increase in the numbers of people using drugs and the quantities consumed.

It is unknown whether the legalisation of drugs with possible taxation would reduce drug costs, but the influence of price on consumption should be considered. American research reveals that the extent of drug use may not vary much in response to changes in price[22] but lower prices may mean that the drug is consumed in greater quantities or more frequently by each individual who does use it. However it can not be extrapolated from this that more people will use the drug.[23] In other words, the prevalence of use may not rise noticeably, but in the instance of dependence forming drugs such as heroin and cocaine, 'dependence' may. From a medical and resourcing standpoint, this would have enormous implications. However, it may be easier to minimise harm to drug users and encourage the uptake of treatment if the illegality were removed and perhaps the stigma of drug use lessened. For instance users might feel more willing to use needle exchanges and attend drug dependency units.

In conclusion, in view of the many complex interrelated factors involved, it will not be possible to predict the consequences of either decriminalisation or legalisation in the UK; we can only try to learn from countries which have taken such steps.

Appendix II

Fitness to drive

Patients may have their driving licenses revoked if they fail to notify the Driver Vehicle Licensing Agency (DVLA) that they are using illicit drugs or substitute prescribed drugs for the treatment of dependence. Failure to notify the DVLA is an offence, and if they have a car accident following which it transpires they are taking drugs, it is possible that the insurance company will refuse to pay costs, as their policy may be declared invalid. It is also an offence under Section 4(1) of the 1988 Road Traffic Act to drive a motor vehicle when unfit through drugs. GPs should be aware of these regulations so that they can inform their patients. However, it is not the responsibility of doctors to ensure that patients notify the DVLA. The DVLA's requirements are as follows, although this guidance is currently being reviewed:

The applicant or licence holder must notify DLVA unless stated otherwise in the text.

Drug misuse and dependency	Group 1 Entitlement*	Group 2 Entitlement*
Cannabis Ecstasy and other 'recreational' psychoactive substances, including LSD and Hallucinogens	The regular use of these substances, confirmed by medical enquiry, will lead to licence revocation or refusal for a 6 month period. Independent medical assessment and urine screen arranged by DVLA, may be required.	Regular use of these substances will lead to refusal or revocation of a vocational licence for at least a 1 year period. Independent medical assessment and urine screen arranged by DVLA, may be required.

Amphetamines Heroin Morphine Methadone** Cocaine Benzodiazepines	Regular use of, or dependency on, these substances, confirmed by medical enquiry, will lead to licence refusal or revocation for a minimum 1 year period. Independent medical assessment and urine screen arranged by DVLA, may be required. In addition favourable Consultant or Specialist report will be required on reapplication. **Applicants or drivers on Consultant supervised oral Methadone withdrawal programmes **may** be licensed, subject to annual medical review and favourable assessment.	Regular use of, or dependency on, these substances, will require revocation or refusal of a vocational licence for a minimum 3 year period. Independent medical assessment and urine screen arranged by DVLA, may be required. In addition favourable Consultant or Specialist report will be required before relicensing.
Seizure(s) associated with illicit drug usage	A seizure or seizures associated with illicit drug usage may require a licence to be refused or revoked for a one year period. Thereafter, licence restoration will require independent medical assessment, with urine analysis, together with favourable report from own doctor, to confirm no ongoing drug misuse. In addition, patients may be assessed against the Epilepsy Regulations.	Vocational Epilepsy Regulations apply.

NB: A person who has been relicensed following illicit drug misuse or dependency must be advised as part of their follow up that if their condition recurs they should cease driving and notify DVLA Medical Branch.

This guidance is reproduced by kind permission from the DVLA's *At a glance guide to the current medical standards of fitness to drive* (Swansea: DVLA, March 1996).

* Group 1: motorcyclists, car and Light Goods Vehicle drivers
 Group 2: Goods Vehicle drivers driving vehicles in excess of 3.5 metric tonnes laden weight and bus and coach drivers. By convention, Group 2 standards are also generally applied to emergency police, firemen and ambulance drivers as well as taxi drivers.

Appendix III

The Task Force to Review Services for Drug Misusers *Report of an independent review of drug services in England*

Summary of recommendations (reproduced by kind permission of the Department of Health)

> The Task Force's report has made an important contribution to establishing the effectiveness of drug services and treatments in England. Although the views expressed have not been endorsed as BMA policy its work is referenced at several points in this BMA report, and its recommendations are therefore reproduced below.

Outreach

1   Better management, monitoring and support systems should be introduced. Outreach services should clearly identify their aims and objectives and collect data on number of contacts made, the effect of contact, costs per contact and on turnover of clients.

Services for young people

2   We recommend that purchasers should consider the needs of young people at risk of drug misuse and those who are misusing drugs within a comprehensive local assessment of need. Meeting the needs of young drug misusers is likely to include:

- youth services which are aware of and responsive to possible drugs problems;

- drugs services specifically dedicated to young people;

- arrangements for access, where appropriate, to "mainstream" drug services.

Social services

3   We endorse the recommendations of the Social Services Inspectorate report.[24] Social Services Departments should build on the positive start which many have made and make sure that adequate priority is given to services for drug misusers and especially young people misusing drugs.

Accident and Emergency Departments

4   All A&E Department staff should receive basic drug awareness training.

5   Purchasers should discuss with A&E providers the practicalities of collecting data on drug misuse attendance at A&E Departments.

6   A&E Departments should display posters and have leaflets available on drug misuse, health promotion and harm minimisation, and where to get help from local drug treatment services.

7   Purchasers should explore with A&E providers the scope for developing needle exchanges in A&E Departments.

Maternity services

8   Maternity staff should receive basic drug awareness training.

9   Purchasers should explore the need for maternity drug liaison workers.

General Practitioners

10 GPs have responsibility for the physical health needs of drug misusers within the provision of general medical services and should be encouraged to identify drug misuse, promote harm minimisation and where appropriate refer to specialist services.

11 The process of "shared care", with appropriate support for GPs, should be available as widely a possible. Health authorities should encourage its expansion to enable GPs to take overall clinical responsibility for drug misusers and agree with a specialist a treatment plan which may involve the GP prescribing substitute opiate drugs.

12 GPs should be sufficiently skilled to identify a problem drug misuser who may be consulting them for other, perhaps related, problems. This may require a programme of specialised training for some GPs.

13 GPs should know to whom they can refer in a crisis and for ongoing support, either from specialist drug workers, such as community psychiatric nurses, regularly attending their clinics, or by access to a named key worker in the local specialist agency.

14 The service provided by the GP should be agreed between the Local Medical Committee and specialist services and should clearly set out the respective roles of the GP and the specialist services, and the support the GP can expect in delivering the service.

15 Purchasers should ensure that GPs have straightforward access to urine testing facilities.

16 Where they have concerns about compliance with consumption arrangements, GPs should have access to facilities where supervised consumption can take place.

17 The agreement between the Local Medical Committee and specialist services for the provision of shared care should include arrangements for referral, assessment and management. Purchasers should monitor local arrangements and ensure adequate controls are in place.

18 Where the service is defined as exceeding the requirements of general medical services, following consultation and agreement with the profession, the question of additional payment for the delivery of specialist service needs to be considered.

Pharmacies

19 We recommend that the Department of Health should consider setting up pilot projects to investigate the potential for pharmacists to expand the range of services they offer to drug misusers, including the supervised consumption of controlled drugs or other medication on the premises where appropriate. Results should be used to draw up guidelines and ensure appropriate training is available for participating pharmacists and their staff.

20 We recommend that Health Authorities:

- ensure a comprehensive coverage of needle-exchange facilities, using pharmacy outlets as well as specialist agency services, outreach workers and potentially A&E departments;

- consider the extent to which participating pharmacies can deliver health promotion messages. These could include advice to protect others as well as drug misusers themselves, for example on storing controlled drugs to prevent harm to children and to educate misusers on the risks of, and methods to avoid, overdose;

- take steps to improve links between pharmacies and prescribers and feedback in both directions, and ensure participating pharmacists have effective links with specialist services for advice.

Police

21 HM Inspectors of Constabulary should take steps to encourage full and consistent use of cautioning of drug misusers by local police.

22 Arrest referral schemes should be provided at each police station. DATs should consider whether there are cost benefits to provision of support from specialist drugs workers.

23 DATs should explore ways of monitoring the effectiveness of cautioning and arrest referral schemes as a means of reducing re-offending.

24 DATs should encourage their police representative to consider training needs of police surgeons so they are equipped with the skills to manage the clinical needs of drug misusers within police custody.

The Probation Service

25 Through their membership of DATs, probation services should consider ways of maximising joint working and, where appropriate, pooling resources with other statutory bodies such as health and local authorities to maximise the benefits for treatment of drug misusers in their care.

Drug misusers in prison

26 In completing their own evaluation, the Prison Service should take full account of our findings on the effectiveness of those interventions with which their pilot projects are concerned.

27 The Prison Service Health Care Directorate should ensure that development of treatment services is consistent with the identified needs of prisoners.

28 Approved treatment pharmacotherapies, including methadone, should be available for people entering the prison system who are opioid dependent.

Throughcare

29 Drug misusers should have immediate access to appropriate treatment programmes on release. This is essential to maximising the treatment opportunity we hope will be available within prisons, as well as to reducing the risk of overdose inherent in a return to use of street drugs after a period of abstinence.

30 In those areas with prisons, DATs should review the arrangements for managing drug misusers on release and ensuring that effective arrangements exist for referring drug misusers to appropriate services.

Self help networks

31 Purchasers should be aware of the possible benefits of self-help networks and should encourage the development of a wide range of self-help groups and self-help treatments.

32 Information about existing groups such as NA and FA, and services such as ADFAM, should be made available in all treatment settings.

33 Where possible, self-help groups should be evaluated more rigorously.

Syringe exchange schemes

34 Purchasers should ensure comprehensive local coverage by syringe exchange schemes.

35 Purchasers should ensure that minimum service specifications for exchange schemes include provision on basic health checks for clients and that exchange scheme staff receive training to enable them to provide these.

36 Purchasers should require all exchange schemes to collect basic client data. They should also collect information on cost, including cost per exchange.

37 Purchasers should agree targets with syringe exchange schemes on volume of clients, frequency of visit, duration of contact and percentage of referrals to treatment. Details of targets should be set locally.

38 The Department of Health should take steps to make sure that current injectors and those at risk of becoming injectors have easy access to hepatitis B vaccinations through specialist drug services, GUM clinics and GPs.

39 Purchasers should review arrangements for delivering hepatitis B vaccinations locally and monitor progress towards universal vaccination of drug service clients.

40 The Department of Health should consider how people who could benefit from treatment for hepatitis B & C could be encouraged to come forward.

Counselling

41 Counselling should be recognised as a core component of drug treatment and not just an optional subsidiary to other treatments.

42 There is a need for purchasers and providers to distinguish clearly between structured counselling approaches, with clearly defined goals, and information and advice giving.

43 Delivery of structured counselling needs training and skills and purchasers should encourage this by requiring services to increase their numbers of accredited counsellors.

44 Further research is needed to evaluate the effectiveness of different counselling approaches.

Opioid detoxification programmes

45 Purchasers should ensure detoxification services are always complemented by counselling and social support.

46 Purchasers should establish outcome criteria for detoxification, based on evidence of safety and minimal discomfort, and the percentages of patients who complete the treatment and who go on to further treatment.

Methadone reduction programme

47 Reduction programmes should review the status of clients and their treatment contract on a regular basis, eg once a month, according to the length of the programme.

48 Purchasers should consider how to ensure clients who have become drug free can have access to appropriate support through further outpatient attendances, community projects or self-help groups such as NA.

Methadone maintenance programmes

49 Purchasers should:

- ensure that the programme content, structure and setting of methadone maintenance programmes reflects the needs of clients;

- expect programmes to review the status of the client on a regular basis (eg every 3 months) to see if they have reached a stage where they are readier to contemplate reduction leading to abstinence;

- monitor the impact of treatment on other problem domains (eg crime, etc);

- study the longer term results from NTORS to see if structured programmes produce better outcomes, and to identify optimum dispensing arrangements.

Pharmacotherapy issues arising from methadone treatment

50 The Department of Health explores ways to ensure that methadone tablets are no longer prescribed for the treatment of drug addicts, but are only prescribed for other indications such as pain control.

51 The Department of Health explores ways to ensure that injectable opioids and other injectable addictive drugs are only prescribed for drug addicts by doctors (including GPs) with appropriate training and expertise working with adequate multidisciplinary input and by specialist drug misuse services. The authority of all doctors to prescribe injectables for other indications such as pain control should be left unaltered.

52 Such services should have in place systems, such as daily instalment dispensing, to safeguard diversion of prescribed injectable drugs into the illicit market.

53 Standards should be set of frequency and approved methods of drug testing which will help to limit diversion of prescribed injectable drugs into the illicit market.

54 The proposed Department of Health clinical guidelines cover the issues of specialist prescribing and the management of more complicated cases.

Residential services: therapeutic communities

55 Purchasers should ensure access to residential care for those likely to benefit.

56 Given the levels of drug related and psychological problems likely to be present in clients in need of residential care, prompt access is likely to be important. Purchasers should ensure admission within a specified time from identification of need.

57 Purchasers need to be able to meet the varied needs of their clients. Given the range of distinct philosophical approaches to rehabilitation adopted by

centres in England, they should have access to centres to the 3 main types: therapeutic communities, 12 step and Christian based houses.

58 Until more comprehensive and longer term outcome data become available from NTORS purchasers will need to look at the rates of retention in the services they purchase. We consider that, as a preliminary measure, more than 50% should remain in treatment at the end of 4 weeks — a target already achieved by some centres. Purchasers should take steps to follow up people who drop out to establish why and thus inform future purchasing strategies.

Residential services: in-patient treatment

59 Purchasers should:

- recognise that specialist in-patient (and residential) detoxification programmes can have significant impact on certain types of drug misusers who may not benefit from outpatient detoxification;

- ensure that those needing detoxification are admitted within a specified time from identification of need. Given the levels of drug related and psychological problems likely to be present in clients in need of residential care, prompt access is likely to be important;

- gather cost information on in and outpatient detoxification programmes and monitor outcomes to inform them of the relative cost-effectiveness of the different approaches;

- health authorities should identify, from local needs assessments, the likely demand for in-patient services, and contract for that level in advance so that such services can undertake proper planning to meet the expected level of need.

Treatment of stimulant misusers

Amphetamines
60 Provision should be made for services to be able to deal with the treatment needs of amphetamine drug misusers heavily dependent on amphetamines.

Cocaine
61 All specialist drug agencies should be prepared to offer treatment to primary cocaine drug misusers.

62 Services should provide rapid access to treatment.

63 Purchasers need to monitor that cocaine drug misusers are getting appropriate and adequate treatment.

Benzodiazepine misuse

64 Purchasers should ensure that provision is made for services to be able to detoxify and withdraw benzodiazepine dependent drug misusers.

Alternative therapies

65 Purchasers should encourage careful monitoring of the effectiveness of any alternative therapies.

Service users' rights

66 Health and social services purchasers should have a dedicated resource to deal with drug misuse and should work with others to ensure organisational barriers do not slow down speed of assessment and response.

67 Contracts between purchasers and providers against which overall performance is assessed should incorporate specific quality standards which ensure individual clients:

- have the right to an assessment of individual need (where appropriate) within a specified number of working days;

- have the right of access to specialist services within a specified maximum waiting time;

- have the right to respect for privacy, dignity and confidentiality, and an explanation of any (exceptional) circumstances in which information will be divulged to others;

- have the right of access to a complaints procedure;

- have the right to full information about treatment options and informed involvement in making decisions on treatment;

- have the right, when referred to a consultant, to be referred for a second opinion, in consultation with their GP;

- can expect the right to an individual care and treatment plan.

68 DATs should initially monitor local performance standards, but this should be with a view to development of national targets.

Opening hours

69 Purchasers should identify when users need services to be open, taking account of the needs of particular groups such as young people, and reflect this in contracts.

70 Opening times should be widely publicised.

Services tailored to individual needs

Gender

71 Purchasers and providers should take account of particular needs (eg, childcare facilities for drug misusing mothers) and reflect these in contracts.

Ethnic minorities

72 Purchasers should establish links with representatives of ethnic minority groups to identify, and take account of, any particular service needs they identify and reflect these in contracts.

Co-existing mental illness

73 Purchasers and providers should ensure that people working in both drugs and mental illness services are aware of the need to identify and respond to problems of combined psychiatric illness and drug misuse.

Alcohol dependence

74 Purchasers and providers should ensure that people working in both drug and alcohol treatment services are aware of the need to identify and respond to overlapping alcohol and drug problems.

Training

75 Professional bodies should review the extent to which they have implemented the ACMD's 1990 recommendations.

76 Purchasers should require providers to examine skill levels of staff working with drug misusers and make sure that service budgets include enough to enable the right training to be undertaken.

Management of drug services

77 People appointed as service directors should have good management skills and in-post training should be made available to them, and other managers, as appropriate.

78 Voluntary sector management committees and NHS Trust line managers should recognise their own responsibilities to ensure these directors perform effectively.

79 The guidance for purchasers which DH is to produce should contain examples of indicators which could be adapted for local use by purchasers and providers as the basis of objective setting and systematic monitoring of the delivery of these objectives.

Effective purchasing

80 The guidance to purchasers which DH is to produce should include the following points:

- purchasers should consider the need for funding periods of adequate length to reflect the need for stability in provision of some services because they aim to address long-term problems;

- purchasers should seek to develop stable working partnerships with providers, based on trust, dialogue, and shared objectives;

- purchasers should establish, monitor, and act on indicators of the impact services are having on drug problems;

- purchasers and providers should also monitor key indicators of treatment, organisation and outcome.

References

Introduction

1   British Medical Association. *The BMA guide to living with risk.* (2nd ed.) Harmondsworth: Penguin, 1990

2   British Medical Association. *Young people and alcohol.* London: BMA, 1986

3   British Medical Association. *The drinking driver.* London: BMA, 1988

4   British Medical Association. *The BMA guide to alcohol and accidents.* London: BMA, 1989

5   British Medical Association. *Alcohol: guidelines on sensible drinking.* London: BMA, 1995

6   British Medical Association. *Driving impairment through alcohol and other drugs.* London: BMA, 1996

7   Parker H, Meaham F, Aldridge J. *Drug futures: changing patterns of drug use amongst English youth.* London: ISDD, 1995

8   Miller P Mc, Plant M. Drinking, smoking and illicit drug use among 15 and 16 year olds in the United Kingdom. *BMJ* 1996;313:394-7

9   Department of Health and Social Security. *Report of the Working Group on Inequalities in Health* (The Black Report). London: DHSS, 1980

10 British Medical Association. *Deprivation and ill-health.* London: BMA, 1987

11 British Medical Association. *Inequalities in health.* London: BMA, 1995

12 British Medical Association, Strategies for national renewal; A British Medical Association commentary on the report of the Commission on Social Justice, London: BMA, 1996

13 Health Education Authority. Personal Communication. 1996

14 Royal College of Physicians. *A great and growing evil: the medical consequences of alcohol abuse.* London: RCP, 1987

15 Government Statistical Service. *Statistical bulletin. Drug misuse statistics.* Issue 1996/24; London: Department of Health, 1996

16 Task Force to Review Services for Drug Misusers. *Report on an independent review of drug treatment services in England.* London: Department of Health, 1996

Chapter 1

1   Barber A, Corkery J, Ogunjuyigbe K. *Statistics of drug seizures and offenders dealt with, United Kingdom, 1995.* Issue 25/96. London: Home Office, 1996

2   Research and Statistics Department. *Statistics of drugs seizures and offenders dealt with, United Kingdom, 1995,* Issue 15/96. London: Home Office, 1996

3   Berridge V. Historical Issues. In: MacGregor S, ed. *Drugs and British society.* London: Routledge, 1989:20-35

4   Spear B. The Early Years of the 'British System' in Practice. In: Strang J, Gossop M, eds. *Heroin addiction and drug policy. The British system.* Oxford: Oxford University Press, 1994:3-28

5   Department of Health, Scottish Office Home and Health Department, Welsh Office. *Drug misuse and dependence. Guidelines on clinical management.* London: HMSO, 1991

6   Glanz A, Taylor C. Findings of a national survey of the role of general practitioners in the treatment of opiate misuse (3 parts). *BMJ* 1986;293:543-545

7   Advisory Council on the Misuse of Drugs. *AIDS and drug misuse. Part 1.* London: HMSO, 1988

8   Scott R, Gruer L, Wilson P et al. Glasgow has an innovative scheme for encouraging GPs to manage drug misusers. (Letter). *BMJ* 1995;310:464-465

9   British Medical Association, General Medical Services Committee. *Core services: taking the initiative.* London: BMA, 1996

10   Fleming P M, Roberts D. Is the prescription of amphetamine justified as a harm reduction measure? *Journal of the Royal Society of Health* 1994;114(3):127-31

11   Department of Health. *Guidelines of good clinical practice in the treatment of drug misuse.* London: HMSO, 1984

12   Ward J, Mattick R, Hall W. *Key issues in methadone maintenance treatment.* Kensington, New South Wales: New South Wales University Press, 1992

13   Farrell M, Ward J, Mattick R et al. Methadone maintenance treatment in opiate dependence: a review. *BMJ* 1994;309:997-1001

14   Robertson J R, Bucknall A B V, Welsby P D. Epidemic of AIDS related (HTLV III/LAV) infection among intravenous drug abusers. *BMJ* 1986;292:527-9

15   Robertson J R, Bucknall A B V, Wiggens P. Regional variations in HIV antibody seropositivity in British intravenous drug users. *Lancet* 1986;i:1435-1436

16   Burns S M, Brittle R, Gore S M et al. The epidemiology of HIV infection in Edinburgh related to the injecting of drugs: an historical perspective and new insight regarding the past incidence of HIV infection derived from retrospective HIV antibody testing of stored samples of serum. *Journal of Infection* 1996;32:53-62

17   Scottish Home and Health Department. *HIV infection in Scotland. Report of the Scottish Committee on HIV infection and intravenous drug use.* Edinburgh: Scottish Home and Health Department 1986

18   Advisory Council on the Misuse of Drugs. *AIDS and drug misuse. Part 1.* London: HMSO, 1988

19   Advisory Council on the Misuse of Drugs. *AIDS and drug misuse. Part 2.* London: HMSO, 1989

20   Advisory Council on the Misuse of Drugs. *AIDS and drug misuse update.* London: HMSO, 1993

21   Skidmore C A, Robertson J R, Roberts J J K. Changes in HIV risk-taking behaviour in intravenous drug users: a second follow-up. *British Journal of Addiction* 1989;84:695-696

22   Advisory Council on the Misuse of Drugs. *AIDS and drug misuse update.* London: HMSO, 1993

23   Advisory Council on the Misuse of Drugs. *AIDS and drug misuse update.* London: HMSO, 1993

24   Advisory Council on the Misuse of Drugs. *Problem drug use: a review of training.* London: HMSO, 1990

25   Advisory Council on the Misuse of Drugs. *Drug education in schools. The need for a new impetus.* London: HMSO, 1993

26   Advisory Council on the Misuse of Drugs. *Drug users and the criminal justice system. Part 2: Police, Drug Misusers, and the Community.* London: HMSO, 1994

27   Lord President of the Council and Leader of the House of Commons, Secretary of State for the Home Department, Secretary of State for Health et al. *Tackling drugs together. A strategy for England 1995-1998.* London: HMSO, 1995

28   Ministerial Drugs Task Force. *Drugs in Scotland: meeting the challenge.* Scottish Home and Health Department, Edinburgh and London: HMSO, 1994

29   Welsh Office. *Forward together. A strategy to combat drug and alcohol misuse in Wales.* Cardiff: Welsh Office, 1996

30   Northern Ireland Office. *Drug misuse in Northern Ireland. A policy statement* (unpublished) 1995

31   Ramsay M, Percy A. *Drug misuse declared: results of the 1994 British Crime Survey.* London: Home Office, 1996

32   Leitner M, Shapland J, Wiles P. *Drug usage and drugs prevention: The views and habits of the general public.* London: HMSO, 1993

33   Balding J. *Young people in 1994.* Exeter: University of Exeter, 1995

34   Parker H, Meaham F, Aldridge J. *Drug futures: changing patterns of drug use amongst English youth.* London: ISDD, 1995

35   Health Education Authority. *Today's Young Adults.* London: HEA, 1992

36   Health Education Authority. *Tomorrow's Young Adults.* London: HEA, 1992

37   Gallup/Wrangler. *The youth report.* London: Wrangler, 1992

38   Grampian Health Board. *Lifestyle survey of young people in Grampian.* Aberdeen: Grampian Health Board, 1993

39   Smith S, Nutbeam D. Adolescent drug use in Wales. *British Journal of Addiction* 1992;87:227-33

40   Southern Health and Social Services Board. *Illicit drug and solvent use: survey of prevalence and opinions in the SHSSB.* Portadown: SHSSB, 1993

41   Health Education Authority, BMRB International. *Drug realities, National Drugs Campaign survey* London: HEA, 1996

42   Leitner M, Shapland J, Wiles P. *Drug usage and drugs prevention: The views and habits of the general public.* London: HMSO, 1993

43   Ramsay M, Percy A. *Drug misuse declared: results of the 1994 British Crime Survey.* London: Home Office, 1996

44   Pritchard C, Cotton A, Cox M. Truancy and illegal drug use and knowledge of HIV infection in 932 14-16 year-old adolescents. *Journal of Adolescence* 1992;15(1):I-A

45   Balding J. *Young People in 1994.* Exeter: University of Exeter, 1995

46   Parker H, Meaham F, Aldridge J. *Drug futures: changing patterns of drug use amongst English youth.* London: ISDD, 1995

47   Leitner M, Shapland J, Wiles P. *Drug usage and drugs prevention: The views and habits of the general public.* London: HMSO, 1993

48   Miller P McC, Plant M. Drinking, smoking and illicit drug use among 15 and 16 year olds in the United Kingdom. *BMJ* 1996;313:394-7

49   Ramsay M, Percy A. *Drug misuse declared: results of the 1994 British Crime Survey.* London: Home Office, 1996

50   Health Education Authority, BMRB International. *Drug realities, National Drugs Campaign survey.* London:HEA, 1996

51   Mid-Glamorgan Social Crime Prevention Unit. *Crime, alcohol, drugs and leisure: a survey of 13,437 young people in Mid-Glamorgan.* Mid-Glamorgan Social Crime Prevention Unit, 1992

52   Ramsay M, Percy A. *Drug misuse declared: results of the 1994 British Crime Survey.* London: Home Office, 1996

53   Baker O, Marsden J. *Drug misuse in Britain 1994.* London: ISDD, 1994

54   Release. *Release National Drugs Survey.* London: Release, 1994

55   Baker O, Marsden J. *Drug misuse in Britain 1994.* London: ISDD, 1994

56   Baker O, Marsden J. *Drug misuse in Britain 1994.* London: ISDD, 1994

57   ISDD. *Drug notes 5: Cocaine and crack.* London: ISDD, 1993

58   Ramsay M, Percy A. *Drug misuse declared: results of the 1994 British Crime Survey.* London: Home Office, 1996

59   Johnson A M, Wadsworth J, Wellings K et al. Sexual lifestyles and HIV risks. *Nature* 1992;360:410-2

60   Forsyth A J M, Farquhar D, Gemmell M et al. The dual use of opioids and temazepam by drug injectors in Glasgow (Scotland). *Drug and Alcohol Dependence* 1993;32:277-280

61   Robertson J R, Treasure W. Benzodiazepine Abuse. Nature and extent of the problem. *CNS Drugs* 1996;5(2):137-146

62   Release. *Release National Drugs Survey.* London: Release, August 1994

63   Balding J. *Young people in 1994*. Exeter: University of Exeter, 1995.

64   Ives R. Sniffing out the solvent users. In: Ives R ed. *Soluble problems: tackling solvent sniffing by young people*. London: National Children's Bureau, 1991:31-50

65   Taylor J C, Norman C L, Bland J M et al. *Trends in deaths associated with abuse of volatile substances 1971-1994*. Report No.9. London: St George's Hospital, 1996

66   Newcombe R. *Raving and dance drugs: house music clubs and parties in north west England*. Liverpool: Rave Research Bureau, 1991

67   Newcombe R. *Official statistics on dance drugs 1986-1992*. Liverpool: Rave Research Bureau, 1993

68   Balding J. *Young People in 1988*. Exeter: University of Exeter, 1989

69   Baker O, Marsden J. *Drug misuse in Britain 1994*. London: ISDD, 1994

70   Kenny C, Unell I. *An epidemiological assessment of anabolic steroid use in Nottingham*. (unpublished), 1993

71   Williamson D J. Misuse of anabolic drugs. *BMJ* 1993;306:61

72   Shapiro H. Adjusting to steroid users. *Druglink* 1992;7(5):16

73   Kenny C, Unell I. *An epidemiological assessment of anabolic steroid use in Nottingham*. (unpublished), 1993

74   Lenehan P, Bellis M, McVeigh J. *Anabolic steroid use in the North West of England*. Liverpool: The Drugs and Sport Information Service, 1996

75   Mc Bride A J, Williamson K, Peterson T. Three cases of nalbuphine hydrochloride dependence associated with anabolic steroid use. *British Journal of Sports Medicine* 1996;30:69-70

76   ISDD. *Drug abuse briefing.* (5th ed.) London: ISDD, 1994

77   Thomas R M. AIDS risks, alcohol, drugs and the sex industry: a Scottish study. In: Plant M, ed. *AIDS, drugs and prostitution.* London, New York:Tavistock/Routledge, 1990:88-108

78   Newcombe R. *Raving and dance drugs: house music clubs and parties in north west England.* Liverpool: Rave Research Bureau, 1991

79   Ashton M. *The ecstasy papers.* London: ISDD, 1993

80   Sheffield Health Board. *Alcohol survey.* Undated (1992?)

81   Measham M, Newcombe R, Parker H. The post-heroin generation. In: ISDD, *National Audit of Drug Misuse in Britain 1992.* London: ISDD, 1993:18-82

82   Government Statistical Service. *Statistical bulletin. Drug misuse statistics.* Issue 1995/2 London: Department of Health, 1995

83   Royal Pharmaceutical Society of Great Britain. *Medicines, ethics and practice: a guide for pharmacists.* (17th ed.) London:Royal Pharmaceutical Society, 1996

84   ISDD. *Drug notes 10: Over the Counter (OTC) medicines.* (revised ed. 1993) London:ISDD, 1991

85   Over-Count Drugs Advice Agency. *Annual Report/Statistical Returns, 1994-95*, Dumfries: Over-Count, 1995

86   Armstrong D J. The use of over-the-counter preparations by drug users attending an addiction treatment unit. (Letter). *British Journal of Addiction* 1992;87:125-128

87   Over-Count Drugs Advice Agency. *Annual Report/Statistical Returns, 1994-95*, Dumfries: Over-Count, 1995

88   Kennedy J G. Over the counter drugs; changing the roles of doctors and pharmacists. *BMJ* 1996;312:593-594

89   Lord Privy Council. *Tackling drug misuse: a summary of the government's strategy.* London: HMSO, 1985

90   Lord President of the Council and Leader of the House of Commons, Secretary of State for the Home Department, Secretary of State for Health et al. *Tackling drugs together. A strategy for England 1995-1998.* London: HMSO, 1995

91   Ministerial Drugs Task Force. *Drugs in Scotland: meeting the challenge.* Scottish Home and Health Department, Edinburgh and London: HMSO, 1994

92   Association of Chief Police Officers' Working Party on Drug Related Crime and the Association of Chief Police Officers' Crime Committee. *The final report of the Working Party on Drug Related Crime*. London: ACPO, 1985

93   Lord President of the Council and Leader of the House of Commons, Secretary of State for the Home Department, Secretary of State for Health et al. *Tackling Drugs Together. A strategy for England 1995-1998*. London: HMSO, 1995

94   HM Inspectorate of Constabulary. *An Examination of Police Force Strategies*. London: Home Office, 1996

95   Task Force to Review Services for Drug Misusers. *Report on an Independent Review of Drug Treatment Services in England*. London: Department of Health, 1996

96   Maden A, Swinton M, Gunn J. Drug dependent prisoners. *BMJ* 1991;302:880-881

97   NHS Executive. *Purchasing Effective Treatment and Care for Drug Misusers*. EL(96) 74 CI (96) 24. 22 August 1996

98   Task Force to Review Services for Drug Misusers. *Report on an Independent Review of Drug Treatment Services in England*. Department of Health, 1996

99   Ministerial Drugs Task Force. *Drugs in Scotland: Meeting the Challenge*. Scottish Home and Health Department, Edinburgh and London: HMSO, 1994

100   Scottish Prison Service. *Guidance on the management of prisoners who misuse drugs*. (unpublished) 1994

101   Association of Chief Officers of Probation. *Addressing the problems of drug and alcohol misuse among offenders: advice on suggested framework to assist local services develop policy and strategy*. London: ACOP, 1995

102   Advisory Council on the Misuse of Drugs. *Drug misusers and the criminal justice system: Part 1 - community resources and the Probation Service*. London: HMSO, 1991

103   Probation Service Division. *Addressing the problems of drug and alcohol misuse among offenders: guidance for probation service management*. London: Home Office, 1994

104   Department for Education, School Curriculum and Assessment Authority. *Drug proof. Drug education: curriculum guidance for schools*. London: Department for Education, 1995

105   Advisory Council on the Misuse of Drugs and the Home Office. *Drug education in schools: the need for a new impetus*. London: HMSO, 1993

106   Home Office. *Drugs Prevention Initiative. Annual progress report 1994-95*. London: Home Office, 1995

107   *National Health Service and Community Care Act*. London: HMSO, 1990

108   Lord President of the Council and Leader of the House of Commons, Secretary of State for the Home Department, Secretary of State for Health et al. *Tackling Drugs Together. A strategy for England 1995-1998*. London: HMSO, 1995

109   Advisory Council on the Misuse of Drugs. *AIDS and Drug Misuse Update*. London: HMSO, 1993

110   CWR Associates for SCODA and Alcohol Concern. *Community care and residential rehabilitation services: the first year. Findings and recommendations*. London: SCODA and Alcohol Concern, 1994

111   Department of Health. *An inspection of social services for people who misuse drugs and alcohol*. London: DH, 1995

112   Task Force to Review Services for Drug Misusers. *Report on an Independent Review of Drug Treatment Services in England*. London: Department of Health, 1996

113   Advisory Council on the Misuse of Drugs. *AIDS and Drug Misuse*. London: HMSO, 1988

114   Lord President of the Council and Leader of the House of Commons, Secretary of State for the Home Department, Secretary of State for Health et al. *Tackling Drugs Together. A strategy for England 1995-1998*. London: HMSO, 1995

115   Commission of the European Communities. *Communication from the Commission to the Council and the European Parliament on a European Union action plan to combat drugs (1995-1999)*, Brussels 23.06.1994. COM (94) 234 Final

116   European Monitoring Centre for Drugs and Drug Addiction. *Annual report on the state of the drugs problem in the European Union*. Lisbon: European Communities, 1996

Chapter 2

1   Zinberg N. *Drug, set, and setting: the basis for controlled intoxicant use.* New Haven: Yale University Press, 1984

2   NHS Health Advisory Service. *Children and young people. Substance misuse services. The substance of young needs.* London: HMSO, 1996

3   Stockwell T. The psychological and social basis of drug dependence: an analysis of drug-seeking behaviour in animals and dependence as learned behaviour. In: Edwards G, Lader M, eds. *The nature of drug dependence.* Oxford: Oxford University Press, 1990:195-210

4   Nutt D J. Addiction: brain mechanisms and their treatment implications. *Lancet* 1996;347:31-36

5   Leitner M, Shapland J, Wiles P. *Drug usage and drugs prevention: The views and habits of the general public.* London: HMSO, 1993

6   Miller P McC, Plant M. Drinking, smoking and illicit drug use among 15 and 16 year olds in the United Kingdom. *BMJ* 1996;313:394-397

7   Elliott T, Elliot B. Physician attitudes and beliefs about use of morphine for cancer pain. *Journal of Pain and Sympton Management*: 1992;7(3):141-8

8   Elliott T, Elliot B. Physician attitudes and beliefs about use of morphine for cancer pain. *Journal of Pain and Sympton Management* 1992;7(3):141-8

9   Easthope G. Perceptions of the causes of drug use in a series of articles in the International Journal of the Addictions. *International Journal of the Addictions* 1993;28(6):559-569

10   Swadi H A. Longitudinal perspective on adolescent substance abuse. *European Child and Adolescent Psychiatry* 1992;1(3):156-70

11   DeJong C, Brink W, Harteveld F M. Personality disorders in alcoholics and drug addicts. *Comprehensive Psychiatry* 1993;34(2):87-94

12   Stowell R. Dual diagnosis issues. *Psychiatric Annals* 1991;21(2):98-104

13   Smith J, Frazer S, Donovan M. Dual diagnosis in the UK. *Hospital and Community Psychiatry* 1994;45(3):280-1

14   Sokolski K N, Cummings J L, Abrams B I et al. Effects of substance abuse on hallucination rates and treatment responses in chronic psychiatric patients. *Journal of Clinical Psychiatry* 1994;55(9):380-7

15   Cantwell R, Harrison G. Substance misuse in the severely mentally ill. *Advances in Psychiatric Treatment* 1996;2:117-124

16   Cantwell R, Harrison G. Substance misuse in the severely mentally ill. *Advances in Psychiatric Treatment* 1996;2:117-124

17   Sokolski K N, Cummings J L, Abrams B I et al. Effects of substance abuse on hallucination rates and treatment responses in chronic psychiatric patients. *Journal of Clinical Psychiatry* 1994;55(9):380-7

18   Selzer J A, Lieberman J A. Schizophrenia and substance abuse. *Psychiatric clinics of North America* 1993;16:401-412

19   Cantwell R, Harrison G. Substance misuse in the severely mentally ill. *Advances in Psychiatric Treatment* 1996;2:117-124

20   Dixon L, Haas G, Weiden P J et al. Drug abuse in schizophrenia patients: clinical correlates and reasons for use. *American Journal of Psychiatry* 1991;148:224-230

21   Cox W. *The addictive personality.* New York: Chelsea House, 1986

22   Patton D, Barnes G E, Murray R P. The reliability and construct validity of two measures of addictive personality. *International Journal of the Addictions* 1994;29(8):999-1014

23   Lavelle T. Is the 'addictive personality' merely delinquency? *Addiction Research* 1993;1:27-37

24   Preble E, Casey J J Jr. Taking care of business - the heroin user's life on the street. (1969) In: South N, ed. *Drugs, crime and criminal justice volume II.* Aldershot: Dartmouth, 1995

25   Schroeder D, Laflin M T, Weis D L. Is there a relationship between self-esteem and drug use? Methodological and statistical limitations of the research. *Journal of Drug Issues* 1993;23(4):645-65

26   Currie C, Todd J. *Health behaviours of Scottish schoolchildren: national and regional patterns.* Edinburgh: University of Edinburgh, 1990

27   Anthenelli R M, Schuckit M A. Genetics. In: Lowinson J H, Ruiz P, Millman R B et al, eds. *Substance abuse - a comprehensive textbook.* Baltimore: Williams and Wilkins, 1992:39-50

28   George F, Ritz M, Elmer G. The role of genetics in vulnerability to drug dependence. In: Pratt J, ed. *The biological bases of drug tolerance and dependence.* London, San Diego: Academic Press, 1991:265-295

29   Schuckit M. Subjective responses to alcohol in sons of alcoholics and control subjects. *Archives of General Psychiatry* 1984;41:879-884

30   Dinwiddie S, Cloninger C. Family and adoption studies in alcoholism and drug addiction. *Psychiatric Annals* 1991;21(4):206-14

31   Remi J, Cadoret M D, Troughton E et al. An adoption study of genetic and environmental factors in drug abuse. *Archives of General Psychiatry* 1986;43(12):1131-1136

32   Barnard M, McKeganey N. *Drug misuse and young people: a selective review of the literature.* Glasgow: University of Glasgow, 1994

33   Stoker A, Swadi H. Perceived family relationships in drug abusing adolescents. *Drug and Alcohol Dependence* 1990;25:293-7

34   McCord J. Long-term perspectives on parental absence. In: Robins L, Rutter M, eds. *Straight and devious pathways from childhood to adulthood.* Cambridge: Cambridge University Press, 1991:116-34

35   Robins L N, Helzer J E, Pryzbeck T. Substance abuse in the general population. In: Barrett J E, Rose R M, eds. *Mental disorders in the community: progress and challenges.* New York: Guildford Press, 1986:9-31

36   Sweeting H, West P. Family life and health in adolescence: a role for culture in the health inequalities debate? *Social Science and Medicine* 1995;40(2):163-75

37   Kandel D. Parenting styles, drug use and children's adjustment in families of young adults. *Journal of Marriage and the Family* 1990;52:183-96

38   Emmelkamp P, Heeres H. Drug addiction and parental rearing style: a controlled study. *International Journal of Addiction* 1988;23(2):201-16

39   Shedler J, Block J. Adolescent drug use and psychological health: a longitudinal inquiry. *American Psychologist* 1990;45:612-30

40   Rounsaville B J, Weissman M M, Wilber C H. Pathways to opiate addiction: an evaluation of differing antecedents. *British Journal of Psychiatry* 1982;141:437-46

41   Bailey G. Current perspectives on substance abuse in youth. *Journal of the American Academy of Child and Adolescent Psychiatry* 1989;28:151-62

42   Mott J, Mirlees-Black C. *Self-reported drugs misuse in England and Wales: findings from the 1992 British Crime Survey.* London: Home Office, 1995

43   Leitner M, Shapland J, Niles P. *Drug usage and drugs prevention: The views and habits of the general public.* London: HMSO, 1993

44   Gorman D, Brown G. Recent developments in life-event research and their relevance for the study of addictions. *British Journal of Addiction* 1992;87:837-49

45   Brown G. Meaning, measurement and stress of life events. In: Dohrenwend B, ed. *Stressful life events: their nature and effects.* New York: Wiley, 1974

46   Gorman D, Peters T. Types of life events and the onset of alcohol dependence. *British Journal of Addiction* 1990;85:71-9

47   Vaillant G. What can long-term follow-up teach us about relapse and prevention of relapse in addiction? *British Journal of Addiction* 1988;83:1147-57

48   Kandel D. On processes of peer influences in adolescent drug use: a developmental perspective. *Advances in Alcohol and Substance Abuse* 1985;4:139-63

49   Swadi H. Drug and substance use among 3,333 London adolescents. *British Journal of Addiction* 1988;83(8):935-42

50   Swadi H. Adolescent drug taking: role of family and peers. *Drugs and Alcohol Dependence* 1988;21:157-60

51   Brook J S, Lukoff I F, Whiteman M. Initiation into marijuana use. *Journal of Genetic Psychology* 1980;137:133-42

52   Graham J, Bowling B. *Young people and crime.* Home Office Research Study 145. London: Home Office, 1995

53   Wilks J. The relative importance of parents and friends in adolescent decision-making. *Journal of Youth and Adolescence* 1986;15:323-34

54   Stein J. An 8-year study of multiple influences on drug use and drug use consequences. *Journal of Personality and Social Psychology* 1987;53:1094-1105

55   Stimson G, Quirk A. *Drugs: the state of the region. A profile of drug and alcohol problems in North West Thames Regional Health Authority 1991.* London: The Centre for Research on Drugs and Health Behaviour, 1992

56   Newman M. *West Midlands Health Regional Drug Misuse Database - Regional report 1/1/93 to 30/6/93.* Birmingham: West Midlands RHA, 1993

57   Jones A. *Mersey Regional Health Authority: an examination of known levels of drug and drug service use in 1992.* Liverpool: Mersey RHA, 1993

58   Pearson G. Social deprivation, unemployment and patterns of heroin use. In: Dorn N, South N, eds. *A land fit for heroin?* London: MacMillan, 1987:62-94

59   Fazey C, Brown P, Batey P. *A Socio-demographic analysis of patients attending a drug dependency unit.* Liverpool: John Moores University, 1990

60   Ramsay M, Percy A. *Drug misuse declared: results of the 1994 British Crime Survey.* London: Home Office, 1996

61   Leitner M, Shapland J, Wiles P. *Drug usage and drugs prevention: The views and habits of the general public.* London: HMSO, 1993

62   Mott J, Mirlees-Black C. *Self-reported drug misuse in England and Wales: findings from the 1992 British Crime Survey.* London: Home Office, 1995

63   Leitner M, Shapland J, Wiles P. *Drug usage and drugs prevention: The views and habits of the general public.* London: HMSO, 1993

64   Cohen P et al. Common and uncommon pathways to adolescent psychopathology and problem behavior. In: Robins L, Rutter M, eds. *Straight and devious pathways from childhood to adulthood.* Cambridge: Cambridge University Press, 1991

65   Health Education Authority. *Today's young adults.* London: HEA, 1992

66   Hastings G B, Aitken P P, MacKintosh A M. *From the billboard to the playground.* Glasgow: Strathclyde University, 1991

67   Health Education Authority. *Tomorrow's young adults.* London: HEA, 1992

68   Leitner M, Shapland J, Wiles P. *Drug usage and drugs prevention: The views and habits of the general public.* London: HMSO, 1993

69   ISDD. *Drug notes 1: Heroin.* London: ISDD, 1992

70   ISDD. *Drug notes 5: Cocaine and crack.* London: ISDD, 1993

71   ISDD. *Drug notes 3: Cannabis.* London: ISDD, 1993

72   ISDD. *Drug notes 2: LSD.* London: ISDD, 1993

73   Lader M. Problem definition: the case of the benzodiazepines. In: Lader M, Edwards G, Drummond D, eds. *The nature of alcohol and drug related problems.* Oxford: Oxford University Press, 1992:161-166

74   Beubler E. Addiction potential of opiates in medical use. In: Loimer N, Schmid R, Springer A, eds. *Drug addiction and AIDS.* Vienna: Springer-Verlag, 1991:149-152

75   Frith S. *Sound effects: youth, leisure and the politics of rock and roll.* London: Constable, 1983

76   South N. 'Drugs: control, crime and criminological studies'. In: Maguire M, Morgan R, Reiner R, eds. *The Oxford Handbook of Criminology.* Oxford University Press, 1994:393-440

77   Hadfield L. *In focus: drugs, alcohol and the workforce.* Health and Safety Monitor, 1992;8:1-2

78   Lader M. Problem definition: the case of the benzodiazepines. In: Lader M, Edwards G, Drummond D, eds. *The nature of alcohol and drug related problems.* Oxford: Oxford University Press, 1992:161-166

79   Ramsay M, Percy A. *Drug misuse declared: results of the 1994 British Crime Survey*. London: Home Office, 1996

80   Seivewright N. Benzodiazepines in the illicit drugs scene - the UK picture and some treatment dilemmas. *International Journal of Drug Policy* 1993;4(1):42-8

81   Dorn N, Ribbens J, South N. *Coping with a nightmare: family feelings about long-term drug abuse*. London: ISDD, 1995

82   Oppenheimer E, Sheehan M, Taylor C. Letting the client speak: drug misusers and the process of help-seeking. *British Journal of Addiction* 1988;83(6):635-47

83   Kandel D. Epidemiological and psychosocial perspectives on adolescent drug use. *Journal of the American Academy of Child Psychiatry* 1982;21:328-47

84   Labour Party. *Drugs: the need for action*. London: Labour Party, 1994

85   Dorn N, Baker O, Seddon T. *Paying for heroin: estimating the financial cost of acquisitive crime committed by dependent heroin users in England and Wales*. London: ISDD, 1994

86   Ministerial Drugs Task Force. *Drugs in Scotland: meeting the challenge*. Scottish Home and Health Department, Edinburgh and London: HMSO, 1994

87   Hammersley R, Forsyth A, Morrison V. The relationship between crime and opioid use. *British Journal of Addiction* 1989;84:1029-43

88   Grapendaal M. Cutting their coat according to their cloth: economic behaviour of Amsterdam opiate users. *International Journal of the Addictions* 1992;27(4):487-501

89   Johnson B D, Goldstein P J, Preble E. *Taking care of business: the economics of crime by heroin users*. Massachusetts: Lexington Books, 1985

90   Graham J, Bowling B. *Young people and crime*. Home Office Research Study 145. London Home Office, 1995

91   Bennett T. Drugs and crime - drug use and criminal behaviour. In: ISDD, *Drugs: your questions answered*. London: ISDD, 1995

92   Gossop M, Griffiths P, Powis B et al. Severity of dependence and route of administration of heroin, cocaine and amphetamines. *British Journal of Addiction* 1992;87(11):1527-36

93   Mott J, Mirrlees-Black C. *Self-reported drug misuse in England and Wales: findings from the 1992 British Crime Survey*. London: Home Office, 1995

94   Advisory Council on the Misuse of Drugs. *AIDS and drug misuse. Part 1*. London: HMSO, 1988

95   Public Health Laboratory Service. The unlinked anonymous HIV prevalence monitoring programme in England and Wales: preliminary results. *Communicable Diseases Report* 1991;1(7)

96   Rhodes T, Quirk A. Drug use, sexual risk and sexual safety. *Druglink* 1995;10(5):15-18

97   Rhodes T, Quirk A. Forbidden pleasures: drugs and sexual desire. *Druglink* 1995;10(6):13-15

98   Rhodes T, Quirk A. Drug use, sexual risk and sexual safety. *Druglink* 1995;10(5):15-18

99   Gossop M, Griffiths P, Powis B et al. Severity of heroin dependence and HIV risk. II: sharing injecting equipment. *AIDS Care* 1993;5(2):159-68

100 Dolan K A, Stimson G V, Donoghoe M C. Reductions in HIV risk behaviour and stable HIV prevalence in syringe exchange patients and other injectors in England. *Drug and alcohol review* 1993;12:133-4

101 Farrell M. Physical complications of drug abuse. In: Glass I B, ed. *The international handbook of addiction behaviour*. London: Routledge, 1991:120-125

102 Waller T, Holmes R. Hepatitis C: the sleeping giant wakes. *Druglink* 1995;10(5):8-11

103 British Medical Association. *A guide to hepatitis C*. London:BMA, 1996

104 Cellar F, Dabs F, Upon M et al. Prevalence and determinants of antibodies to hepatitis C virus and markers for hepatitis B virus infection in patients with HIV infection in Acetin. *BMJ* 1996;313:461-464

105 Stark K, Bienzle U, Hess G et al. Detection of the hepatitis G virus genome among injecting drug users, homosexual and bisexual men, and blood donors. *Journal of Infectious Diseases* 1996; 174(6):1320-3

106 Farrell M. Physical complications of drug abuse. In: Glass I B, ed. *The international handbook of addiction behaviour*. London: Routledge, 1991:120-125

107   Gossop M, Griffiths P, Powis B et al. Frequency of non-fatal heroin overdose: survey of heroin users recruited in non-clinical settings. *BMJ* 1996;313:402

108   Gossop M, Griffiths P, Powis B et al. Frequency of non-fatal heroin overdose: survey of heroin users recruited in non-clinical settings. *BMJ* 1996;313:402

109   Farrell M. Physical complications of drug abuse. In: Glass I B, ed. *The international handbook of addiction behaviour.* London: Routledge, 1991:120-125

110   Caplan G A, Brigham B A. Marijuana smoking and carcinoma of the tongue: is there an association? *Cancer* 1990;66(5):1005-6

111   Gold M S. Cocaine (and crack): clinical aspects. In: Lowinson J H, Ruiz P, Millman R B et al, eds. *Substance abuse - a comprehensive textbook.* Baltimore: Williams and Wilkins, 1992:205-221

112   Jenkins A J, Keenan R M, Henningfield J E et al. Pharmacokinetics and pharmacodynamics of smoked heroin. *Journal of Analytical Toxicology* 1994;18(6):317-30

113   Senay E C. *Substance abuse disorders in clinical practice.* Bristol:John Wright, 1983

114   ISDD. *Drug notes 5: Cocaine and crack.* London: ISDD, 1993

115   Redda K, Walker C A, Barnett G. *Cocaine, marijuana, designer drugs: chemistry, pharmacology and behaviour.* Boca Raton: CRC Press, 1989

116   O'Connor D. *Glue sniffing and volatile substance abuse. Case studies of children and young adults.* London:Gower, 1983

117   Elliott D C. Frostbite of the mouth: a case report. *Military Medicine* 1991;156 (1):18-19

118   Shepherd R T. Mechanism of sudden death associated with volatile substance abuse. *Human Toxicology* 1989;8(4):287-91

119   British Medical Association. *Driving impairment through alcohol and other drugs.* London: BMA, 1996

120   Simon E. Opiates: neurobiology. In: Lowinson J H, Ruiz P, Millman R B et al, eds. *Substance abuse - a comprehensive textbook.* Baltimore: Williams and Wilkins, 1992:195-204

121   Goldstein A, Barrett R, James I. Morphine and other opiates from beef brain and adrenal. *Proceedings of the National Academy of Science USA* 1985;82:5203-7

122   Shapiro H. Illicit drugs and their effects. In: ISDD, *Drugs: your questions answered.* London: ISDD, 1995

123   Jaffe J. Opiates: clinical aspects. In: Lowinson J H, Ruiz P, Millman R B et al, eds. *Substance abuse - a comprehensive textbook.* Baltimore: Williams and Wilkins, 1992

124   Shapiro H. Illicit drugs and their effects. In: ISDD, *Drugs: your questions answered.* London: ISDD, 1995

125   West R. Psychological theories of addiction. In: Glass I, ed. *The international handbook of addiction behaviour.* London Routledge, 1991.

126   Robertson J R, Treasure W, Benzodiazepine Abuse. Nature and Extent of the Problem. *CNS Drugs* 1996;5(2):137-146

127   Hallstom C, Lader M. Benzodiazepine withdrawal phenomena. *Int Pharmacopsychiat.* 1981;16(4): 235-244

128   Ungerleider J T, Pechnick R N. Hallucinogens. In: Lowinson J H, Ruiz P, Millman R B et al, eds. *Substance abuse - a comprehensive textbook.* Baltimore: Williams and Wilkins, 1992:280-289

129   Ungerleider J T, Pechnick R N. Hallucinogens. In: Lowinson J H, Ruiz P, Millman R B et al, eds. *Substance abuse - a comprehensive textbook.* Baltimore: Williams and Wilkins, 1992:280-289

130   Ungerleider J, Pechnick R N. Hallucinogens. In: Lowinson J H, Ruiz P, Millman R B et al, eds. *Substance abuse - a comprehensive textbook.* Baltimore: Williams and Wilkins, 1992:280-289

131   ISDD. *Drug notes 2: LSD.* London: ISDD, 1993

132   Bowers M. The role of drugs in the production of schizophreniform psychoses and related disorders. In: Meltzer H, ed. *Psychopharmacology: the third generation of progress.* New York: Raven Press, 1987:819-23

133   Ungerleider J, Pechnick R N. Hallucinogens. In: Lowinson J H, Ruiz P, Millman R B et al, eds. *Substance abuse - a comprehensive textbook.* Baltimore: Williams and Wilkins, 1992:280-289

134   Baker O, Marsden J. *Drug misuse in Britain 1994.* London: ISDD, 1994

135   Ungerleider J, Pechnick R N. Hallucinogens. In: Lowinson J H, Ruiz P, Millman R B et al, eds. *Substance abuse - a comprehensive textbook*. Baltimore: Williams and Wilkins, 1992:280-289

136   Abraham H D, Aldridge A M. Adverse consequences of lysergic acid diethylamide. *Addiction* 1994;89(6):762-3

137   ISDD. *Drug notes 3: Cannabis*. London: ISDD, 1993

138   Grinspoon L, Bakalar J. Marihuana. In: Lowinson J H, Ruiz P, Millman R B et al, eds. *Substance abuse - a comprehensive textbook*. Baltimore: Williams and Wilkins, 1992:236-246

139   Thornicroft G. Cannabis and psychosis: is there epidemiological evidence for an association? *British Journal of Psychiatry* 1990;157:25-33

140   Johnson B A. Cannabis. In: Glass I B, ed. *The international handbook of addiction behaviour*. London: Routledge, 1991:69-76

141   ISDD. *Drug notes 3: Cannabis*. London: ISDD, 1993

142   Ashton CH. Cannabis: dangers and possible uses. *BMJ* 1987;294:141-142

143   Wu T C, Tashkin D P, Djahed B et al. Pulmonary hazards of smoking marijuana as compared with tobacco. *N Engl J Med* 1988;318:347-51

144   Wu T C, Tashkin D P, Djahed B et al. Pulmonary hazards of smoking marijuana as compared with tobacco. *N Engl J Med* 1988;318:347-51

145   Mason A, McBay A . Ethanol, marijuana and other drug use in 600 drivers killed in single-vehicle crashes in North Carolina 1978-81. *Journal of Forensic Sciences* 1984;29:788-92

146   World Health Organization, Addiction Research Foundation. *Report of an ARF/WHO Scientific Meeting on the adverse health and behavioural consequences of cannabis use*. Toronto:Addiction Research Foundation, 1981

147   Yesavage J A, Leirer V O, Denari M et al. Carry-over effects of marijuana intoxication on aircraft pilot performance: a preliminary report. *American Journal of Psychiatry* 1985;142(11):1325-9

148   Leirer VO. Yesavage JA. Morrow DG. Marijuana carry-over effects on aircraft pilot performance. *Aviation Space and Environmental Medicine* 1991;62(3)221-7

149   Government Statistical Service. *Drug misuse statistics: for the six months ending 31 March 1993 - England*. London: Department of Health, 1994

150   ISDD. *Drug notes 4: Amphetamines*. London: ISDD, 1993

151   Home Office. *Statistics of the misuse of drugs: seizures and offenders dealt with, United Kingdom, 1994. Issue 25/1995*. London: Home Office, 1995

152   King G, Ellinwood E. Amphetamines and other stimulants. In: Lowinson J H, Ruiz P, Millman R B et al, eds. *Substance abuse - a comprehensive textbook*. Baltimore: Williams and Wilkins, 1992:247-270

153   ISDD. *Drug notes 4: Amphetamines*. London: ISDD, 1993

154   Gawin F, Ellinwood E. Cocaine and other stimulants. *New England Journal of Medicine* 1988;318:1173

155   Darke S, Cohen J, Ross J et al. Transitions between routes of administration of regular amphetamine users. *Addiction* 1994;89:1077-1083

156   Davis J, Schlemmer R. The amphetamine psychosis. In: Caldwell J, Mule S J, ed. *Amphetamines and related stimulants: chemical, biological, clinical and sociological aspects*. Boca Raton: CRC Press, 1980:161-173

157   ISDD. *Drug notes 4: Amphetamines*. London: ISDD, 1993

158   ISDD. *Drug notes 5: Cocaine and crack*. London: ISDD, 1993

159   Gold M S. Cocaine (and crack): neurobiology. In: Lowinson J H, Ruiz P, Millman R B et al, eds. *Substance abuse - a comprehensive textbook*. Baltimore: Williams and Wilkins, 1992:205-221

160   Baker O, Marsden J. *Drug misuse in Britain 1994*. London: ISDD, 1994

161   Gold M S. Cocaine (and crack): neurobiology. In: Lowinson J H, Ruiz P, Millman R B et al, eds. *Substance abuse - a comprehensive textbook*. Baltimore: Williams and Wilkins, 1992:205-221

162   Druglink. Ecstasy update. *Druglink* 1995;11(1): factsheet

163   ISDD. *Drugs - your questions answered*. London: ISDD, 1995

164   ISDD. *Drug notes 8: Ecstasy*. London: ISDD, 1993

165 Winstock A. Chronic paranoid psychosis after misuse of MDMA. *BMJ* 1991;302:6785

166 Henry J, Jeffreys K T. Toxicity and deaths from 3,4-methylenedioxymethamphetamine ('ecstasy'). *Lancet* 1992;340:384-7

167 Milroy C M. Clark J C. Forrest A R. Pathology of deaths associated with 'ecstasy' and 'eve' misuse. *Journal of Clinical Pathology* 1996;49(2):149-53

168 Gorard D, Davies S E, Clark M L. Misuse of ecstasy (Letter) *BMJ* 1992;305:309.

169 Shearman J, Chapman R W G, Satsangi J. Misuse of ecstasy (Letter) *BMJ* 1992;305:309

170 Weil A. The love drug. *Journal of Psychedelic Drugs* 1976;8(4):336

171 Colado M I, Green A R. A study of the mechanisms of MDMA ('ecstasy')-induced neurotoxicity of 5-HT neurones using chlormethiazole, dizocilpine and other protective compounds. *British Journal of Pharmacology* 1994;111(1):131-6

172 Colado M L, Williams J L, Green A R. The hyperthermic and neurotoxic effects of 'Ecstasy' (MDMA) and 3,4 methylenedioxyamphetamine (MDA) in the Dark Agouti (DA) rate, a model of the CYP2D6 poor metabolizer phenotype. *British Journal of Pharmacology* 1995;115(7):1281-9

173 ISDD. *Drugs - your questions answered.* London: ISDD, 1995

174 Parliamentary Office of Science and Technology. *Common illegal drugs and their effects - cannabis, ecstasy, amphetamines and LSD.* London:POST, 1996

175 ISDD. *Drug notes 8: Ecstasy.* London: ISDD, 1993

176 Milroy C M, Clark J C, Forrest A R W. Pathology of deaths associated with 'ecstasy' and 'eve' misuse. *J Clin Pathology* 1996;49:149-153

177 Baker O, Marsden J. *Drug misuse in Britain 1994.* London: ISDD, 1994

178 Druglink. The effects of E on harm minimisation. *Druglink* 1995;11(1):4

179 Bahrke M S, Yesalis C E. Anabolic-androgenic steroids. Current issues. *Sports Medicine* 1995;19(5):326-40

180 Malone D A Jr, Dimeff R J, Lombardo J A et al. Psychiatric effects and psychoactive substance use in anabolic-androgenic steroid users. *Clinical Journal of Sports Medicine* 1995;5(1):25-31

181 Pope H G J, Katz D L. Psychiatric and medical effects of anabolic-androgenic steroid use. A controlled study of 160 athletes. *Archives of General Psychiatry* 1994;51(5):375-82

182 Burnett K F, Kleiman M E. Psychological characteristics of adolescent steroid users. *Adolescence* 1994;29(113):81-9

183 Choi P Y, Pope H G Jr. Violence towards women and illicit androgenic-anabolic steroid use. *Annals of Clinical Psychiatry* 1994;6(1):21-5

184 Lenehan P, Bellis M, McVeigh J. *Anabolic steroid use in the North West of England.* Liverpool: The Drugs and Sport Information Service, 1996

185 Burnett K F, Kleiman M E. Psychological characteristics of adolescent steroid users. *Adolescence* 1994;29(113):81-9

186 Pope H Q J, Katz D L. Psychiatric and medical effects of anabolic-androgenic steroid use. A controlled study of 160 athletes. *Archives of General Psychiatry* 1994;51(5):375-82

187 Ferenchick G S, Hirokawa S, Mammen E F et al. Anabolic-androgen steroid abuse in weight lifters: evidence for activation of the hemostatic system. *American Journal of Hematology* 1995;49(4):282-8

188 Lenehan P, Bellis M, McVeigh J. *Anabolic steroid use in the North West of England.* Liverpool: The Drugs and Sport Information Service, 1996

189 McBride A J, Williamson K, Petersen T. Three cases of nalbuphine hydrochloride dependence associated with anabolic steroid use. *British Journal of Sports Medicine* 1996;30:69-70

190 ISDD. *Drug abuse briefing.*(6th ed.) ISDD, 1996

191 Society calls for 'poppers' crackdown. *Pharmaceutical Journal* 1997;258(6927):114

192 Leitner M, Shapland J, Wiles P. *Drug usage and drugs prevention: The views and habits of the general public.* London: HMSO, 1993

193 Druglink. Ecstasy: 'one stop shop' to polydrug use? *Druglink* 1996;11(1):4

194   Hammersley R, Cassidy M T, Oliver J. Drugs associated with drug-related deaths in Edinburgh and Glasgow, November 1990 to October 1992. *Addiction* 1995;90:959-965

195   ISDD. *Drug notes 10: Over the Counter (OTC) medicines.* London: ISDD, 1991 (revised ed. 1993)

196   Cascade. *Over-the-counter substances.* Bristol: Cascade, 1990

197   Pearson G, Gilman M, Traynor P. The limits of intervention. *Druglink* 1990;5(3):12-13

198   Chasnoff I. Chemical dependency and pregnancy. *Clinics in perinatology* 1991;18:1-191

199   ISDD. *Drugs, pregnancy and childcare: a guide for professionals.* London: ISDD, 1995

200   Liepman M, Goldman R E, Monroe A et al. Substance abuse by special populations of women. In: Gomberg E, Nirenberg T, eds. *Women and substance abuse.* Norwood N J: Ablex Publishing, 1993:214-257

201   Koren G, Shear H, Graham K et al. Bias against the null hypothesis: the reproductive hazards of cocaine. *Lancet* 1989;2(8677):1440-2

202   Chasnoff I J, Burns W J, Schnoll S H et al. Cocaine use in pregnancy. *New England Journal of Medicine* 1985;313:666-669

203   Pritchard J A, MacDonald P C, Grant N F et al. *William's obstetrics.* (17th ed.) Norwalk, CT: Appleton-Century-Crofts, 1985

204   ISDD. *Drug notes 5: Cocaine.* London: ISDD, 1993

205   Udell B. *Cocaine addiction in the neonate. Cocaine babies. Evidence to the Select Committee on Narcotics Abuse and Control.* Washington D C: USGPO, 1995

206   Fried P. Marijuana and human pregnancy. In: Chasnoff I J, ed. *Drug use in pregnancy: mother and child.* Norwell, Ma: MTP Press, 1986:64-74

207   Fried P. Postnatal consequences of maternal marijuana use in humans. *Annals of the New York Academy of Science.* 1989;562:123-32

208   Edelin K C, Gurganious L, Golar G et al. Methadone maintenance in pregnancy: consequences to care and outcome. *Obstetrics and Gynecology* 1988;71(3):399-404

209   Rementaria J L, Nuang N N. Narcotic withdrawal in pregnancy - still-birth incidence with a case report. *Am J Obst Gynec* 1973;116:1152-1156

210   Banks A, Waller T. *Drug misuse: a practical handbook for GPs.* Oxford: Blackwell Scientific Publications, 1988

211   Little B, Snell L A, Gilstrap L C. Methamphetamine abuse during pregnancy: outcome and fetal effects. *Obstetrics and Gynecology* 1988;72(4):541-4

212   Flanagan R J, Ruprah M, Meredith T J, Ramsey J D. An introduction to the clinical toxicology of volatile substances. *Drug Safety* 1990;5(5):359-83

213   Toutant C. Lippmann S. Fetal solvents syndrome. (Letter) *Lancet* 1979;1(8130):1356

214   Tucker GT, Lennard MS, Ellis SW, Woods HF, Cho AK, Lin LY, Hiratsuka A, Schmitz DA, Chu TY. The demethylenation of methylenedioxymethamphetamine ('ecstasy') by debrisoquine hydroxilase (CYP2D6). *Biochemical Pharmacology* 1994;47(7):1151-6

Chapter 3

1   Advisory Council on the Misuse of Drugs. *Treatment and rehabilitation.* London: HMSO, 1984

2   Advisory Council on the Misuse of Drugs. *AIDS and drug misuse update.* London: HMSO, 1993

3   Department of Health. *Health of the nation.* London: HMSO, 1992

4   Ministerial Drugs Task Force. *Drugs in Scotland: meeting the challenge.* Scottish Home and Health Department, Edinburgh and London: HMSO, 1994

5   NHS Executive. *Purchasing effective treatment and care for drug users. Guidance for health authorities and social service departments.* (Draft) 22nd August 1996

6   Strang J. The roles of prescribing. In: Strang J, Stimson G, eds. *AIDS and drug misuse*. Routledge: London, 1990:142-152

7   Wilson P, Watson R, Ralston GE. Methadone maintenance in general practice: patients, workload, outcomes. *BMJ* 1994;309:641-644

8   Task Force to Review Services for Drug Misusers. *Report of an independent review of drug treatment services in England*. London: Department of Health, 1996

9   NHS Executive. *Purchasing effective treatment and care for drug users. Guidance for health authorities and social service departments*. (Draft) 22nd August 1996

10 MacGregor S, Ettore B, Coomber R et al. *The Central Funding Initiative and the development of drug services in England*. London: Birkbeck College, University of London, 1990

11 Cook C. The Minnesota model in the management of drug and alcohol dependency: Miracle, method or myth. Part I - The philosophy and the programme. *B.J. Addiction* 1988a;83:625-634

12 Cook C. The Minnesota model in the management of drug and alcohol dependency: Miracle, method or myth. Part II - Evidence and conclusions. *B.J. Addiction* 1988b;735-748

13 Gerstein D R, Harwood H J. *Treating drug problems. Vol 1. A study of evolution, effectiveness, and financing of public and private drug treatment systems*. Washington: National Academy Press, 1990

14 Task Force to Review Services for Drug Misusers. *Report of an independent review of drug treatment services in England*. London: Department of Health, 1996

15 Gerstein D R, Harwood H J. *Treating drug problems. Vol 1. A study of evolution, effectiveness, and financing of public and private drug treatment systems*. Washington: National Academy Press, 1990

16 Mangtani P, Kovats S, Hall A. Hepatitis B vaccination policy in drug treatment services. *BMJ* 1995;311:1500

17 British Medical Association. *Medical ethics today: Its practice and philosophy*. London: BMJ, 1993

18 Department of Health. *Guidelines for pre-test discussion on HIV testing*. London: Department of Health, 1996

19 The Task Force to Review Services for Drug Misusers. *Report of an independent review of drug treatment services in England*. Department of Health: London, 1996

20 Stimson G V. AIDS and injecting drug use in the UK. 1987-1993. The policy response and the presentation of the epidemic. *Social science in medicine* 1995;41(5)699-716

21 Stimson G V. Has the United Kingdom averted an epidemic of HIV-1 infection among drug injectors? *Addiction* 1996;91(8):1085 - 1088

22 Task Force to Review Services for Drug Misusers. *Report of an independent review of drug treatment services in England*. London: Department of Health, 1996

23 Task Force to Review Services for Drug Misusers. *Report of an independent review of drug treatment services in England*. London: Department of Health, 1996

24 Waller T, Holmes R. Hepatitis C: Time to wake up. *Druglink* 1993;10(5):7-9

25 Healey C J, Chapman R W, Fleming K A. Liver histology in hepatitis C infection: a comparison between patients with persistently normal and abnormal transaminases. *Gut.* 37(2):274-8

26 Dusheiko G M, Khakoo S, Soni P et al. A rational approach to the management of hepatitis C infection. *BMJ* 1996:312-357-364

27 Renton A, Main J. *Hepatitis C among injecting drug users*. London:The Centre for Research on Drugs and Health Behaviour, 1996

28 Banks A, Waller T A N. *Drug misuse - a practical handbook for GPs*. Oxford:Blackwell Scientific in association with the Institute for the Study of Drug Dependence, 1988

29 Gossop M, Griffiths P, Powis B et al. Frequency of non-fatal heroin overdose: survey of heroin users recruited in non-clinical settings. *BMJ* 1996;313:402

30 Gossop M, Griffiths P, Powis B et al. Frequency of non-fatal heroin overdose: survey of heroin users recruited in non-clinical settings. *BMJ* 1996;313:402

31 General Medical Services Committee. *Combating violence in general practice, guidance for GPs*. GMSC, 1995

32   More W, Maguire J. *Handling aggression and violence in health services*. Birmingham: British Medical Association and Pepar, 1995

33   Kintz P, Tracqui A, Jamey C et al. Detection of codeine and phenobarbital in sweat collected with a sweat patch. *Journal of Analytical Toxicology* 1996;20(3):197-201

34   Cone E J, Hillsgrove M J, Jenkins A J et al. Sweat testing for heroin, cocaine and metabolites. *Journal of Analytical Toxicology* 1994;18(6):298-305

35   Brewer C. Naltrexone in the prevention of relapse and detoxification. In Brewer C, ed. *Treatment options in addiction*. London: Gaskell, 1993:54-62

36   Farrell M, Ward J, Mattick R et al. Methadone maintenance treatment in opiate dependence: a review. *BMJ* 1994;309:997-1001

37   Farrell M, Ward J, Mattick R et al. Methadone maintenance treatment in opiate dependence: a review. *BMJ* 1994;309:997-1001

38   Binchy J M, Molyneaux E M, Manning J. Accidental ingestion of methadone by children in Merseyside. *BMJ* 1994;308:1335-1336

39   Robertson J R. Dihydrocodeine - a second strand of treatment for drug misusers. (Letter) *Drug and alcohol Review* 1996;15(2):200-201

40   Cairns A, Roberts I S D, Benbow E W. Characteristics of fatal methadone overdose in Manchester, 1985-94. *BMJ* 1996;313:264-5

41   Farrell M, Ward J, Mattick R et al. Methadone maintenance treatment in opiate dependence: a review. *BMJ* 1994;309:997-1001

42   Wilson P, Watson R, Ralston GE. Methadone maintenance in general practice: patients, workload, outcomes. *BMJ* 1994; 309:641-644

43   Liese B S, Franz R A. Treating substance use disorders with cognitive therapy: lessons learned and implications for the future. In Salkovskis P, ed. *Frontiers of Cognitive Therapy*. New York: Guildford (In press)

44   Ball J, Ross A. *The effectiveness of methadone maintenance treatment: patients, programmes, services and outcome*. New York: Springer-Verlag, 1991

45   Joe G W, Simpson D D, Hubbard R L. Treatment predictors of tenure in methadone maintenance. *Journal of Substance Abuse* 1991;3:73-84

46   Robertson J R. Dihydrocodeine - a second strand of treatment for drug misusers. (Letter) *Drug and Alcohol Review* 1996;15(2):200-201

47   Marks J. Who killed the British System? *Druglink* 1995;10(4):3-4.

48   Johns A. Is there really a London Connection? *Druglink* 1995;10(5):p14

49   Hartnoll R L, Mitcheson M C, Battersby A et al. Evaluation of heroin maintenance in controlled trial. *Archives of General Psychiatry* 1980;37:877-884

50   Derks J T M. *The dispensing of injectable morphine in Amsterdam. Experiences, results and implications for the Swiss Project for medical prescription of narcotics*. In The Medical Prescription of Narcotics, Fribourg: Huber Verlag (In press), 1996

51   Lewis D A. Methadone and caries. *British Dental Journal* 1990;168(6):231

52   Strain E C, Stitzer M L, Liebson I A et al. Comparison of buprenorphine and methadone in the breakout of opioid dependence. *Am. Journal of Psychiatry* 1994;151(7):1025-1030

53   Task Force to Review Services for Drug Misusers. *Report of an independent review of drug treatment services in England*. London: Department of Health, 1996

54   Task Force to Review Services for Drug Misusers. *Report of an independent review of drug treatment services in England*. London: Department of Health, 1996

55   Strang J, Seivewright N, Farrell M. Intravenous and other novel abuses of benzodiazepines: the opening of Pandora's box? *British Journal of Addiction* 1992;87:1373-1375

56   Klee H, Faugier J, Hayes C et al. AIDS related risk behaviour, polydrug use and temazepam. *British Journal of Addiction* 1990;85:1125-1132

57   Klee H. A new target for behavioural research: amphetamine research. *Addiction* 1992;87:289-297

58   Fleming P M, Roberts D. Is the prescription of amphetamine justified as a harm reduction measure? *Journal of The Royal Society of Health* 1994;114(3):127-31

59   Task Force to Review Services for Drug Misusers. *Report of an independent review of drug treatment services in England.* London: Department of Health, 1996

60   Ter Riet G, Kleijnen J, Knipschild P. A meta-analysis of studies into the effect of acupucture on addiction. *British Journal of General Practice* 1990;40:379-382

61   Hatrick J A, Dewhurst K. Delayed psychosis due to LSD. *Lancet* 1970; ii:742-744

62   O'Conner B. Hazards associated with the recreational drug ecstasy. *Br. Journal Hosp. Med.* 1994;52(10)507:510-4

63   McGuine P K, Cope H, Fahy T A. Diversity of psychopathology associated with use of 3,4 methylene-dioxymethamphetamine (Ecstasy). *Br.J. Psychiatry* 1994;165(3):391-5

64   Wootton J, Miller S I. Cocaine: a review. *Pediatrics in Review* 1994;15(3):89-92

65   Preston K L, Sullivan J T, Strain E C, Bigelow G E. Enhancement of cocaine's abuse liability in methadone maintenance patients. *Psychopharmacology* 1996;123:15-25

66   Gossop M. Griffiths P, Powis B et al. Frequency of non-fatal heroin overdose: survey of heroin users recruited in non-clinical settings. *BMJ;*1996(313):402

67   Armstrong D J. The use of over-the-counter preparations by drug users attending an addiction treatment unit (Letter). *British Journal of Addiction* 1992;87:125-128

68   Tyrer S. Psychiatric assessment of chronic pain. *British Journal of Psychiatry* 1992;161:422

69   Siney C. Management of pregnant women who are drug-dependent. In Siney C, ed. *The pregnant drug addict.* Hale: Books for Midwives Press, 1995:1-8

70   Siney C. Management of pregnant women who are drug-dependent. In Siney C, ed. *The pregnant drug addict.* Hale: Books for Midwives Press, 1995:1-8

71   Jarvis M A, Schnoll S H. Methadone treatment during pregnancy. *J. Psychoactive Drugs* 1994;26(2):155-161

72   Barton S J, Harrigan R, Tse A M. Prenatal cocaine exposure: Implications for practice, policy development and needs for future research. *Journal of Perinatology* 1995;15(1):10-22

73   Greenfield S F, Weiss R D, Tohen M. Substance abuse and the chronically mentally ill: a description of dual diagnosis treatment services in a psychiatric hospital. *Community Mental Health Journal* 1995;31(3):265-77

74   Butler R W. Jenkins M A, Braff D L. The abnormality of normal comparison groups: the identification of psychosis proneness and substance abuse in putatively normal subjects. *American Journal of Psychiatry* 1993;150(3):1386-91

75   Bartles S J, Drake R E, Wallach M A. Long-term course of substance use disorders among patients with severe mental illness. *Psychiatric Services* 1995;46(3):248-52

76   Haywood T W, Kravitz H M, Grossman L S et al. Predicting the 'revolving door' phenomenon among patients with schizophrenic, schizoaffective, and affective disorders. *American Journal of Psychiatry* 1995,152(6):856-61

77   Grossman L S, Haywood T W, Cavanaugh J L et al. State psychiatric hospital patients with past arrests for violent crimes. *Psychiatric Services* 1995;46(8):790-5,

78   Cantwell R, Harrison G. Substance misuse in the severely mentally ill. *Advances in Psychiatric Treatment* 1996;2:117-124

79   Cantwell R, Harrison G. Substance misuse in the severely mentally ill. *Advances in Psychiatric Treatment* 1996;2:117-124

80   Adapted from British Medical Association and Association of Police Surgeons. *Health Care of Detainees in Police Stations.* London: BMA, 1994

81   UK Health Department. *Substance misuse detainees in police custody. Guidelines for clinical management.* London: HMSO, 1994

82   UK Health Departments. *Substance misuse detainees in policy custody. Guidelines for clinical management.* London: HMSO, 1994

83   Task Force to Review Services for Drug Misusers. *Report of an independent review of drug treatment services in England*. London: Department of Health, 1996

84   Turnbull P. *Drug use and injecting risk behaviour in prison*. London: The Centre for Research on Drugs and Health Behaviour, 1996

85   H M Prison Service. *Drug misuse in prison*. London: H M Prison Service, 1995

86   Gore S M, Bird A G, Ross A J. Prison rights: mandatory drugs tests and performance indicators for prisons. *BMJ*;1996;312:1411-3.

87   H M Inspectorate of Prisons for England and Wales. *Patient or prisoner? A new strategy for health care in prisons*. London: Home Office, 1996

88   Ford C, Drug users and people with HIV need better care in prison (Letter). *Brit Med J*. 1996;312:1671

89   Gore S M, Bird A G, Burns S M et al. Drug injection and HIV prevalence in inmates of Glenochil prison. *Brit Med J*. 1995;310:293-296

90   Donoghoe M, Power R. *Efficacy of household bleach as a disinfecting agent for injecting drug users*. London: The Centre for Research on Drugs and Health Behaviour, 1993

91   Advisory Council on the Misuse of Drugs. *Drug misusers and the criminal justice system Part II: Drug misusers and the prison system - an integrated approach*. London: HMSO, 1996

92   Advisory Council on the Misuse of Drugs. *Drug misusers and the criminal justice system Part II: Drug misusers and the prison system - an integrated approach*. London: HMSO, 1996

93   Gill O N, Noone A, Heptonstall J. Imprisonment, injecting drug use, and bloodborne viruses. *Brit Med J* 1995;310:275-276

94   Dolan K, Hall W, Wodak A, Methadone maintenance reduces injecting in prison (Letter). *Brit Med J* 1996;312:1162

95   Advisory Council on the Misuse of Drugs. *Drug misusers and the criminal justice system Part II: Drug misusers and the prison system - an integrated approach*. London: HMSO, 1996

96   Lord President of the Council and Leader of the House of Commons, Secretary of State for the Home Deparment, Secretary of State for Health et al. *Tackling drugs together. A strategy for England 1995-1998*. London: HMSO, 1995

97   Task Force to Review Services for Drug Misusers. *Report of an independent review of drug treatment services in England*. London: Department of Health, 1996

Chapter 4

1   Task Force to Review Services for Drug Misusers. *Report of an independent review of drug treatment services in England*. London: Department of Health, 1996

2   *Misuse of Drugs Act 1971*. London: HMSO, 1971

3   Rettig RA, Yarmolinsky A. *Federal Regulation of Methadone Treatment*. Washington D C: National Academy Press, 1995

4   Department of Health, Scottish Office Home and Health Department, Welsh Office. *Drug Misuse and Dependence. Guidelines on Clinical Management*. London: HMSO, 1991

5   Rettig RA, Yarmolinsky A. *Federal Regulation of Methadone Treatment*. Washington D C: National Academy Press, 1995

6   *Misuse of Drugs Regulations 1985*. London:HMSO, 1985

7   *The Mental Health Act 1983*. London:HMSO, 1983

8   *The Children Act 1989*. London: HMSO, 1989

9   The NHS Health Advisory Service. *Children and young people: substance misuse services*. London: HMSO, 1996

10 Department of Health, Scottish Office Home and Health Department, Welsh Office. *Drug misuse and dependence. Guidelines on clinical management.* London: HMSO, 1991

11 Strang J, Sheridan J, Barber N. Prescribing injectable and oral methadone to opiate addicts: results from the 1995 National Postal Survey of Community Pharmacies in England and Wales. 1996;313:270-2

12 Sheridan J. Unpublished data from the 1995 National Postal Survey of Community Pharmacies in England and Wales.1995

13 Sell LA, Farrell M, Robson PJ. *Prescription of diamorphine, dipipanone and cocaine in England and Wales.* 1996. in press

14 Hall W, Solowij N, Lemon J eds. The health and psychological consequences of cannabis use. National Drug Strategy Monograph Series No. 25, Canberra: Australian Government Publishing Service, 1994

15 General Medical Council. *Good medical practice.* London: GMC, 1995

16 Waller T. *Working with GPs.* London:Institute for the Study of Drug Dependence, 1993

17 General Medical Council. *HIV infection and AIDS: the ethical considerations.* General Medical Council, London, 1995

18 SCODA and Alcohol Concern. *Building confidence- advice for alcohol and drug services on confidentiality patients.* London: SCODA, 1994

19 Advisory Council on the Misuse of Drugs. *Problem drug use: A review of training.* London: HMSO, 1990

20 General Medical Council. *Tomorrow's Doctors.* London: GMC, 1993

21 Department of Health, Scottish Office Home and Health Department, Welsh Office. *Drug misuse and dependence. Guidelines on clinical management.* London: HMSO, 1991

22 Wilson P, Watson R, Ralston G E. Methadone maintenance in general practice: patients, workload, outcomes. *BMJ;*1994;309(6995):641-644

23 Task Force to Review Services for Drug Misusers. *Report of an independent review of drug treatment services in England.* London: Department of Health, 1996

24 Advisory Council on the Misuse of Drugs. *Problem drug use: A review of training.* London: HMSO, 1990

25 Task Force to Review Services for Drug Misusers. *Report of an independent review of drug treatment services in England.* London: Department of Health, 1996

26 Boys A, Strang J, Homan C et al. *How well trained are drugs workers? 1995 baseline data from a survey of workers in drug agencies in England.* In preparation

27 The Task Force to Review Services for Drug Misusers. *Report of an independent review of drug treatment services in England.* London: Department of Health, 1996

28 Atkin K, Lunt N, Parker G et al. *Nurses Count: A national census of practice nurses.* York:Social Policy Research Unit University of York, 1993

29 Advisory Council on the Misuse of Drugs. *Problem drug use: a review of training.* London: HMSO, 1990

30 Central Council for Education and Training in Social Work. *Substance misuse. Guidance notes for the diploma in social work.* London: CCETSW, 1992

31 British Medical Association. *A code of practice for the safe use and disposal of sharps.* (revised ed) London: BMA, 1995)

32 British Medical Association. *A code of practice for: Implementation of the UK hepatitis B immunisation guidelines for the protection of patients and staff.* London: BMA, 1995

33 Task Force to Review Services for Drug Misusers. *Report on an independent review of drug treatment services in England.* London: Department of Health, 1996

34 Medical Research Council Field Review. *The basis of drug dependence.* London:MRC, 1994

35 102/97/EC of the European Parliament and of the Council adopting a programme of community action on the prevention of drug dependence within the framework for action in the field of public health (1996-2000). Brussels 29th October 1996 COD October 1996

36 NHS Executive. *Purchasing Effective Treatment and Care for Drug Misusers.* EL(96) 74 CI (96) 24. 22 August 1996

37 Home Office. *Statistics of drug addicts notified to the Home Office, United Kingdom, 1994.* Home Office Statistical Bulletin Issue 17/95. London: Home Office, 1995

38   Magregor S, Smith L, Flory P. *A report on a mapping exercise of drug treatment services in England.* London: University of Middlesex, 1994

39   Office of Population Censuses and Statistics. *Morbidity statistics from general practice: fourth national study, 1991-1992.* Series MB5 no.3. London: HMSO, 1995

40   Office of Population Censuses and Statistics. *The prevalence of psychiatric morbidity among adults aged 16-64, living in private households, in Great Britain.* London: HMSO, 1995

41   Coyle D, Godfrey C, Hardman G et al. *Costing substance misuse services.* YARTIC Occasional Paper 5. York: Centre for Health Economics and Leeds Addiction Unit, University of York, 1994

42   Department of Health Statistic Division 1e Prescription Cost Analysis System. Private Communication 1996

43   NHS Executive. *HCHS revenue resources allocation: weighted capitation formula.* Leeds: NHS Executive, 1994

44   Ramsay M, Percy A. *Drug misuse declared: findings from the 1994 British Crime Survey.* London: Home Office, 1996

45   British Medical Association, General Medical Services Committee. *Core services: Taking the initiative.* London:BMA, 1996

46   Dorn N, Baker O, Seddon T. *Paying for heroin: estimating the financial cost of acquisitive crime committed by dependent heroin users in England and Wales.* London: ISDD, 1994

47   Task Force to Review Services for Drug Misusers. *Report on an independent review of drug treatment services in England.* London: Department of Health, 1996

Chapter 5

1   Lord President of the Council and Leader of the House of Commons, Secretary of State for the Home Department, Secretary of State for Health et al. *Tackling drugs together. A strategy for England 1995-1998.* London: HMSO, 1995

2   The Royal College of Psychiatrists. *Drug Scenes.* London: Gaskell, 1987

3   The Royal College of Psychiatrists. *Drug Scenes.* London: Gaskell, 1987

4   Lord President of the Council and Leader of the House of Commons, Secretary of State for the Home Department, Secretary of State for Health et al. *Tackling drugs together. A strategy for England 1995-1998.* London: HMSO, 1995

5   Ministerial Drugs Task Force. *Drugs in Scotland: meeting the challenge.* Scottish Home and Health Department, Edinburgh and London: HMSO, 1994

6   Welsh Office. *Forward together. A strategy to combat drug and alcohol misuse in Wales.* Cardiff: Welsh Office, 1996

7   Northern Ireland Office. *Drug misuse in Northern Ireland. A policy statement* (unpublished) 1995

8   Her Majesty's Inspectorate of Prisons for England and Wales. *Patient or prisoner? A new strategy for health care in prisons.* London:Home Office, 1996

9   Medical Research Council Field Review. *The basis of drug dependence.* London:MRC, 1994

10   Task Force to Review Services for Drug Misusers. *Report on an independent review of drug treatment services in England.* London: Department of Health, 1996

11   Lord President of the Council and Leader of the House of Commons, Secretary of State for the Home Department, Secretary of State for Health et al. *Tackling drugs together. A strategy for England 1995-1998.* London: HMSO, 1995

12   Ministerial Drugs Task Force. *Drugs in Scotland: meeting the challenge.* Scottish Home and Health Department, Edinburgh and London: HMSO, 1994

13   Welsh Office. *Forward together. A strategy to combat drug and alcohol misuse in Wales.* Cardiff: Welsh Office, 1996

14   Northern Ireland Office. *Drug misuse in Northern Ireland. A policy statement* (unpublished) 1995

15   Commission of the European Communities. *Communication from the Commission to the Council and the European Parliament on a European Union action plan to combat drugs (1995-1999)*, Brussels 23.06.1994. COM (94) 234 Final

16   *102/97/EC of the European Parliament and of the Council adopting a programme of Community Action on the prevention of drug dependence within the framework for action in the field of public health (1996-2000).* Brussels 29th October 1996 COD October 1996

17   European Monitoring Centre for Drugs and Drug Addiction. *Annual report on the state of the drugs problem in the European Union.* Lisbon: EMCDDA, 1996

Appendices

1   Research and Statistics Department. *Statistics of drugs seizures and offenders dealt with, United Kingdom, 1994.*Issue 25/1995. London: Home Office, 1995

2   Misuse of Drugs Act 1971. London: HMSO, 1971

3   United Nations. *Commentary on the Single Convention on Narcotic Drugs, 1961.* New York: UN, 1973

4   Dorn N, Jepsen J, Savona E. *European drug policies and enforcement.* London: Macmillan, 1996

5   Smith R. The war on drugs: prohibition isn't working - some legalisation will help. *BMJ* 1995;311:1655-1656

6   Release. *A Release white paper on reform of the drug laws.* London:Release publications Ltd, 1992

7   Research and Statistics Department. *Statistics of drugs seizures and offenders dealt with, United Kingdom, 1994.*Issue 25/1995. London: Home Office, 1995

8   Parker H, Meaham F, Aldridge J. *Drug futures: changing patterns of drug use amongst English youth.* London: ISDD, 1995

9   Balding J. *Young people and illegal drugs 1989-1995. Facts and predictions.* Exeter: University of Exeter, 1994

10   Lord President of the Council and Leader of the House of Commons, Secretary of State for the Home Deparment, Secretary of State for Health et al. *Tackling drugs together. A consultation document on a strategy for England 1995-1998.* London: HMSO 1994

11   Task Force to Review Services for Drug Misusers. *Report of an independent review of drug treatment services in England.* London: Department of Health, 1996

12   Lord President of the Council and Leader of the House of Commons, Secretary of State for the Home Deparment, Secretary of State for Health et al. *Tackling drugs together. A consultation document on a strategy for England 1995-1998.* London: HMSO, 1994

13   Lord President of the Council and Leader of the House of Commons, Secretary of State for the Home Department, Secretary of State for Health et al. *Tackling drugs together. A strategy for England 1995-1998.* London: HMSO, 1995

14   Payne G. Why drugs must be made legal. *Police Review* 1992;100(5154):388-389

15   Release. *A Release white paper on reform of the drug laws.* London:Release publications Ltd, 1992

16   Lord President of the Council and Leader of the House of Commons, Secretary of State for the Home Deparment, Secretary of State for Health et al. *Tackling drugs together. A consultation document on a strategy for England 1995-1998.* London: HMSO 1994

17   Sifaneck S, Kaplan C D. Keeping off, stepping on and stepping off: the stepping stone theory re-evaluated in the context of the Dutch cannabis experience. *Contemporary Drug Problems* 1995;22:483-512

18   British Medical Association. Alcohol: guidelines on sensible drinking. London: BMA, 1995

19   Payne G. Why drugs must be made legal. *Police Review* 1992;100(5154):388-389

20   Anonymous. *The myth of legalisation - a heroin addict replies to Sergeant Gordon Payne.* Police Review, 1992;100(5155):442-443

21   Shapiro H. Only way - or no way? *Druglink.* 9(1):12-15

22   Reuter P, Kleiman A. Risks and prices: an economic analysis of drug enforcement. In: Tonry M, Morris N, eds. *Crime and justice. Volume 7.* Chicago: University of Chicago Press, 1986

23   Mishan E. Legalising drugs. *The Salisbury Review.*1990;9:4-9

24   Department of Health. Social Services Inspectorate. *Inspection of Social Services for people who misuse alcohol and drugs.* London: Department of Health, 1995

Index